CROSS-COUNTRY SKI ROUTES OF OREGON'S CASCADES

Mt. Hood • Bend
(and Southern Washington)

KLINDT VIELBIG

The Mountaineers/Seattle

THE MOUNTAINEERS: Organized 1906
". . .to explore, study, preserve, and enjoy
the natural beauty of the Northwest."

©1984 by Klindt Vielbig

First edition; first printing January 1984, second printing September 1984

Published by The Mountaineers
306 2nd Avenue W., Seattle, Washington 98119

Published simultaneously in Canada by Douglas & McIntyre, Ltd.
1615 Venables Street, Vancouver, British Columbia V5L 2H1

Book design by Marge Mueller
Photos and maps by the author unless otherwise credited
Edited by Stephen Whitney
Manufactured in the United States of America

Cover photo—Elk Meadows, Mt. Hood
Photo opposite—Upper White River valley with medial moraine visible below
the valley rim

Library of Congress Cataloging in Publication Data

Vielbig, Klindt.
    Cross-country ski routes of Oregon's Cascades.

    Includes index.
    1. Cross-country skiing—Cascade Range—Guide-books.
2. Cascade Range—Description and travel—Guide-books.
I. Title.
GV854.5.C27V53   1983   917.97'46   83-22050
ISBN 0-89886-083-0

For Preston, Brett and Kurt, my sons,
who share some of my visions and tolerate my idiosyncrasies,
and for Elizabeth, who didn't

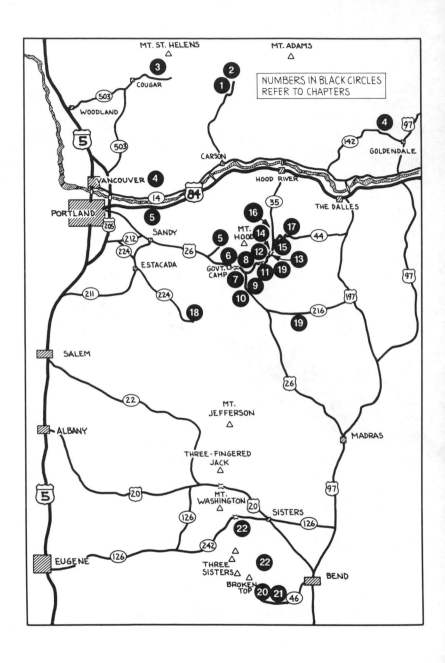

Table of Contents

Acknowledgments

I wish to express appreciation to the following individuals for providing information: Warren Seaward, Dave Kruger, David B. Marshall, Betty Jones Marshall, Jack Grauer, Ty Kearney, Jerry Igo, Doug Newman, Wendy Evans, Steve Couche, Ken Davis, Bob Mathews, Homer Blackburn, James C. Davidson, Russell Plaeger, Harold Lange, Darryl Lloyd, Bill Boyce, Jim Nieland, Carter Harrison, and Bill Kerr.

Thanks also to the following people who have, in other ways, contributed to this guidebook: Nancy Chapman, Jeff Jendro, Bill Kerr, Jan Carpenter, Brett Vielbig, Otto Rode, Lou Isaacs, and Barbara Fox.

I want to express my gratitude to the editorial staff of The Mountaineers Books, who shared my vision of a definitive guidebook. My thanks to Donna DeShazo, Ann Cleeland, and in particular Steve Whitney, the editor who worked most closely with me. In addition, thanks to Marge Mueller, and Phil Jones of Portland, for advice regarding map design, and to Nancy Chapman for assistance in the final drawing of maps. Also, thanks to Barry Wright who did all the photographic work and over a period of a year or so offered much needed advice on winter photography and equipment. Thanks also to Kurt Vielbig who in the final months provided help in many ways.

A special word of appreciation goes to John S. Day of Central Point, Oregon, who introduced Nordic skiing in the state in 1965. Since then, John Day's vision of citizen skiing for the general public as a life sport has become a reality. He directed his unfailing enthusiasm, resources, and considerable efforts to the promotion of Nordic skiing in those early years, and has ever since maintained close touch with the sport's growth. His own life, dedicated to a wide range of sports, has set an example for all of us who have had the privilege of knowing him. He is a charter member of the Oregon Nordic Club.

I would also like to extend recognition to the following people, who have made significant contributions to the growth of modern Nordic skiing in Oregon: Bill Pruitt, Jay Bowerman, Virginia Meissner, Jack Meissner, Ernie Meissner, Ron Radabaugh, Owen and Ruth Bentley, Ed Park, John Craig, Peggy Stone, Dorothy Rich, Homer Blackburn, Vilho Bjorn, George Korn, Emil Nordeen, Tom Gibbons, Birgit Hanssen, Gary Grimm, Doug Newman, Connie Wilson, Frank Moore, and Bob Venner.

Klindt Vielbig
Portland, Oregon

Introduction

This is a guidebook born out of both necessity and purpose. The necessity? There is at this time no other guide that accurately and thoroughly describes the skiing areas of Mt. Hood, Southern Washington and the Central Cascades of the Bend area. The purpose? To disperse skiers from presently crowded areas to less-used areas. In addition, this guidebook will assist in selecting tours that suit your interests and skill level, thereby minimizing the chance of getting onto trails that are too difficult or of little interest.

All guidebooks have the potential for increasing the use of areas described and should therefore be concerned with the inevitable problem of crowding. Considering the independent spirit of many Nordic skiers, however, it is not surprising that many of them seek isolation and an outdoor experience inconsistent with crowded trails. This type of skier has little reason to be alarmed because most skiers seldom venture farther than three miles from the trailhead. And there are over 800 miles of trails and loops described here! The guidebook includes a number of areas and trails that are little used. Even experienced Mt. Hood skiers will find "new" tours and areas to try their next time out.

This guidebook also encourages loop skiing, not only to disperse skiers but to make each trip more interesting. And although many skiers are in the habit of skiing out and back on the same track, most should find the concept of loop skiing refreshing and challenging. Loops and connector trails are included wherever possible to encourage different and more efficient use patterns in some of the more popular areas.

Although the thorough coverage of this guidebook may lead you to conclude that it covers every road, trail, and viewpoint, leaving nothing to the imagination, be assured that there are a number of interesting places that have not been included. In every aspect of life or sport, there should be left a little mystery.

For the first-time skiers to our region the descriptions and trail ratings should serve to make your initiation a pleasant one. No more wasting time on dull, snow-covered roads that lead nowhere, or skiing to within a few yards of a fine viewpoint but missing it because you didn't know it was there and didn't ski quite far enough. For help in choosing tours appropriate for you, see Appendix A.

The growth of Nordic skiing in the Pacific Northwest has outpaced the development of skiing areas, trails and sno-parks. It is in the interest of all skiers to be concerned with the future planning for Nordic skiing by the Forest Service and outdoor clubs. Without suitable additions and improvements to existing areas, the problem of crowding will worsen, resulting in a reduction in skiing quality.

People who have skied in several states will attest that each region has its own special mood and physical qualities. Those who have skied the

mountains of Washington and Oregon almost always speak of the unique natural beauty and variety of the areas covered in this guidebook. No other skiing region offers more variety or a greater concentration of skiing routes. Our Northwest volcanoes, extensive and beautiful forests, and accessible backcountry are remarkable assets to be valued.

Nomenclature

The lack of names for natural features in some areas has made it necessary to apply names for convenience in descriptions. Some may think that assuming such a prerogative is pretentious. To them I can only say that doing so was unavoidable. In selecting names, I have attempted to remain within the bounds of accepted practice and good taste, using logical associations or, as in the case of the Trillium Basin, using names from Norse mythology. Examples of such place names following geographical or historical guidelines are Barlow Saddle, Weygandt Basin, Trillium Pass, Knebal Pass, Wy'east Trail, Boy Scout Ridge. Only the test of time will tell whether these will be accepted. I hope that skiers will find such names appropriate and relevant.

Trail Difficulty and Skill Level

Each trail has been rated according to the level of skill required to ski it comfortably. These skill levels are as follows:

Novice. Can be skied with reasonable ease and safety by a first-time skier of average athletic ability. The trail is easy to follow, often marked, and seldom longer than three or four miles. It is restricted to gentle terrain. A novice skier often has little stamina, partly from lack of efficient skiing technique, and has little or no knowledge of winter survival. The novice has little ability to ski down hill, turn, or control speed.

Intermediate. Can be skied by skiers who have mastered basic gliding, turning, slowing, and stopping techniques. The trail may involve some minor route finding, downhill skiing on moderate to moderately steep slopes, and distances up to ten miles round trip. An intermediate skier has some knowledge of map reading, route finding, and winter survival. He or she is comfortable in the snow by having suitable equipment and clothing and by having developed a good sense of skiing and skiing conditions.

Advanced. Can be skied only by skiers with good stamina and highly developed skiing skills. The advanced skier is able to ski in all snow conditions and to ski safely and with control on most slopes. He or she is skilled with map and compass and is able to travel safely in all weather conditions and over all types of terrain and understands avalanche safety and conditions.

A word of caution in rating one's own skill level: the number of times or years one has skied is by itself not an indication of skill. Skill lies in technique and probably relates to the number of miles skied and type of

Trailside cascade in Upper Pocket Creek, Mt. Hood area

terrain on which one has skied. Most skiers tend to consider themselves intermediates after only a few times on skis, whereas they really lack the skills to qualify for that category. Many self-appointed intermediates are truly advanced novices. A flat-terrain expert is rarely more than a novice in varied terrain. Many times around Trillium Lake does not an intermediate make!

Terrain Steepness

Although skiing uphill can be taxing, most people find skiing down the same hill more difficult to master. Therefore, the following categories describe slope steepness in terms of downhill difficulties.

Gentle. Only average athletic ability required to handle this terrain with ease, but under fast conditions may exceed a novice's ability.

Moderate. Too fast for most novice skiers, and under fast conditions may challenge the ability of intermediates. The intermediate skier can easily handle moderate steepness in average snow.

Moderately Steep. Usually too fast for most skiers skiing straight downhill. Skills demanded to control speed are the use of turns, stems or snowplow maneuvers, and effective use of edging. On open slopes, descending traverses and kick turns are often used.

Steep. Cannot be skied straight downhill under control by any skier. Dangerous for novices and very difficult for intermediate skiers. Advanced skiers may have difficulty. Descent is usually with traverses and kick turns, sidestepping or walking down. Turns are very difficult unless conditions are perfect.

These terms are used in all tour descriptions and are uniformly applied so that you can compare the terrain of various trails. You will find that skis and body easily and quickly come to learn these terms.

At best, however, such terms are difficult to apply because of the large number of factors that affect slope conditions and skiing speed. The same slope may change greatly from one day to the next, or even from early morning to late afternoon. Insofar as possible the trail descriptions attempt to recognize and comment on such changes when they seriously affect slope conditions along a particular trail.

Maps

Each trail description lists the U.S.G.S. topographic maps for the trip. These maps are available from local mountaineering, backpacking, and skiing shops or may be ordered by mail from the U.S. Geological Survey, Federal Center, Denver, Colorado 80225. Southern Washington and the Mt. Hood region are also covered by Green Trails maps, which are based on U.S.G.S. topographic maps, but which are revised periodically to show recent changes in roads, trails, and other human features. These maps are often more useful than the U.S.G.S. maps for skiing on logging roads and clearcuts. Forest Service maps are also more up to date than

U.S.G.S. maps and show all but the most recent roads and facilities. They do not, however, show the very latest logging roads, which can complicate route finding on some tours. The best policy is to take several maps, preferably the most recent edition of each. For serious route finding both U.S.G.S. and Forest Service maps are necessary. In using maps, however, be cautious and thorough. Compare maps and evaluate information carefully. Then double-check the details before your final route-finding decision is made.

To complicate matters, the Forest Service initiated an entire new system of road numbering in 1982, and the new numbers have no relationship to the old. If you are using an old forest map, you may have problems. Be sure to carry the latest edition. The new road numbers are used throughout this book.

The maps in this guidebook are not always precisely to scale, and proportions are occasionally slightly distorted for improved readability. Yet while these sketch maps are not appropriate for compass work, they often include information not found on any of the maps described above. For some tours the maps in this guidebook are the only ones showing critical route-finding details.

As a general rule we advise everyone to carry appropriate maps, even novices engaged in simple circuits near a sno-park. In practice many novice tours can be enjoyed in safety without a topographic map, yet it is good to get in the habit of never being without one. On intermediate tours a map not only is helpful for identifying landmarks, judging distances, and general route finding, but adds to your knowledge and enjoyment of an area. On advanced tours skiers should never be without appropriate maps and a good compass to use in conjunction with them. Leaving maps at home or in the car has ruined more than one potentially good tour. The best advice to all skiers is to always carry a map of the area in which you plan to ski.

Sno-Parks

Oregon operates a sno-park program between November 15 and April 30. Washington has the same program during unspecified dates, but for the duration of heavy snow accumulation. During those periods, most parking lots and plowed roadside areas in the snow zone require sno-park permits. In Oregon you can obtain sno-park permits at all Motor Vehicles Division offices and at many sporting goods stores, ski shops, and other facilities near winter recreation areas. Both daily and annual permits are available. In Washington you can obtain sno-park permits at outdoor equipment stores or by mail from the:

Office of Winter Recreation
Washington State Parks and Recreation Commission
7150 Clearwater Lane KY-11
Olympia, Washington 98505

Parking in designated sno-parks without a permit will result in a fine. Oregon and Washington have reciprocal agreements wherein each state honors the other's sno-park permits. Parking outside sno-parks is *sometimes* possible if the vehicle is outside the roadside fog line, is not on a curve, and does not obstruct normal snow plowing.

To reduce the chance of someone breaking into your parked car do not leave possessions inside. Instead, lock them in the trunk. But since even trunks are easily popped open, carry your billfold, cash, checks, and credit cards with you on your ski tour. The best place to park in a sno-park is near the highway, where the presence of passing cars discourages break-ins.

Cascade Weather

To the uninitiated, particularly skiers from the Rockies, the mild winter weather of the Cascades may be both a surprise and a disappointment. Typical Cascade winters are overcast with air temperatures often hovering near freezing. The result is wet snowfalls, particularly at 3500-foot to 4500-foot elevations, where most Nordic skiing is done. These warm conditions on occasion cause problems with staying dry but also with waxing skis. On the other hand, every winter has many fine skiing days, so it balances out well if you are prepared with the proper clothing and attitude.

Although there are many days of cold snow and weather, there are others when air temperatures allow occasional rain. Depending on weather conditions on the west side of the Cascades—for example at Government Camp on Mt. Hood—it is sometimes worth altering skiing plans to seek out better weather. By driving to Timberline Lodge, for example, you may get above the damp weather into snowfall, or even above the clouds. With threatening forecasts and weather, driving to the east side of Hood—to the White River or Pocket Creek areas, or perhaps even to Clear Lake or even farther to Foreman Point—often results in improved weather. Sometimes the difference in weather is startling: from cloudy with rain to broken skies with no rain. Of course, this is not always the case, but it is often enough to justify driving east to look for better conditions.

Skiing on Mt. Hood does develop in some skiers the ability to make at-home weather forecasts. These can often result in an exceptional day of skiing even when outward conditions would indicate otherwise. Do not always judge the area where you plan to ski, which probably has its own microclimate, by local forecasts for nearby lowlands or other mountain areas. It is often worth taking a chance and going skiing in spite of bad forecasts. Careful attention to snow level, freezing level, weather reports, ski area reports, common sense, and knowledge of basic weather patterns and cloud forms over a period of time, will lead one to quite accurate analysis of the mountain weather. Oddly, some of the best skiing days have been when weather in Portland was at its worst.

Recent years have seen unusual weather patterns for much of each winter in the Cascades. The normal low maritime cloud masses, predictable and solid, seem to have given way to atypical patterns, with thunderstorms, rapidly changing weather fronts, and cloud forms of surprising variety. The winter of 1982-83 saw heavier than average snowfall above 5000 feet, but less than average below, in the Nordic skiing zone. The previous winter, with above average snowfall at all elevations (eight feet at Summit Meadows in mid-April), contrasted with the five preceding snow-drought winters, when the maximum depth at Government Camp was five feet and the average was less than two feet, with many periods of bare ground.

The snow line on Mt. Hood and in the Bend area is typically near the 3500-foot elevation, fluctuating up or down on a short-term basis. Above 3500 feet, the depth of snow increases rapidly. As there are no sno-parks in the Clackamas area, and therefore no snow plowing above the snow line, fluctuations in the 2000 to 3000 foot zone will affect your skiing plans more than in other areas. The Mt. St. Helens and Upper Wind River areas, also subject to snow-line fluctuations in recent years due to unstable weather patterns, typically have a lower snow line than Mt. Hood. Southern Washington has an average 3000-foot snow line. All areas in the guidebook generally have good skiing into April and, in the Bend backcountry, into May. Spring skiing on Mt. St. Helens is shorter, however, as most of the ski routes on south-facing slopes have less protective tree cover. Fluctuations and snow depth are often unpredictable, however, and therefore there is no sure way of knowing exact conditions until you go to the area you want to ski   more often than not a risk worth taking.

The west slopes of the Cascades receive heavier snowfall and experience more cloudy weather than the east slope. As moist air from the Pacific Ocean reaches the Cascades, it rises and cools, producing heavy precipitation. The east side of the Cascades receives less precipitation and enjoys fairer weather. The Bend area benefits from this advantage and is considered by many skiers to be a haven from the damper weather and snows of the west side.

To make the most out of a given set of skiing and weather conditions, particularly when changing rapidly, will demand all your skills. Each snowfall, each weekend, each winter presents us with a new set of problems and opportunities. It is usually possible by careful planning, to turn most conditions to an advantage. Doing so is just part of the excitement of skiing.

Avalanches

Avalanches are rare in most areas covered by this book. Unlike the precipitous North Cascades, where avalanches are commonplace, the

Cascades of southern Washington and Oregon feature quite gentle terrain at skiing elevations—generally from 3500 feet to 6000 feet. Most of the ski routes described here are through forest and on trails and roads below timberline. Of course, many of these ski routes do ultimately lead to open slopes and high country, where cornices and slab avalanches pose a threat. Where danger exists, it has been duly noted in the trail descriptions. Where avalanches are not mentioned, the potential can be considered low to nil.

Infrequent evidence of avalanches, however, does not mean that they never occur on some of the ski routes described here. Skiers should always be alert to possible avalanche danger. Any slope steeper than 25 degrees is vulnerable to avalanches, but most slides occur on slopes of 30 degrees to 45 degrees. Any slope, however, may avalanche under the right conditions, and it is imperative that all skiers have some knowledge of those conditions and of what to do should an avalanche bury a fellow skier. Such knowledge may save your life or that of a friend.

The time of greatest avalanche activity is during or immediately following a storm. Eighty percent of all slides occur at this time. At such times skiers should avoid steep slopes, especially those on the leeward side of a ridge, where wind-blown snow can form large, unstable drifts and cornices. Ridge tops are generally safer than the slopes on either side, but skiers must avoid venturing, perhaps unwittingly, onto cornices. Stay well away from the edge of cliffs and steep, leeward slopes, where the extent, location, and stability of cornices may not be apparent.

When skiing in valleys, stay on the flat, well away from the slopes. Learn to recognize avalanche signs, such as fracture lines and steep, open chutes through the forest. If hard-packed snow sounds hollow, keep off!

If you must travel on a dangerous slope, do so one person at a time. Before proceeding, loosen your equipment. Avoid traversing the slope; if possible, ski directly up or down. And under no circumstances should you cross a convex slope. If you must traverse, stay as near to the top of the slope as possible and use dense woods or scattered trees as islands of safety. As each person ventures onto the slope, others in the party should watch and wait, staying alert to the sights and sounds that may signal an imminent slide.

If you are caught, get rid of whatever equipment you can. Skis, poles, and pack can trap you. Make a vigorous effort to swim, staying near the top and side of the flow. When you come to rest, keep snow from packing against your face. Try to form an air pocket as the movement decreases. If buried, try to stay calm to conserve air and strength.

If you have seen someone swept away, mark the spot where the person was last seen. Search directly downhill from there. If there are several survivors, one should go for aid while the others organize a systematic search. Use the handle end of your ski poles to probe carefully into the snow. Remember, after one hour, the victim has only a fifty percent survival rate.

If planning a tour in avalanche-prone terrain, be sure to call the North-west Avalanche Center (503) 221-2400 for current avalanche information. Avalanche forecasts speak of low, moderate, high, and extreme avalanche hazard, which refers not to terrain, but to weather conditions. In periods of low hazard the snow is mostly stable. Moderate hazard means that there are areas of unstable snow on steep slopes, in snow chutes, and other avalanche-prone terrain. High avalanche hazard means the snow is very unstable and that avalanches are likely. Extreme avalanche hazard indicates that most mountain travel is unsafe.

Icing Up

Because the vast majority of Northwest cross-country skiers use wax-less skis, it may seem strange to devote space to the subject of waxing. Actually, this subject is of concern to many skiers because the typical, warm, moist winter weather of the Cascades creates special problems for owners of waxless skis, particularly when temperatures hover near 32° F. Rapid changes in both weather and temperature, often from cold to warmer conditions, also create problems. These are particularly frustrating to skiers using waxable skis, but to a lesser degree skiers using waxless skis are also affected.

In such weather waxless skis often benefit from some form of waxing, which can improve both grip and glide. This is particularly important if you are planning a long ski tour or lots of climbing. For better performance while skiing, an appropriate wax for prevailing conditions can be rubbed on rapidly and corked smooth, even over the gripping surface. The additional grip provided by the wax conserves energy and permits a faster, steeper ascent.

"Icing up" refers to the formation of frost-like patches on ski bases. These patches usually grow in size and depth as you ski. Since even one small patch significantly affects gliding, increased icing becomes disabling if the situation is not remedied.

Icing up occurs when moisture penetrates the pores of the base material, then freezes. Skis can pick up the moisture either from the air—when riding atop the car—or from the snow surface itself. It is then necessary to carefully scrape off all the frosty patches. Even then, however, the base will probably continue to ice up as you ski unless additional preventive measures are taken. To prevent further icing up, apply cross-country wax or paraffin, an easy-to-apply hard wax, and cork it smooth. This remedy often helps, but the entire process often has to be repeated because the skis will continue to experience some icing.

When the air temperature hovers near freezing, all skis, regardless of type of base, are affected by moisture. If skis are waxed at home, moisture is less likely to penetrate the base material and is therefore less likely to ice up on the snow. For waxless skis, any wax will do: cross-country wax, paraffin, even spray-on waxes for furniture.

Herringboning on the lower slopes of Mt. St. Helens. (Photo by Nancy Chapman)

Your regular touring pack should include a good scraper, such as a flexible putty knife, a selection of waxes and paraffin, and a cork. Severe icing up does not happen often, but when it does you must have the right tools to make your skis glide. Even the slightest icing will be frustrating and energy consuming, and more than a few tours have been ruined by the lack of a good scraper. Unfortunately, on some days nothing you do eliminates icing. With a good "de-icing" kit, however, you can continue your tour even on those difficult days when icing is unavoidable.

Setting a Track

Always set a good ski track for yourself and those who follow. Maintain or improve the tracks you are on. Years ago, when there were only a few Nordic skiers, a ski tour usually meant breaking tracks in deep snow — slow going and hard work! Today, it always seems that someone has been out ahead, breaking trail and setting a track. This makes skiing certainly easier, but the tracks you find often do not permit pleasureable skiing. If *you* are breaking trail, look back to observe the line of your tracks. If they wander or waiver, then you are skiing inefficiently— using excess energy and not leaving an enjoyable track for those behind you, or even for your own return trip.

Learn to make a good track: as straight as possible, with the skis about eight inches apart. If tracks ahead are bad, improve them by smoothing out wobbles and establishing proper width. A group of skiers should all ski in one set of tracks, each improving the track ahead as required. Tracks that overlap, crisscross, and randomly wander are difficult to ski and destroy the rhythm of forward movement.

Clothing

The clothing you wear is the most basic item of all your cross-country equipment. Your comfort and enjoyment to a large extent depend on what you wear. In severe weather proper clothing can ensure your survival. Yet clothing selection is also a personal matter, and a wide range of styles will be seen on the trails. Whatever style you prefer, your clothing should keep you warm and dry while permitting maximum freedom of movement.

As a general rule avoid cotton, which absorbs moisture and dries out slowly. Instead dress in wool or suitable synthetic fabrics. Keep your clothing light and flexible, dressing in layers for warmth rather than relying on heavy, cumbersome garments. In the Northwest it is also important to carry good rain gear. If your jacket is light, it can double as a windbreaker. Coated nylon or breathable waterproof materials seem to work best.

What to Take

Winter is fickle, a season of rapid and often unpredictable weather changes. Every skier should hope for the best weather and prepare for the worst. For winter, while beautiful, is quick to punish the ill prepared. Each ski pack should include at least the ten essentials.

1. Extra clothing, 2. Extra food, 3. Sunglasses, 4. Knife, 5. First aid kit, 6. Fire starter, 7. Matches in a waterproof container, 8. Flashlight, 9. Map, and 10. Compass.

An eleventh essential for ski tours is a repair kit (see below for what to take and how to use them).

In addition to the above, day skiers should also have the following items in their pack: closed-cell foam seating pad, lunch and full water bottle (water is often hard to come by in winter), snow scraper, paraffin or wax, toilet paper, litter bag, rain suit, extra mitts and socks, and a light sweater. For day tours that are rated advanced, take the following items in addition to the above: survival food, whistle, two plastic garbage bags for emergency cover, container for melting snow, small nylon-tarp shelter, heat tabs or stove, heavy sweater or pile or down jacket.

Repair Kit and How to Use It

There should be at least one complete repair kit with every party. Carry in a compact stuff sack or other container. You may not have to repair your own equipment or that of some member of your party, but someone else—a stranger on the trail—may be eternally grateful for your repair kit. It does not add significant weight to your pack and will inevitably be required at some time or another. The repair kit should include the following items:

- spare ski pole basket (If necessary, use tape or wire to attach baskets firmly.)
- plastic ski tip
- binding bail (For rugged skiing, some skiers tie the binding bail to the binding to eliminate accidental loss. They may also run a "runaway strap" from the binding to the boot or ankle to secure the ski in the event the binding opens on a steep slope.)
- Swiss Army knife (It must include an awl for drilling screw holes. A binding torn from a ski may have to be placed elsewhere on the ski to ensure a snug fit. Use an awl for making new screw holes. For a tighter fit stuff the holes with steel wool or match sticks. In extreme situations, drive bolts through the ski to hold the binding. This will certainly make skiing difficult, but it will ensure your retreat to the trailhead.)
- needle-nose pliers (Choose a small size, with wire cutter. An essential tool for cutting and manipulating wire.)
- screw driver (The stubby type is best. Make sure the head fits the screws on your skis.)
- screws (Carry a small assortment. You will need at least three to fit the usual binding.)
- nuts and bolts (For use where screws fail.)
- steel wool (Good for reinforcing screw holes.)
- wire (Use to attach binding, support broken pole or basket, attach new basket, or splint a cracked ski.)
- fiber tape (May be used for same jobs as wire. In addition it is essential for mending torn clothes or boots.)
- nylon cord (This is useful for tying a shelter together, repairing clothing, holding a boot into a binding, dangling a container over a snowbank for water, and for other uses. Where friction would wear out a cord or where elasticity is undesirable, use wire instead.)
- short nylon strap (For replacing broken pole strap.)
- 2 long (30-inch) nylon straps (These are useful for attaching boot to ski if a bail breaks and is lost.)
- large safety pins

Skiing with a full pack may seem troublesome, but the lack of just a piece of tape or spare pole basket can make the difference between an

Meadow near Todd Lake, with Mt. Bachelor in the distance

easy return to your car and a difficult, tiring, even dangerous experience. The extra ounces of repair equipment are an important investment in your enjoyment, peace of mind, and perhaps survival.

Trail Courtesy

The quality and enjoyment of the skiing experience can be maintained if we all show sensitivity to other skiers and minimize the effects of our passage through the silent winter landscape.

If you stop to rest, eat or wax, step off to the side without damaging the continuity of the track. When skiing in a group, do not block the track.

If you fall, fill in the depression (sitzmark) your body makes and re-establish the track. A sitzmark may cause others to fall. Just scrape snow into it and tamp the snow down.

Step aside to permit faster skiers to pass.

Avoid walking across or in an established track. Snowshoers and snow players should not walk on ski tracks. Snowmobiles should not run on ski tracks.

When skiing uphill, always give the right of way to the skier coming downhill by stepping out of the track.

Litter should not be dropped on the snow or buried. Carry out your own litter and that of others. Use a plastic bag. Practice no-trace skiing. Litter diminishes the outdoor experience for all.

Enjoy the quiet outdoor world without yelling, shouting or whistle blowing, except to solicit aid.

Avoid downhill runs in ski areas. If you must cross one, do so rapidly, or try to stay near their margins.

If there is more than one set of tracks, ski in the right hand track. If trails are marked for skiing direction, proceed in that direction only. Keep poles close to the body when near another skier.

If an accident occurs, everyone should render assistance. If several skiers are involved, witnesses should establish their identity.

Fires should be discouraged. Those requiring a warm meal on day tours should use a thermos bottle or carry a stove. If a fire is absolutely necessary, keep it small and use only lower, dead limbs. Do not cut trees or boughs. Also do not cut dead snags, which are a picturesque part of the winter scene.

Pets

The Forest Service discourages pets in cross-country areas. Dogs get in the way on narrow trails and usually walk on ski tracks. They not only ruin the tracks but also pose a hazard to skiers, particularly novices, who cannot easily maneuver out of their way. Dogs also chase wildlife and mess skiing areas with their urine and feces.

Skiers who insist on bringing their dogs should ski in areas that are not heavily used and should hold them when other skiers approach. Dog owners also should clean up after them. Dogs should not be permitted to urinate or defecate on or near ski tracks. If possible, leave your dog at home.

Sanitation

One of the most conspicuous abuses of the winter scene is uncovered human waste. People who urinate and defecate at random not only create a health hazard, but mar otherwise beautiful areas. When relieving yourself, always dig a hole with your boot or ski pole. Toilet paper must be burned or carried out in a plastic bag. Remember, toilet paper will remain long after the spring thaw. When selecting a toilet site, avoid lakes and streams, frozen or otherwise, and always get well away from trails, roads, and other facilities.

Flexibility

If you take each day by itself and carefully select your tour based on weather and snow for that day, there is a good chance that you will have a successful trip. If you are out for distance skiing and the snow is bad, use the day or route to its best advantage: enjoy the views or take short side trips to explore previously unvisited areas. If the snow is excellent but clouds block the views, forget the panoramas and enjoy the exercise and sheer fun of skiing for its own sake. If you learn to adapt to conditions as you find them, your skiing will be more rewarding. You will have more "good days" and fewer disappointments.

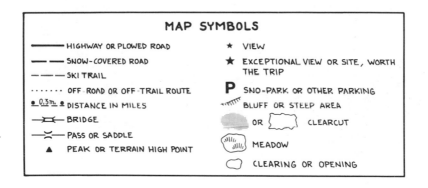

Steam and ash eruption of Mt. St. Helens. Several such emissions occur each year, along with frequent ash releases that cover the snow with thin layers.

Part I
Southern Washington Cascades

The Cascades of southern Washington—from near the town of Goldendale in the east to Larch Mountain (Washington) in the west— offer several destinations for skiers that provide variety to the usual type of Northwest skiing. They include Larch and Silver Star mountains, the incomparable Mt. St. Helens, the Upper Wind River-Crazy Hills region, and far to the east of these the Simcoe Mountains. The Trout Lake–Mt. Adams area has not been included because of its remoteness and the lack of scenic rewards for the average skier.

The two principal ski touring areas of southern Washington are the south side of Mt. St. Helens and the Upper Wind River, both located in the Gifford Pinchot National Forest. To ski at the very foot of an active volcano is in itself exciting, particularly if it is steaming on the day you are there. In addition, due to extensive logging, the south side offers many views, not only of the mountain, but off in many directions over the lower forests and ridges.

Chapter 1
UPPER WIND RIVER

The Upper Wind River ski trail complex, 76 miles from Portland and 26 miles north of the Columbia River at Carson, offers many trails and views in generally rolling, heavily clearcut and forested areas. This is a little-known Nordic skiing area with many scenic surprises and superb views of Mt. Adams, Mt. St. Helens, and Mt. Rainier.

Crossing Outlaw Creek, Mt. St. Helens in distance

Because of the ski area's relatively low elevation (3000 feet to 4000 feet), you should verify snow depth in winters of light snowfall by calling the Wind River Ranger Station before making the trip. Still, the area generally has more snow than might be expected for its modest elevation.

Special recognition should be accorded Harold P. Lange, District Ranger, Wind River Ranger District, and his recreation specialist Russell Plaeger for the exceptional variety of marked ski trails in the Upper Wind River area. Mr. Lange had the unusual foresight in 1975 to recognize the growing need for Nordic ski trails and in annual increments developed an outstanding area with assistance from local skiers, and with considerable sensitivity separated snowmobiles from skiers in most areas. It is interesting to note that in the entire state of Oregon, where Nordic skiing has grown with exceptional speed since 1966, there is only one comparable ski-trail complex: the Swampy Lakes-Dutchman Flat area near Bend.

From downtown Portland to Carson, Washington is 50 miles, and from Carson to the Upper Wind River Sports Area is 26 miles. Drive east on I-80, cross the Columbia River on the Bridge of the Gods at Cascade Locks, and drive east on Highway 14 for 6.7 miles to the Carson exit. After exiting, enter Carson and drive northwest on the Wind River road (the street on which you enter town) past a fish hatchery 13 miles north of town. Just past the hatchery, at a junction, turn right onto Road 30 and drive 13 miles to Old Man Pass. The road is paved, but the last five miles to the pass are fairly steep, gaining 1500 feet elevation.

Road and snow information is available from the Wind River Ranger Station, which is 12 miles from Carson, off the Wind River road. A small 76 gas station 8.3 miles from Carson temporarily serves as a map and information center for skiers. The station is often closed but has an outside bulletin board and map holder. If snow depth or road conditions are questionable, telephone the ranger station during weekday business hours for more information. Leave home with a full tank of gas.

Road 30 is generally plowed Monday through Friday only, rarely on weekends. Be prepared to drive through snow. Tire chains are often required, and a shovel is always handy. During heavy snowfall at lower elevations, county plows may not be able to plow Road 30 because residential areas have priority, a good reason to call the ranger station for current road conditions.

There are seven sno-parks in the area. Six have been labeled A through F by the Forest Service. For whatever reason, the sno-park at Hardtime Creek road has no letter. The Upper Wind River sno-parks are as follows (numbers indicate vehicle capacity):

A	Point 3670	5—share with snowmobiles
B	Old Man Pass	25—skiers only
C	Access to McClellan Meadows, Pete Gulch, Outlaw Creek Clearcuts	7—skiers only
–	Hardtime Creek Trail and Loop	4—skiers only
D	Outlaw Creek Clearcuts	6—skiers only
E	Outlaw Creek Clearcuts	25—share with snowmobiles
F	Crazy Hills	25—share with snowmobiles

Parking is permitted only in sno-parks, which are located along a six-mile section of road. A Washington or Oregon sno-park permit is required. Please do not block snowmobile unloading ramps. On weekends and holidays, parking may be crowded so please always use space efficiently. Car pooling is encouraged. Several sno-parks are maintained during midweek. A toilet is located at Old Man Pass. Due to high snow banks, some side-road trails may not be obvious.

The most useful maps of this area are, first, the Forest Service map of trails and roads and, second, the Green Trails maps. The latter, using USGS maps as a base, indicate roads in black and summer trails in green, making them more complete, up to date, and easier to read and use than the standard USGS quadrangles. The Green Trails Lone Butte and Wind River sheets cover the entire area and are the same scale. It takes three USGS maps to cover the same area, and their scales do not match. Moreover, the scale of the USGS Wind River quad is so small as to be almost useless.

The Upper Wind River area, with more than 50 miles of ski trails, of which 21 miles are marked, offers tours for all tastes and skill levels. The trails are well marked with blue diamonds. (The Forest Service is changing trail markers from the now fading orange signs to the standard blue diamond. Until this change is completed, both types will be seen.) In some open areas, tall poles with markers are used to show ski routes. Novices can glide along short, easy trails on gentle terrain. Advanced skiers can enjoy extended tours requiring downhill and route-finding skills. Numerous loops are possible by joining various trails. Some of the trails are identified by Forest Service numbers; others are not. All are shown on the map on page 27.

OLD MAN TRAIL: TRAIL 148

Main loop Intermediate, shortcut loop Novice
Marked trails and roads
Round trip main loop 5.3 miles, shortcut loop 1.5 miles
Elevation gain main loop 400 feet
High point 3200 feet
USGS Burnt Peak, Wind River

Map—page 27

This scenic and varied loop west of Road 30 offers forest trails, meadows, and a vast, flat clearcut with views of Mt. Adams. There is also some gentle downhill skiing. The loops should be skied counter-clockwise to keep steep grades to a minimum.

The trail is well marked but you may have to take a few moments to find your way back into the forest from the large clearcut at the north end of the loop.

The usual trailhead is sno-park B at Old Man Pass, 3000 feet. Or you may hike 200 yards north of sno-park C to find a connector route leading west to the northern end of the main loop. A shortcut side trail on a road 0.5 mile from the trailhead permits a shorter loop for those with limited time or experience.

The main loop is one of the finest tours in the area, with a diversity of landscape. A huge clearcut at the north end offers unique views.

The Old Man Trail goes north from the sno-park, paralleling the road. For the first 2 miles it meanders through dense woods on trails and old skid roads. When the trail reaches the north end of the loop, it turns left onto a narrow road that leads west into clearcuts. In the largest clearcut there is an interesting foot bridge. From this bridge a 0.5-mile off-trail tour through open country leads to the Hardtime Creek road (see Hardtime Creek). This unmarked route is for aggressive skiers wishing to expand their horizons. It will be marked in the future. After crossing the foot bridge the Old Man Trail re-enters the forest, passes through a meadow with cottonwood trees, and follows a long, moderate, uphill, zigzag course onto a high, rolling area (3200 feet), where a future clearcut will provide views. The route then bridges a stream, shortly reaching a junction with the shortcut loop. Turn uphill to the right, skiing over a

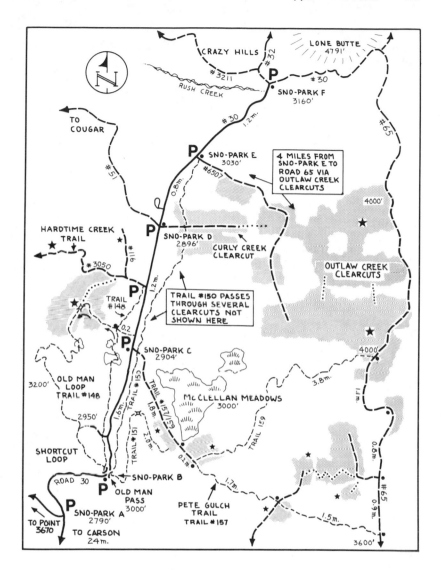

low divide and then gently downhill to Old Man Pass.

The Shortcut Loop, only 1.5 miles long, is suitable for novices. It offers scenic forest skiing, with easy uphill and downhill stretches. Follow the Old Man Trail north to where it crosses an obvious, wide road. Turn left here and follow the road uphill to its end, where it joins the west leg of the Old Man Trail coming from the north. There, both trails join and climb to a low divide, followed by a gentle descent to the trailhead.

WIND RIVER/McCLELLAN MEADOWS TRAIL: TRAIL 151

Intermediate
Round trip 4 miles
Marked trail
Elevation loss 150 feet

High point 3000 feet
USGS Burnt Peak, Wind River

Map—page 27

Of the two trails into McClellan Meadows this is the most challenging. It first descends to the Wind River, which it crosses on a foot bridge, then enters a large clearcut climbing finally to the south end of the meadows. The trailhead is across the road from the Old Man Pass sno-park. Take the right-hand trail which immediately heads east on a gentle descent through forest. Do not take the left-hand trail—the Old Man Connector Trail—which here goes north.

After several hundred yards the McClellan Meadows Trail makes an abrupt left turn to the north, traversing the slope and descending to the river, which here is just a creek. Cross the river on a foot bridge. The trail shortly turns southeast and enters a long clearcut, following its bottom edge to near the south end. There, the trail turns uphill and climbs steeply through cleared brush. Near the top of this clearcut the trail dodges into the trees for a short distance then emerges onto a road—Trail 157—at the south end of McClellan Meadows. After exploring the meadow, you may

Clearcut near Road 65 and top of trail 151

return to the trailhead by retracing your tracks. Or you may follow Trails 157 and 150 (See map on page 27) back for an interesting 5.4 mile loop. An even longer loop is possible by going uphill on Trail 159 for 4 miles to Road 65, then downhill through the Outlaw Creek clearcuts to Road 30, and finally, south along Trail 150 paralleling Road 30 to Old Man Pass for an eventful 13-mile loop. Before deciding on such an ambitious undertaking, however, consult your maps, snow, and weather. If you are unfamiliar with the area, the 5.4 mile loop is quite satisfying. If 13 miles is too long and 5.4 miles too short, consider skiing to sno-park C, hiking north 200 yards to an obscure side road going west, then join the northern end of the Old Man Trail Loop for an 8-mile loop back to your car.

McCLELLAN MEADOWS/INDIAN HEAVEN TRAIL: TRAIL 157/159

To meadows Novice, to Road 65 Intermediate
Round trip to meadows 3.6 miles, to Road 65 11.6 miles
Marked road and trail
Elevation gain to meadow 100 feet, to Road 65 1100 feet
High point 4000 feet
USGS Lone Butte, Wind River

Map—page 27

This trail is the most popular route to McClellan Meadows. And from there it climbs 3.8 miles through forest, with a gain of 1000 feet, to Road 65, where grand views are enjoyed from the upper ends of immense clearcuts. Indian Heaven is a roadless, backcountry area above and east of Road 65. Not recommended for the average skier, Indian Heaven is a confusing area to ski because there are few landmarks. Experienced off-trail skiers entering this area should start with a compass bearing and topographic maps.

From Old Man Pass drive north 1.6 miles to sno-park C. Follow a snow-covered road southeast up a long, gentle hill to flat terrain near the meadows and past a long clearcut to the right, about 1.2 miles from sno-park C. For a fine view ski into the clearcut to its northwest corner. You are now at the top of a long cliff forming the western edge of the clearcut, and here are the best views of the area. Look directly down into a lower clearcut and into the forested valley of the Wind River. The view south down the valley is impressive. Ski with care along the edge of the cliff, then turn eastward toward the meadows, where the top of Mt. Adams may be seen to the northeast, above a forested ridge.

A challenging tour for advanced skiers begins at the south end of the clearcut. Descend the steep hill and pick up Trail 151. Then cross the

Wind River, climb to Old Man Pass, and turn right onto Trail 150 to sno-park C, for a loop of 5.4 miles.

Back on Trail 157, the road continues into another clearcut and ends there beyond the south edge of the meadows. From there turn left onto Trail 159, climbing the southeast edge of the clearcut to its top, where Mt. St. Helens comes into view. Entering forest, the trail winds and twists tightly across rough terrain and through dense growths of alder and cedar. After a 0.5 mile or so, however, the trail enters semi-open second-growth and from there to Road 65 becomes most attractive, climbing through beautiful forest of various types. About halfway up, the trail switchbacks (site of a future clearcut) providing the only views from the trail until the top end is reached. From McClellan Meadows to Road 65 and the Outlaw Creek clearcuts is 4.0 miles.

When you leave the forest at the upper end of the trail, you will be at the south edge of the Outlaw Creek clearcuts, a vast treeless area offering wide views, through which you may descend to form an interesting loop by way of sno-park E and Trail 150 (see Outlaw Creek Clearcuts). Although the trail above the meadows was designed for cross-country skiing, the descent can be difficult if icy or crusted.

PETE GULCH TRAIL: Trail 157

Advanced	High point 3600 feet
Round trip 6.4 miles	USGS Wind River
Marked trail	
Elevation gain 600 feet	Map—page 27

From McClellan Meadows the Pete Gulch Trail climbs along narrow, winding summer trail 157 to Road 65, where it ends. The trail is only partially marked at this time and there are some minor problems following it. Furthermore, it is not an easy trail to descend in fast snow, for several places are moderately steep. As a result this trail is for only experienced skiers with route-finding skills.

The trail starts at the bottom of the clearcut just south of McClellan Meadows, where the Trail 157 road ends. From there the trail enters forest and winds gently to moderately upward through second-growth, along the way crossing three bridged streams. At 1.7 miles the trail crosses the top edge of a clearcut. Turn right 100 yards for a view of Mt. St. Helens. After more forest travel where the trail is easy to miss in places, it eventually reaches Road 65. You can turn left onto Road 65 and ski 0.9 mile north to a side road leading 200 yards into several clearcuts with fine views—a side trip worth taking.

A shorter, more interesting route to this area begins back at the clearcut 1.7 miles up the Pete Gulch Trail. From there turn left and follow the clearcut road uphill into the forest to a large clearcut with a view of St.

Helens. Along the upper edge of the clearcut is an opening into a yet higher one, with direct access to Road 65, 400 feet above and 1.5 miles from where you left the Pete Gulch Trail. A clearcut to the south—and through a screen of trees—from the upper clearcut has a fine view of Mt. Hood, Mt. Jefferson, and nearby Red Mountain in Indian Heaven. For a loop tour ski north on Road 65 to the upper end of the Outlaw Creek clearcuts, returning to sno-park C either by way of Trail 159, or by Trail 150 from sno-parks D or E.

OLD MAN CONNECTOR TRAIL: TRAIL 150

Novice
Round trip to sno-park C 3.2 miles,
  to sno-park E 7.2 miles
Elevation gain to sno-park E 240 feet

High point 3020 feet
USGS Lone Butte, Wind River

Map—page 27

This trail, 3.6 miles long, closely parallels Road 30 from Old Man Pass to sno-park E. The first 1.6 miles follow a beautiful primitive road to sno-park C; the remainder is a trail through both forest and clearcuts. The Old Man Connector Trail joins with Trail 157 and with the Old Man Trail for loop tours. The purpose of the trail is to serve as a connecting leg for several loop systems and to provide access to trails all along Road 30. Due to lack of funds, however, the Forest Service has not been able to provide the full maintenance the trail requires. Even so, it is now skiable for its full length. The future of this trail possibly depends on volunteer maintenance. In the meantime it can be skied either from end to end (using a car shuttle) or as one leg in a variety of interesting loops. Starting from the trail's north end at sno-park E, there is a slight elevation drop to Trail 157, then a gentle ascent of 100 feet to Old Man Pass.

HARDTIME CREEK TRAILS AND LOOP

Novice
Round trip to principal viewpoint
  5 miles
Unmarked road
Elevation loss and gain 300 feet

High point 3000 feet
USGS Lone Butte, Wind River

Map—page 27

There are striking vistas of three volcanoes, as well as other fine views, along this road. The combination of large clearcuts, forest, valley, and mountains make this one of the most scenic tours of the area. To reach the trailhead ski or drive to Road 3050, Hardtime Creek road, 0.5 mile north of sno-park C. From the small sno-park at Road 3050 ski west into a large clearcut. This sno-park is connected to the north end of Old Man Trail Loop by a 0.5-mile trail. From Road 30 the ski route drops 300 feet in 1 mile to Hardtime Creek, then climbs gradually through alternating stands of old-growth timber and clearcuts. In clear weather there are stunning views of Mt. Rainier across deep valleys and distant ridges, plus views of nearby Mt. St. Helens and Mt. Adams. The best views are from a steep clearcut on the road 2.5 miles from Road 30. The road end is another 1.5 miles but the additional distance does not offer better views.

Only 0.3 mile along Road 3050 from the trailhead Road 116 branches north for 1 mile, at first level then descending gently and ending in a clearcut overlooking Hardtime Creek. Traveling both past clearcuts with tall, charred snags and through dense stands of pole forest, this road offers an unusual skiing and scenic experience, including views of Mt. St. Helens.

The Hardtime Loop. This interesting 2.5-mile tour can be skied by taking a connector trail (Trail 148) starting 50 yards west of the Road 3050 trailhead. This trail heads south 0.5 mile through trees, then crosses a clearcut to a primitive road, the north leg of the Old Man Trail Loop. Turn right on this road and ski west to the foot bridge in the large clearcut. Do not cross the bridge, but turn right (north), cutting across the 0.5-mile clearcut to Road 3050, returning to the trailhead for a beautiful, adventurous loop of 2.5 miles. To reverse the loop ski west on Road 3050 for about 100 yards past Road 116, where you can see an opening through the forest screen to the south. Ski through this opening into the old, large clearcut and south 0.5 mile to the foot bridge on the Old Man Trail Loop. The Hardtime Loop requires some easy route finding from the foot bridge so save this trip for times of good visibility.

OUTLAW CREEK CLEARCUTS

Intermediate

Round trip up to 8 miles

Unmarked roads and clearcuts

Elevation gain 1000 feet

High point 4000 feet

USGS Lone Butte

Map—page 27

This tour is a unique opportunity to ski through vast open areas with an almost ethereal quality. There are views of distant ridges and a superb view of Mt. St. Helens.

From Old Man Pass drive north on Road 30 for 3.6 miles to sno-park E. Ski the snow-covered road eastward as it gently climbs through forest, then along the edge of a clearcut, then briefly back into the forest. The second clearcut you enter is the bottom (west end) of a system of huge, connecting clearcuts that you can follow upward to excellent views of Mt. St. Helens and the high, forested ridges west of the Wind River area. Road 65, a major forest road, crosses near the upper end of these clearcuts at the

4000-foot level, 1000 feet above the trailhead. The immense Outlaw Creek clearcuts should be of sufficient interest to hold your attention for an entire day: hills to ski, streams to cross, and an ever-changing spectacle of distant forest borders silhouetted against ridges and sky.

For a loop trip find the top end of Trail 159 and ski southwest to McClellan Meadows. From there you can ski Trail 151 to Old Man Pass, then north on Trail 150 to sno-park E. Or you can continue on Trail 157/159 to sno-park C and from there ski Trail 150 to sno-park E, for a total distance of 11.8 miles.

The giant clearcuts are difficult to navigate accurately in poor visibility, however, particularly if you have a precise destination. As in all clearcuts, beware of buried objects if the snow is shallow. Snowmobiles often use this area so be alert when they are near.

POINT 3670

Advanced
Round trip 16 miles
Unmarked road
Elevation gain 644 feet

High point 3670 feet
USGS Burnt Peak, Wind River

Map—page 27

Along the side of a circuitous ridge, through forest and clearcuts, this long road tour leads to outstanding views of three volcanoes and the deep Lewis River valley. The trailhead is sno-park A located 1.1 miles south of Old Man Pass. This is the first sno-park you reach in the Wind River area. The route to point 3670 heads west along a winding ridge road with little elevation gain or loss, first on Road 31 then on Road 3103. There are numerous road junctions along the way where road signs will be buried by snow. A Forest Service map is necessary to select the correct direction. Green Trails maps are even more detailed.

The view from the road's end—at the head of Swift Reservoir, almost 3000 feet below—across to nearby Mt. St. Helens is inspiring. You can clearly see the high country northeast of the volcano that was devastated by the May 18, 1980 eruption. The road to the viewpoint does not receive heavy snowmobile use.

Chapter 2
CRAZY HILLS

The Crazy Hills comprise an unusually compact area north of the main Upper Wind River trail system. This little known but remarkable area offers a number of surprises: road skiing, off-road skiing, a variety of loops, excellent viewpoints, passes, and a beautiful hidden valley. The entire area is encircled by a gentle, easy-to-follow road that forms the longest loop. The fascinating area also invites off-road exploration.

None of the ski routes in the Crazy Hills is marked but all are on roads, so there is generally no problem in route finding unless you try off-road skiing on the ridges. The area is so compact, however, that skiing downhill in any direction will always take a disoriented skier to the perimeter road, which is obvious and ultimately leads back to the sno-park.

Avalanche danger is almost nonexistent in the Crazy Hills. The steepest route described here is the south side of Skookum Peak, up a moderately steep clearcut where you should always be alert to possible danger.

The Crazy Hills are open to snowmobiles and see a lot of such use. Fast-moving snowmobiles are always a danger to skiers. Step aside and watch their approach and be sure they are aware of your presence. Until you are familiar with the Crazy Hills, carry maps of the area. There is only one sno-park for all the Crazy Hills tours: sno-park F, the northernmost in the upper Wind River skiing area. To reach sno-park F from Old Man Pass drive Road 30 north for 4.8 miles to its end.

RUSH CREEK TOUR

Novice
Round trip up to 3 miles
Unmarked road
Elevation gain 60 feet

High point 3220 feet
USGS Lone Butte

Map—page 36

If you are looking for a ski tour that offers maximum open space and views for the least effort, then this is the tour for you. Exceptional, sweeping views are a unique aspect of the tour. From sno-park F, ski along Road 32 (the road on the left at the sno-park) 0.2 mile and turn left onto Road 3211. You will soon be looking down and across several unusual, interesting open draws and the Rush Creek valley to an unfolding scene to the south. As you progress along the level, sidehill road, the view becomes more and more striking, and soon the entire Upper Wind River basin comes into view. The gently sculptured and forested basin sweeps up to a ridge of minor tree-clad peaks to the west, and in a bold,

Ski tours through meadows

long curve upward to the east ends in the massive ridge of the Indian Heaven backcountry. Ski along Road 3211 as far as you like before returning to sno-park F. To the north, above the road, are open slopes leading to a ridge crest. For a description of this area see Lower Loco Pass/ South Peak.

LONE BUTTE MEADOWS

Novice
Round trip 4 miles
Unmarked road
Elevation gain 160 feet total

High point 3280 feet
USGS Lone Butte

Map—page 36

At the west foot of Lone Butte there are a series of meadows and marshes that offer off-road, exploratory skiing for those interested in a short, undemanding tour. From sno-park F ski Road 32 north through forest and past several clearcuts for about 1.5 miles to where the road levels out. Then descend through a screen of trees into the meadows below the road. The road continues north, paralleling the meadows, so enter them wherever you find it convenient. Brushy areas, marshes, and small streams are the only obstacles. This is a tranquil area to enjoy at leisure. The tour is best when there are three feet or more of snow on the ground to cover the brush and marshes completely.

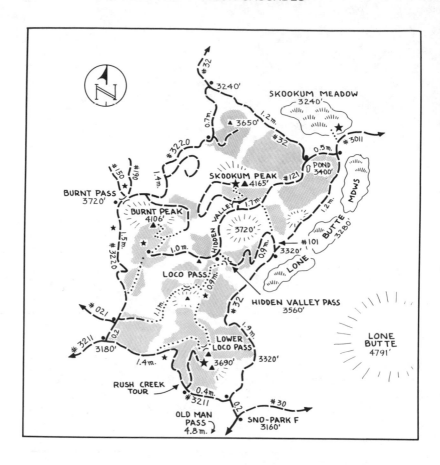

SKOOKUM MEADOW

Intermediate
Round trip 8 miles
Unmarked road
Elevation gain 440 feet cumulative

High point 3320 feet
USGS Lone Butte

Map—page 36

This tour skirts the east foot of the Crazy Hills, an 8-mile round trip offering views, streams, and meadows. From sno-park F ski north on Road 32. This major road offers many views and provides a direct, essentially level route to the meadow once the first mile of gentle up and down is behind you. At 3.0 miles, views open out onto Lone Butte Meadows, a wide valley of streams and marshes. Continuing north, you eventually reach Skookum Meadow as you ski into a wide, open area with many views. *Skookum* is Chinook jargon meaning large, a fitting name for this valley. Skookum Meadow offers a good view of Mt. St. Helens, and from the west end of the meadow the top of Mt. Adams can be seen. For skiers wanting still better views, ski into the open areas above and south of the meadows.

LOWER LOCO PASS/SOUTH PEAK

Intermediate	**High point 3690 feet**
Round trip 3 miles	**USGS Lone Butte**
Unmarked road	**Map—page 36**
Elevation gain 530 feet	

This short tour provides unexcelled views for skiers not interested in the longer loops, or who want to do more than one tour a day. The route follows a moderately climbing road to views of Mt. Hood, Mt. Adams, the Goat Rocks and Mt. St. Helens. From sno-park F ski north on Road 32 for 0.2 mile, then turn left onto Road 3211 following the Rush Creek Tour route. At 0.4 mile from the trailhead you will reach a 200-foot-wide level spot in the road and a large stand of old-growth trees just south of the road. Opposite this spot is an obscure side road heading north into well-established second-growth conifers. Follow this road upward for a 490-foot vertical climb to the two open knobs of South Peak. The northern knob has the best view and is immediately beside and just 80 feet above and south of the pass. From there you have an unobstructed view of Mt. St. Helens, Mt. Adams, and the Goat Rocks, 15 miles north of Adams. The upper part of Mt. Hood also is visible, and the entire Upper Wind River basin is spread out at your feet. Peaks of the Indian Heaven backcountry are seen to either side of the massive, hunchbacked cone of Lone Butte, which dominates the region. To the north, across Lower Loco Pass, are connecting clearcuts leading to Loco and Hidden Valley passes. Beyond is the scalped top of Skookum Peak. This high area of clearcuts lends itself to exploring and there are several ski routes to enjoy.

CRAZY HILLS LOOP

Advanced	**High point 3720 feet**
Round trip 10.8 miles	**USGS Lone Butte**
Unmarked roads	**Map—page 36**
Elevation gain 560 feet cumulative	

Surrounding the Crazy Hills is a 10.8-mile loop road, much of it nearly level, but with several long, gentle hills on the west side, where it crosses Burnt Pass (3720 feet). Roads 32, 3220, and 3211 comprise the loop. The best views are at the north end and from high on the west side, near the pass.

From sno-park F ski Road 32 north to Skookum Meadow, where the easy-to-follow road turns west. Climb slightly to the start of the Hidden Valley route (Road 121), then turn to the right on Road 32 and continue through vast, scenic, logged areas. Here, at the northern end of the loop, is the impressively wide, open valley of the Skookum Meadow-Big Creek basin. Farther west the road passes through attractive forest and rounds the most northern point of the loop. Then, on Road 3220 the route goes south through forest for about 2 miles to Burnt Pass, 7.1 miles from the trailhead. There is a low, clearcut ridge at the pass atop which a short side trip leads to views. From the pass, skiing southward, there is a long downhill run past a good view of Swift Reservoir and the country far to the west. After a 600-foot drop, the road passes the side road to Loco Pass, and from there it is generally level to the trailhead. For skiers not wishing to ski the entire loop, it is only 3.7 miles from sno-park F to Burnt Pass on Roads 3211 and 3220, along the west side of the Crazy Hills—a worthwhile tour in itself.

LOCO PASS LOOP

Intermediate
Round trip 9.7 miles
Unmarked roads and off-trail
Elevation gain 520 feet

High point 3680 feet
USGS Lone Butte

Map—page 36

The Loco Pass Loop is the most scenic tour of the Crazy Hills, offering a great variety of terrain and vistas, crossing two passes, and providing some off-road route-finding. From sno-park F ski north on Road 32 for 3.8 miles past clearcuts and through forest with occasional glimpses eastward of the meandering Lone Butte meadows at the foot of nearby Lone Butte, a prominent volcanic cone and landmark in the area. At the north end of the loop turn left (south) on Road 121, skiing through vast open areas and past a small pond, then gently upward through stands of old-growth timber and past steep hillside clearcuts. This is Hidden Valley, offering a delightful, scenic tour as the road winds gently upward into an ever-narrowing defile.

At the upper (south) end of Hidden Valley, 5.7 miles from the trailhead, the road turns right (west) and climbs into forest. At the turn, leave the road and climb up and to the left to wide, flat Hidden Valley Pass. Then climb to the upper west edge of the clearcut in the pass, where a road enters the forest. Follow the road as it passes through a short forest corridor, and descends to a large clearcut. From there the route climbs open slopes to the broad saddle of Loco Pass (3680 feet), directly above.

Near the north end of Crazy Hills Loop

The road through this large, open area is often totally lost in the covering snow. West of the pass the road generally follows the edge of the forest. After crossing the pass, follow the road downward through another large clearcut to Road 3220, where you turn left to follow it southward as it circles back to the trailhead.

BURNT PEAK

Intermediate
Round trip 9 miles to 14 miles
Unmarked roads and off-trail
Elevation gain 946 feet

High point 4106 feet
USGS Lone Butte

Map—page 36

The 4106-foot summit of Burnt Peak, site of a former lookout, on the west edge of the Crazy Hills, offers panoramic views. It is a road tour to the large clearcut just under the summit, where good views can be enjoyed by those who do not want to go the last steep slopes to the top. There are two routes to the summit of Burnt Peak: the scenic route through Hidden Valley (7.0 miles each way) and the direct route over Hidden Valley Pass (4.5 miles each way). *Direct route:* from sno-park F follow Road 32 north for 2.1 miles to Road 101, an obvious corridor cut in the forest on the left. Climb to a clearcut, but turn left with the road and wind upward around a shoulder to Hidden Valley Pass. Cross the pass and traverse left onto Road 121 and follow it into the forest. Climbing steadily, ski to a large clearcut 1.0 mile from the pass. This clearcut lies directly below the summit. Climb westward for the best views: south across miles of the Upper Wind River forests, east to the Indian Heaven backcountry, and west to the Swift Reservoir and distant ridges and peaks. The summit itself is only a short distance up steep slopes through a silvered forest of old, burned snags. From the small snow dome on the summit an almost unrestricted panorama includes Mt. Adams, Mt. Hood, Mt. St. Helens only eighteen miles away, and Mt. Rainier. *Scenic route:* follow the Loco Pass Loop (which see) to the point on Road 121 just below Hidden Valley Pass. Instead of climbing to the pass, stay on the road, following it west (right) to the summit clearcut, as described above.

SKOOKUM PEAK

Advanced
Round trip 6 to 11 miles
Unmarked roads and off-trail
Elevation gain 1005 feet

High point 4165 feet
USGS Lone Butte

Map—page 36

The ridge-like summit of this 4165-foot peak is the highest point in the Crazy Hills, and clearcutting permits good views to the north and south from the saddle between two highest points. Although the view to the west is blocked, the summit is a worthwhile goal attained by a rugged climb up steep clearcut slopes on the south side.

The most scenic approach is to follow the Loco Pass Loop (which see) into Hidden Valley to a point on Road 121 just below Skookum Peak. Then turn right and climb in a side draw up into a steep clearcut. Traverse the clearcut to the summit ridge. Then ski to the highest point of the saddle for the best view, as scattered trees on the north partially block the view of Mt. St. Helens and Mt. Rainier. In addition to the Goat Rocks, north of Mt. Adams, a number of small, rugged peaks also appear to the north. The view of Mt. Adams is spectacular, and in Indian Heaven several peaks are seen—Sawtooth, Bird Butte, Lemei, and others. Take off your skis and climb to the highest point on the east end of the ridge and look down on Skookum and Lone Butte Meadows. A road connects this high ridge with a clearcut to the west (out of sight), where access to Burnt Peak provides an alternate return route with a lot of adventure.

The most direct route to Skookum Peak is by Roads 32 and 101. Turning left off Road 32 onto Road 101, climb into the clearcut straight ahead and stay on the right (north) side of the creek as you ski toward Skookum Peak, which is straight ahead and easily identified by prominent rock formations near its eastern summit. Cross to the upper end of the clearcut while paralleling the creek, then cross Road 121 to the steep clearcut that leads directly to the top of Skookum Peak. Caution should be exercised in climbing this steep slope as there could be avalanche potential if there is much new snow.

Chapter 3
MT. ST. HELENS

On May 18, 1980 a devastating volcanic explosion destroyed the beautiful symmetry of St. Helens, removing some 1300 feet of the summit, reshaping the mountain in a few moments to a somewhat squat, domelike peak. The incredible blast destroyed miles of roads and leveled 150 square miles of forest. Nordic skiing on the mountain's north side was eliminated due to subsequent closure of large areas for public safety.

Skiing interest was then diverted to the south side of the mountain, which is readily accessible to the Vancouver, Washington/Portland, Oregon metropolitan area. Excellent roads lead to the skiing areas, only 65 miles from the Columbia River bridges at Portland. The most direct route from Portland is via Highway I-5 north to the Woodland/Highway 503 exit (Exit 21), thence east on 503 to the small town of Cougar. From there, drive 6.7 miles east on Road 90, then turn left onto Road 83, which provides access to most of the ski tours.

The south side of Mt. St. Helens offers a variety of unique tours and scenery grouped in two general skiing areas, both accessible from Road 83. These are the Ape Cave–McBride Lake–Goat Marsh area, and the Marble Mountain–Muddy River area. Due to snowline fluctuation the length of the tours can vary considerably. When the snowline is low, some destinations require additional miles of skiing. In general, a snowline of 2500 feet to 3000 feet provides closer access to the more distant points such as Goat Marsh, North Cinnamon Peak, Marble Mountain, and Muddy River.

Sno-parks are maintained near Ape Cave on Road 83, their precise location depending on the snowline. Washington or Oregon sno-park permits are required.

The entire south side of St. Helens outside of the restricted area near the summit is open to snowmobiles. Indeed, some of the trails are even machine groomed. There are no areas closed to off-road vehicles in winter at this time, and the Forest Service has no plans to do so in the future. Consequently, skiers and machines will continue to mix on many of the tours. Although under consideration for the future, there are no marked ski trails on the mountain.

Although most tours in this area are on gentle terrain and grades, rating their skill levels is difficult because of fluctuating snow line. The location of parking areas and trailheads, and thus the length of the tours, depends on the snow line. When the snow line is lower, tours are longer, often thereby pushing their rating into the advanced category even though the terrain may be gentle.

Tours of the Marble Mountain-Muddy River areas offer amazing variety and in general are more open than other areas, with many off-

Mt. St. Helens and steam cloud, as seen from the summit of Marble Mountain. Muddy River is on the right.

road routes available to more experienced skiers. To comfortably ski either Marble Mountain or the Muddy River area, Road 83 should be snow free or plowed for logging. Both areas are excellent for springtime tours. Road 83 has a snow gate at its junction with Road 81 and is generally open only when there is winter logging or in the spring months. To the north of Road 83 are several hilly side valleys, heavily clearcut, beckoning the off-road skier. Surprisingly, there is nothing in Oregon to compare with the extensive logging here, which has created vast, open spaces and sweeping panoramas. The finest tours here are Marble Mountain and the Muddy River outwash plain at the southeast foot of Mt. St.

Helens 7.5 miles from the snow gate.

For up-to-date information on snowline elevation, snow, and road conditions, call the St. Helens Ranger District at Amboy, Washington. An automatic telephone information line is also available.

Heavy snowmobile use on some roads requires alertness. A fast moving snowmobile suddenly whipping around a bend can be dangerous to inattentive skiers. Ski to the sides of roads when machines are about.

With the continuing volcanic activity of the mountain, the Forest Service has established a restricted zone posted with signs. Familiarize yourself with the boundaries of this zone and stay out. Trespassers are subject to a healthy fine. The zone is occasionally patrolled both on land and by air.

The closed zone is established to protect recreational visitors from possible danger from ash, gasses, slides, and other hazards related to the mountain's continuing volcanic activity. Ash on the snow surface can cause several problems for skiers. If you are on waxed skis, you may find gliding impossible. It does not take much ash to seriously slow down or even stop a skier, resulting in major changes in skiing plans. Ash falls are not frequent, however, and usually cover only a portion of the skiing areas, depending on wind direction. If you must take waxable skis with you to Mt. St. Helens, also take waxless skis, which are affected less by ash.

Although most skiing is done on main roads, be alert to the many confusing side roads in the area.

APE CAVE TO NORTH CINNAMON PEAK

Novice to Intermediate
Round trip from Ape Cave 13.2 miles
Unmarked road
Elevation gain 2000 feet
High point 4000 feet

USGS Mount St. Helens,
   Mount St. Helens SW, Cougar NE

Map—page 45

The road above Ape Cave provides many sweeping vistas of the southern part of the state and of Mt. St. Helens, Mt. Adams, and Mt. Hood. For shorter tours there is also open skiing upslope on the lava flows above the cave.

Drive up Road 83 as far as possible, turning left on Road 8303, the side road to the cave area. Ape Cave is 1.1 miles from Road 83. From there the road travels through thick second-growth for about 3.0 miles, where clearcuts open up the tour to impressive views that improve as you ski higher. The road continues to the somewhat steep final open slopes at the summit of the peak. From the summit Goat Peak and Mt. St. Helens dominate the scene, while in the distance Mt. Hood and Mt. Adams appear over countless ridges and blue hills.

McBRIDE LAKE

Novice to Intermediate
Round trip 8.2 miles
Unmarked road
Elevation gain 740 feet
High point 3040 feet

USGS Mount St. Helens,
   Mount St. Helens SW, Cougar NE

Map—page 45

This is one of the finest tours in the area, with numerous roadside open areas, views, and access to backcountry and timberline skiing. The small lake is 4.1 miles from the junction of Roads 81 and 83.

From the sno-parks on Road 83 take Road 81 uphill through thin forest growth, with numerous views of Mt. St. Helens, past a side road leading into the closed zone to the northeast. Continue upward on the gentle grades and cross a flat pass, where off-road skiing is possible. It is 1.3 miles from the pass to the lake. By continuing on Road 81 to Road 8123, you can visit Goat Marsh and the even more distant Sheep Canyon-Toutle River Overlook.

GOAT MARSH

Intermediate
Round trip 12.2 miles or more
Unmarked roads and off-trail
Elevation gain 1230 feet cumulative
High point 3040 feet

USGS Cougar NE,
   Mount St. Helens, Mount St. Helens SW

Map—page 45

Goat Marsh is a most unusual open area. Extending more than a mile from south to north, it contains several shallow lakes and large marshes, and serves as a headwater stream for the Toutle River, which flows to the north. Protected as a Natural Research Area, the marsh has an exotic beauty quite unlike that of any other area described in this guidebook: the irregular shoreline of the lakes, the stands of dark firs that penetrate the flats, the surrounding high, forested ridges, and on the west the imposing, near-vertical Goat Mountain plunging down to the marsh. Stands of ghost trees in the marsh lend an eerie mood, while overall, Mt. St. Helens dominates the entire scene. North of the marsh a ridge road leads to viewpoints, including the Sheep Canyon overlook of the Toutle River valley.

Follow directions for McBride Lake, and ski 0.9 mile beyond the lake to the junction of Roads 81 and 8123. Turn right onto 8123 and ski north 0.5 mile through lodgepole forest to a side road (070) on the left. Descend this primitive road (open to snowmobiles) for 300 yards to a small quarry. Cross the stream bed, turn right, and go uphill into the forest,

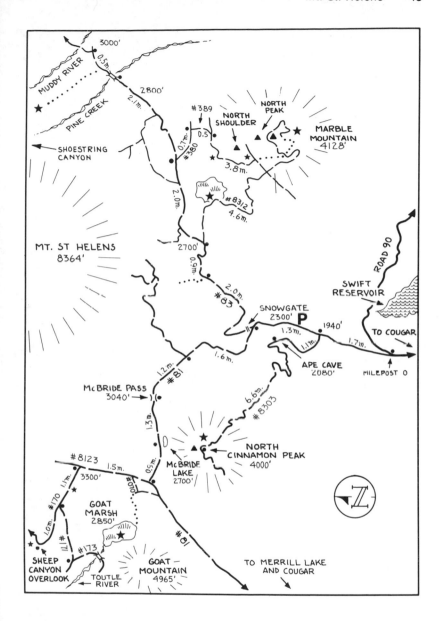

Telemark turns on ash-covered snow of Mt. St. Helens

following a primitive road through lovely forest. The road is soon lost, but continue through the rolling forest for 0.5 mile from the quarry to the edge of the southern lake. A wonderful view of Mt. St. Helens and the marsh greets you here.

If the lake is frozen you are free to explore the extensive marshes and meadows. Along the west shore of the marsh 0.5 mile north are stands of immense noble firs. If the marsh and lakes are not frozen, a ski route around the west shore is possible, but considerable snow depth is required farther along to cover the brush and downed trees.

From the north you can reach the marsh only during deep-snow winters by using Roads 8123, 170, 171, and 173 for access to the bridge on the Toutle River about 0.5 mile north of the meadows. Stay on the west side of the creek for the best skiing.

SHEEP CANYON

Advanced
Round trip from Road 83 17.2 miles
Unmarked roads
Elevation gain 1980 feet cumulative
High point 3600 feet

USGS Mount St. Helens,
   Mount St. Helens SW, Cougar NE

Map—page 45

From the junction of Roads 81 and 8123 (see McBride Lake) ski north on 8123 and in 1.5 miles of gentle climbing reach a Y. Turn left at the fork on Road 170. Ski 0.6 mile to a view of Goat Mountain and the marsh from a logged hillside. Continue 1.5 miles on this road to the Overlook, which is 3.6 miles from the 81/8123 junction. There are views to the west and north of the upper Toutle River valley and nearby clearcut hills and ridges. Beyond the Overlook the road crosses several very steep slopes where further travel is not recommended. At this time the area to the east of the upper part of Road 8123 (beyond Road 170) is a restricted zone, closed to all travel.

MARBLE MOUNTAIN

Advanced
Round trip 10 to 18 miles
Unmarked roads
Elevation gain at least 1228 feet
High point 4128 feet

USGS Mount St. Helens,
   Mount St. Helens SE, Mount St. Helens SW,
   Mount St. Helens NE

Map—page 45

This partly forested, partly clearcut mountain is a major viewpoint on the south side of Mt. St. Helens. Panoramic views await those who follow the gentle roads to the summit. St. Helens, of course, is spectacular, and Mt. Adams, Mt. Rainier, and Mt. Hood are all in view. Vast areas of both forest and clearcuts form a patchwork pattern. Countless ridges, minor peaks, and two major reservoirs all contribute to the exceptional scene.

Because this tour is a long one in times of low snowfall, it is best done during periods of high snow line (2300 feet or higher), when Road 83 is plowed for logging, or in springtime as the snow line recedes. Marble Mountain is an excellent spring tour as most slopes are north-facing, en-

Goat Mountain and the lower slopes of Mt. St. Helens from Marble Mountain

suring deeper and better quality snow later into the spring than in the Ape Cave–McBride Lake areas.

There are two routes to the summit, and they join just beneath it. Your choice will depend on the snow line. If low, the Road 8312 route is shortest, a round trip of 17.6 miles from the 1940-foot level at the junction of Roads 83/8303 (Ape Cave turnoff). If the snow line is higher than, or if Road 83 is plowed beyond Road 8312, the Road 380 route is shortest: only 10 miles round trip from Road 83.

If you determine that the Road 380 route (north side) is best, drive Road 83 as far as possible, with luck as far as Road 380 itself, 6.2 miles from the Ape Cave turnoff. South from Road 380, the highest visible peak is Marble Mountain's north summit, behind which the main one is hidden. The north shoulder is closer yet and below the north peak but not apparent. It is a fine viewpoint for skiers who want a shorter tour.

Located near milepost 8 (from Road 90) Road 380 heads off at an angle to the southeast for 0.7 mile to Road 389, an obscure side road in second-growth, just past a stream with large beaver dams. Road 389 is opposite a large, level clearcut. Follow this road uphill for 0.5 mile to another junction, where you turn right (west). Continue uphill along the winding road crossing mostly open hillsides with many views, which improve as you ski higher.

The other route to the summit—the shortest during low snow line periods—follows Road 8312 from the west. Ski up Road 83 through second-growth to the Road 81/83 junction at 2300 feet, where there is a snow gate that may or may not be closed, depending on conditions and season. Take the right fork, remaining on Road 83, and gently descend 100 feet in 0.5 mile to a gully crossing. Then climb through uninteresting second-growth past milepost 5 at 2450 feet, 1.9 miles beyond the snow gate at the 81/83 junction. Continue for 0.6 mile to a culvert stream crossing, then another 0.4 mile to Road 8312 (milepost 6) at 2700 feet, where there is an obvious, wide Y-junction.

Take the right fork, onto Road 8312. Go downhill, dropping 100 feet in about a half-mile to a creek crossing. Then ski up and around a right turn past a truly beautiful scene—alpine, park-like meadows on Marble Mountain's lower slopes. The area is worth exploring, and there is a permanent log jam for crossing Swift Creek into the splendid meadow area. The road continues climbing a sidehill with many fine views to the east and of Mt. St. Helens. It then winds around onto a steep north-facing hillside, reaching a gentle area at the west foot of the mountain. Pick up the Marble Mountain route here and climb west and southwest slopes to the summit. Or follow a road that sweeps around the north side of the summit near the top then around to the steep east face and circles to the summit. Road 8312 is a regular snowmobile route.

In years of deep snow it might be difficult to find road junctions as you get higher, but this should pose no problem in clear weather as the terrain is open and skiable in all directions. Off-road skiing should be limited to the north and west sides of the mountain as the east slopes are steep. Use your maps to locate the roads higher up. If they are not to be found, climb to the summit by traversing the west and southwest slopes under the highest point.

MUDDY RIVER/SHOESTRING CANYON

Novice to Advanced
Round trip up to 15 miles
Unmarked road and off-road
Elevation gain up to 700 feet
High point at least 3000 feet

USGS Mount St. Helens,
Mount St. Helens NE,
Mount St. Helens SW

Map—page 45

Most skiers will agree that this is the crowning ski touring area of Mt. St. Helens, with distant views and magnificent open areas totally dominated by the towering mass of the often steaming and puffing volcano. Truly a superb area to visit.

The Muddy River outwash plain is 7.5 miles from the junction of Roads 81 and 83. Only advanced skiers should go this far. If Road 83 is plowed or snow free, however, the tour will be shorter. You may even start at the very outwash plain of the Muddy River (3000 feet), the normal starting point for spring tours. Although you can ski in all directions

Skiing one of the canyons formed by mud avalanches during the 1980 Mt. St. Helens eruption. (Photo by Nancy Chapman)

on the river plain, the obvious lure of the mountain leads you uphill along gently inclined flats for almost 3 miles to the restricted zone closure signs. Several shallow but interesting canyons crease the flats, which climb to the very base of the mountain.

The mountain itself is split by the prominent Shoestring Glacier canyon, the upper end of which deeply notches the summit crater rim. This canyon experiences occasional warm-weather, wet-snow avalanches that descend down the canyon far into the ski area. *Stay out of this twenty-foot deep canyon.*

The main touring area of the flats extends across the almost one-mile-wide valley and 3 miles to the closure zone. South of the road there are also large clearcut areas to explore. Mt. Adams, Mt. Hood and Marble Mountain are prominent features along the horizon.

Chapter 4
OTHER TOURS

LARCH MOUNTAIN (Washington)

Intermediate
Round trip 5.6 miles
Unmarked road
Elevation gain 1496 feet

High point 3496 feet
USGS Camas

Map—page 52

Appearing as a complex series of prominent ridges and crests, Larch Mountain and Silver Star Mountain, connected by the Grouse Creek Vista Saddle, are part of an isolated massif only 25 miles northeast of Portland. Larch Mountain offers an outstanding viewpoint for skiers not wishing to attempt the steepness of Silver Star Mountain or just seeking a remarkable view with a minimum of effort. The south view to the Columbia River, up the Columbia Gorge, and over the Portland area is quite exciting on a clear day. The summit is a fine overnight camp spot from which to witness the impressive light show of the large urban area to the southwest. From the I-5 bridge it is 29 miles to the summit and from the I-205 bridge, 22 miles.

From I-5 or I-205 drive east on Washington Highway 14. Take the Camas exit and enter town. Go straight ahead onto 6th Avenue, then uphill to N.E. Garfield, which leads uphill to N.E. Everett. Follow Everett to a right turn, about 2 miles from town, then left onto N.E. 267th Avenue past the airport. At Fern Creek Market turn right onto N.E. 19th Street and drive 0.4 mile, turning left onto 277th Avenue. The road winds around to N.E. 292nd Avenue to a Y-junction. Take the right branch onto N.E. Livingstone Road, which winds upward steeply. At 8.5 miles from Camas the pavement ends (1600 feet), but good gravel continues to the next junction, the Larch Mountain road. This last junction, 2000 feet high and 11.6 miles from Camas, is a good place to park your car as there are no turnarounds above.

From here it is only 2.8 miles to the summit up moderate, then moderately-steep grades, through dense, immature forest, with views only on the last mile. The summit has excellent, tree-protected campsites for winter campers who want to witness the light spectacle of the greater Portland area.

The view from the summit on a clear day encompasses a vast forested area to the south. To the northeast the rugged outline of Silver Star is impressive. Immense denuded areas attest to the Yacolt Burn of 1902, which caused street lights in Olympia, Washington, to be used at midday. Over 100 square miles of forest burned, and over thirty lives were lost.

Because of dense brush and second-growth forest, there are few places

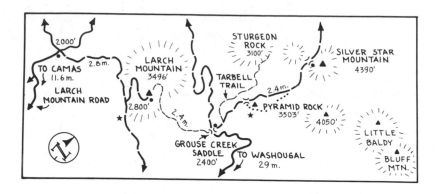

to leave the final summit section of road. There is, however, one side road of note. It branches off the main road at a switchback (2800 feet) only 1.4 miles down from the summit, going southeast for seven miles. The first mile along the steep south slope of Larch Mountain is almost level and offers excellent views. This is a short side trip well worth taking on skis or on foot. From the summit of Larch Mountain there is a 2.4-mile road leading to the Grouse Creek Vista Saddle, but it is difficult to find and follow.

SILVER STAR MOUNTAIN

Advanced above Grouse Creek Saddle,
   Novice to Intermediate below
Round trip 5 miles from saddle
Unmarked road
Elevation gain 1990 feet from saddle

High point 4390 feet
USGS Camas, Bridal Veil

Map—page 52

Silver Star Mountain has absolutely the best view of all the southern Washington summits in this guide, with all the great volcanoes and the Columbia River visible in fair weather. Open areas offer an opportunity to advanced-level skiers for exploratory tours. The Tarbell Trail and roads near Grouse Creek Saddle, a deep pass between Larch and Silver Star mountains, offer tours for less experienced skiers.

Drive Washington Highway 14 east to Washougal, 17 miles east of the I-5 bridge and 9.9 miles east of I-205 bridge across the Columbia River. Driving distance from the I-205 bridge to Grouse Creek Saddle is 29 miles. From Highway 14 enter Washougal at the Highway 140 exit sign. Continue onto 15th Street which changes to 17th Street, which becomes S.E. Washougal River Road. Leave this road and turn left onto N.E. Hughes Road, 6.6 miles from Highway 14. Hughes Road leads to N.E.

New snow and forest shadows

392nd Avenue, which climbs a long hill to a T-junction, where you turn right. In a short distance turn left off Skye Road onto 412th Avenue (Yacolt Recreation Area sign), then drive north to a nearby Y-junction 10 miles from Highway 14. Take the right fork at the Y and from here, at 1000 feet elevation, drive 2.7 miles to a second Y-fork. Go left 5.7 miles to Grouse Creek Saddle.

At the saddle a very steep 2.4-mile road goes west to the summit of Larch Mountain, a climb of 1100 feet. Opposite this road, at the saddle, is another very steep road going almost 3.0 miles to Silver Star summit. At 3100 feet the steep road to Silver Star eases off, as forest is left behind for open hillsides and ridge top meadows with wide views. At the 3400-foot saddle below Pyramid Rock, a prominent minor peak beside the upward road, the easiest and safest route to the summit is to ski along the east side of the ridge you are on. The summit is not the rocky buttress on the left skyline, which appears highest, but the rounded ridge crest straight ahead and east of the buttress.

If the steep roads are intimidating, the Tarbell Trail may be for you. Go up the Silver Star road 180 yards from the saddle to two large firs on the left, where the gentle Tarbell Trail contours for several miles into the basin on the west side of Pyramid Rock.

If the snowline is low and the tour to Grouse Creek Saddle seems too long, an alternative may be the old hiking route to the top of Silver Star. On the road to the saddle, only 2.4 miles beyond the second Y-fork, find a wide place with an old road going west and an obscure one going east. The road to the east is the old route to the top of Silver Star. Either of these roads may offer some skiing.

Due to the area microclimates it is not possible to judge what type of snow you will find. Under some circumstances the upper open slopes may be subject to avalanche danger, and in the mornings the west slopes may be crusty or icy. If so, traverse around the *east* side of Pyramid Rock. Beware of frosty or icy surfaces on the blacktop road, especially in shady areas, while driving to the snow zone.

SIMCOE MOUNTAINS

Intermediate to Advanced
Round trip up to 10 miles
Unmarked roads and off-road
Elevation gain up to 2000 feet
High point 5822 feet

USGS Stagman Butte, Hagerty Butte,
Goldendale

Map—page 55

The Simcoes are a massive, plateau-like Cascade spur rising north of Goldendale, Washington. The top is treeless, offering wide-open skiing and striking vistas of several volcanoes and north to the Yakima Indian Reservation. Some of the gentle, rolling summit area is on reservation land.

The town of Goldendale, 35 miles northeast of The Dalles, Oregon, is the jump-off point for this unusual tour. To reach Goldendale drive to The Dalles, cross the Columbia River and follow Highway 97. A scenic alternative route is to cross the Columbia at Hood River, drive east to Lyle, then north on Highway 142 through Klickitat. High range country, rolling forests, and distant views make this a beautiful drive on paved roads.

If you drive to Goldendale, take Columbus Avenue and drive northwest about 11.5 miles to the end of the maintained road. Continue several

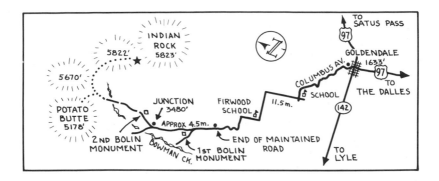

miles past the first Bolin monument as far as snow or road conditions permit. At 3480 feet (Goldendale is 1633 feet) the road forks with both ways leading to the high country. The right fork leads to a cattleman's cabin and a small monument marking the place where agent A.J. Bolin was killed in 1885 by Indian renegades. This fork is the shortest route to the high country, leading to the basin and open slopes southeast of Potato Butte (5178 feet). Numerous logging roads on the approach may lead to some confusion. Be prepared to carry your skis to the snowline.

USGS maps are absolutely necessary to find the most direct route to the best skiing. Trips here have been ruined by not having proper maps, and as this tour is a commitment in time and distance be fully prepared to ensure success. The tops of Potato Butte and point 5670, 1.5 miles east, offer open plateau skiing. This plateau undulates for long distances, inviting exploration. From there several volcanoes are visible, and the impressive east face of Mt. Adams some 35 miles away is especially imposing.

From point 5670, it is about 2 miles southeast to Indian Rock (5823 feet), the highest point of the Simcoes, which is capped by a fifty-foot plug-like rock formation rearing above the snowfield. On the way to Indian Rock, pass point 5822 on its west side to avoid doghair growth. Or drop down to the open lakebeds on the east side for open touring terrain. The best time to ski this area is in early spring, when roads are drier and the snow more consolidated.

The Simcoes may also be approached by starting at Satus Pass, at the east end of the range. From there, follow a primitive road west. Because of long distance, however, this route is best suited to multi-day trips. Dense stands of lodgepole pine in places require map and compass to negotiate.

Southeast side of Mt. Hood from the White River valley

Part II
Mt. Hood
and Vicinity

The inspiring symmetry of Mt. Hood as seen from Portland is that of a classic volcano, possibly the most beautiful of all the Northwest peaks. At 11,239 feet, the mountain is a splendid landmark for Nordic skiers. In winter Hood's eleven glaciers are shrouded in deep snow that smooths out the mountain's upper contours to form a distinctive profile—an eternal guardian of all that lies below.

To reach Mt. Hood from Portland, drive east to Gresham, a suburban town, then follow Highway 26 to the mountain. Many skiers find it convenient to drive east on I-84 to the Wood Village-Gresham exit, about 13 miles from downtown Portland. From here drive south 3 miles to East Burnside Street, a major intersection, where a left turn puts you on Highway 26 to Hood. Government Camp is 55 miles from Portland.

From Salem and the Willamette Valley skiers drive north on I-5 then follow Highway 205 toward the east side of Portland. Some 5 miles north of Oregon City, pick up Highway 212 and drive east through Damascus and Boring, ultimately joining Highway 26 5 miles west of the town of Sandy. Total distance from Salem to Government Camp is about 92 miles, only a few miles more than the drive to ski areas at Santiam Pass.

From the north the town of Hood River on the Columbia River is the only access point to the Mt. Hood region. It is 43 miles by Highway 35 from Hood River to Government Camp, although several fine skiing areas such as Cooper Spur, Pocket Creek and Bennett Pass are passed on the way.

The forested terrain at the mountain's base is gentle, sloping into major valleys on all sides. Fortunately for skiers, the most suitable terrain for skiing is also the most accessible—the west, south and east sides. Surprisingly, in most areas evidence of logging is not troubling and much of the skiing zone between 3500 feet and 6000 feet elevation is covered with attractive forests. On the other hand, in areas such as the Trillium Basin, Lolo Pass and Frog Lake, clearcuts contribute to a sense of openness and freedom. Several lakes and numerous rolling ridges offer viewpoints and variety.

Between the few major creek and river canyons there are miles of forest for skiing, penetrated by logging roads and summer forest trails. Due to the dense forests there is not much off-road skiing except for clearcuts, but the variety, the viewpoints and the meadows more than compensate for this circumstance.

Although the three sides of Hood that skiers frequent are essentially gentle, ridges and valleys break up the terrain into a number of distinctive, separate skiing areas. These are described in separate chapters to follow.

Fortunately, most of these areas are connected to one another by ski routes that are not always marked but are easily skied. The connectors also provide exceptional opportunities to ski longer, more challenging loops, a concept presented in this guidebook as an efficient way to enjoy many areas. Connectors also can be linked together for long-distance trails, the finest example being the Wy'east Trail, extending from west of Government Camp to lower Pocket Creek, a distance of some 20 miles.

The first section covers lowland ski tours, including the Old Maid Flat—Ramona Falls and Rhododendron areas, which several times in a normal winter have sufficient snow for skiing. On the west side, the spectacular Lolo Pass area, remote in mid-winter but easily accessible in spring, offers grand views.

On the south side the Government Camp and Timberline areas, which are treated together, offer several excellent trails for novices together with a variety of challenging routes for experienced skiers. Being the first of the major skiing areas reached by road from Portland, many casual skiers stop here at one of the several sno-parks to enjoy the easy trails.

The next areas east of Government Camp on Highway 26 are Snow Bunny and the Trillium Basin, both popular with novice skiers and close to Government Camp. Both areas have many novice trails, and in the basin there are two scenic ridge routes and numerous loops, short and long, including the scenic Trillium Lake tour. The Salmon River area to the east features unmarked tours on the old pioneer road and a visit to a stand of giant noble firs. South of this area the Frog Lake and Clear Lake areas offer views, lakeshore tours, and miles of gentle, rolling terrain.

Barlow Pass, just east of the Salmon River area, has a wide range of tours, mostly for intermediates. From the pass skiers can climb a ridge to the north or south or ski down a road to Devils Half Acre. Connector trails go north to Barlow Ridge, paralleling Highway 35, and unmarked connectors continue on to White River and to Bennett Pass.

White River, an immensely popular area in good weather, provides scenic views in all directions, being a flat, wide, open river valley, the only such area on Mt. Hood. Bennett Pass, to the north, offers a ridge-top trail, a descending trail to Pocket Creek, and access to the Sahalie Falls Trail and Hood River Meadows. The Bennett Ridge Trail goes east-ward to Gunsight Ridge from where challenging scenic tours go both north and south for miles.

Pocket Creek, just below Bennett Ridge, has many open areas with views. It features a good novice trail as well as connector trails that provide numerous loops in the upper basin adjoining Gunsight and Bennett ridges.

Cooper Spur, on the northeast side of the mountain, and the Brooks Meadow—Lookout Mountain areas, across the deep Hood River valley, offer miles of forest roads to ski and spectacular viewpoints to enjoy. From these areas the land drops rapidly in elevation to the north. The only two lowland tours in this area—Laurance and Lost Lakes—are scenic destinations when the snow is sufficient.

Chapter 5
HOOD LOWLANDS

This group of tours is for skiers who want to try areas that are closer to home. The days following low-elevation snowfall are generally best for these tours, which at other times often lack adequate snow cover. Even then, you may have to gamble on snow depth, not knowing for sure until you are actually there to study the skiing possibilities. In most cases, however, you can, if necessary, easily alter your plans and, with little time lost, head for higher regions.

LARCH MOUNTAIN (Oregon)

Novice to Intermediate	High point 4056 feet
Round trip 8 miles from snow gate	USGS Bridal Veil
Unmarked roads	Map—page 60
Elevation gain 1500 feet	

The summit of Larch Mountain, overlooking the Columbia River Gorge only 30 miles east of Portland, offers outstanding views in many directions. Snowmobiles and low elevation make this trip unpopular for ski touring. But it is near Portland, and under the right conditions can be worthwhile. Most of the skiing is on roads.

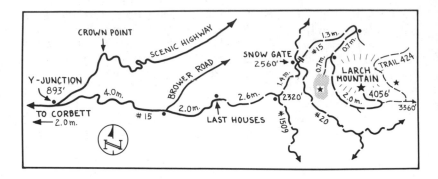

In some years conditions for skiing Larch Mountain are suitable only two or three times during the winter. The road, when snow is low, is normally plowed to the last houses, about eight miles from the summit. The snow line, however, is often above this level. The upper reaches of Larch Mountain have a reputation for being cold and windy so dress appropriately. Although the road to the summit is easy to follow, it is always wise to carry a Forest Service map. Although the only viewpoints are in the clearcut and at the top, do not let this drive you onward in bad weather. This could be a long tour, so turn back if the weather and snow are not what you can handle comfortably.

From Portland drive east on I-84 to either the Lewis and Clark State Park exit or Exit 22 (Corbett). Drive uphill to the small town of Corbett, then east 2 miles to a Y-junction, 893 feet. Turn right at the Y onto the Larch Mountain road. From there it is 14 miles to the end of the road near the summit. A snow gate is located 10 miles up the road and depending on the snow level, skiing may start before or beyond this gate, elevation 2560 feet.

Two miles past the gate, just beyond the 12-mile marker, 3200 feet, a side road to the right descends gently then levels out into a large clearcut—with good views—only 0.7 mile from the main road. Lower Bull Run Reservoir is one of the sights visible far below. From the start of this side road it is only 2 miles uphill to the summit parking lot.

From the snow line the road to the top is a gentle climb, changing to moderate grades in the last mile or so and providing a good return glide. As you climb higher, the snow often becomes lighter and drier, and with recent snowfall the roadside trees can be quite beautiful. The road tour is totally enclosed by forest until the top. If possible, cross by trail 100 yards to the highest point northeast of the road end. In fair weather you can enjoy exceptional, sweeping views of the gorge, Mt. Hood, and the rolling country to the south.

From the sharp bend 0.4 mile below the end of the road, adventurous intermediate skiers can follow summer Trail 424 down moderate grades

The joy of untracked snow

for about 1 mile, then turn left onto Trail 444, which is a most unusual and beautiful level route along an abandoned railroad bed. Although there is only one viewpoint along this trail, the trail itself is picturesque and worthwhile if snow conditions are good. These trails are not marked for skiing.

RAMONA FALLS/OLD MAID FLAT

Old Maid Flat Novice,
 Ramona Falls Intermediate
Round trip up to 12 miles
Unmarked roads and trails
Elevation gain up to 1450 feet

High point, falls 3450 feet
USGS Bull Run Lake

Map—page 63

A beautiful, 100-foot-high waterfall, hidden in a forest grotto, is a prime scenic attraction. When snow depth is adequate, this is a lovely tour through stands of lodgepole pines. If you do not ski to the falls, Old Maid Flat offers miles of almost level skiing through beautiful and unusual stands of stunted trees not unlike those found in tundra areas of the Far North.

From Zigzag on Highway 26 drive 4.2 miles north on the Lolo Pass Road to Road 1828 then 0.6 mile to Road 1825, where you cross a bridge. The snow gate at the bridge may or may not be open, depending on the snow level. Normally, you will park at the gate. From the snow gate it is 3.3 miles to the trail bridge, the road end and summer trailhead at Old Maid Flat.

From the bridge and snow gate follow Road 1825 eastward past several side roads to campgrounds, and Horseshoe Canyon road (see following tour), and ski the road up gentle grades. At 2.1 miles from the snow gate a side road goes left (north) for 0.2 mile to the Ramona Falls trailhead and parking area. Do not follow this side road. Instead, continue straight ahead on the main road for 1.2 miles to its end near the trail bridge across the Sandy River.

Cross the trail bridge, turn right, and continue several hundred feet to a junction. Both trails lead to the falls, but the one on the right is slightly shorter. If you prefer a loop trip, ski the left trail on your return. For now, follow the right hand trail, which climbs moderately along and near the Sandy River. At 1.9 miles beyond the bridge you come to the junction with the Pacific Crest Trail. Turn left and in just over 0.5 mile enter the dense forest enshrouding the beautiful falls.

Return the same way or ski the loop by crossing the creek at the base of the falls and keeping left at the nearby junction. Then follow the trail downhill beside Ramona Creek. Impressive rock cliffs soon appear on the right, and in about 1.5 miles from the falls you leave the stream to enter a stand of lodgepole pines. At the next trail junction turn left and ski 0.5 mile to the trail bridge. Depending on snow depth, creek crossings on the loop trail may present minor problems. Also, be sure to carry a trail map to prevent confusion at trail junctions.

HORSESHOE CANYON

Novice to Intermediate
Round trip 8 to 10 miles
Unmarked roads
Elevation gain 1190 feet

High point 3190 feet
USGS Bull Run Lake

Map—page 63

This is entirely a road tour, climbing steadily to only a few limited viewpoints of the rugged upper canyon. An excellent tour for exercise with a good return glide. If the snow is hard packed or icy, however, the downhill will be dangerous.

Follow road directions for Ramona Falls tour. From the bridge and snow gate ski 0.5 mile and turn right (south) onto Road 382, the Horseshoe Canyon road. After crossing Lost Creek, the road starts to climb, gently at first, then moderately, offering a good gliding return if the snow is right and you have set a good track uphill.

The ascent is unrelieved as the road winds along the east wall of the canyon with the forest dropping steeply to your right. The road is hemmed in by both evergreen and deciduous trees, which effectively block the view.

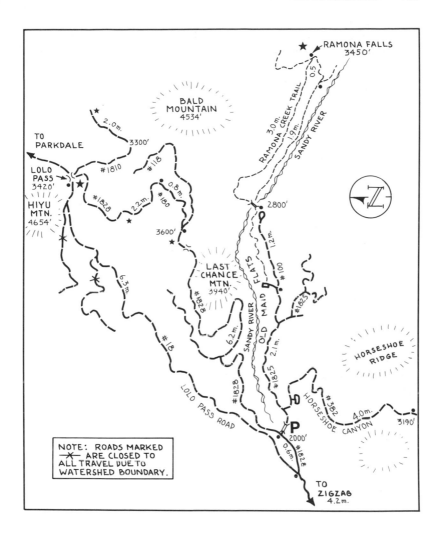

It is about 4 miles from the Old Maid Flat road to the end of this tour, and the last 0.5 mile of the tour, once you have reached the clearcut, is nearly level. The clearcut is an old one, heavily regrown, and not skiable. The road through the clearcut area is almost tunneled by overhanging alder tree limbs, providing an interesting effect, and forming a screen of trunks and branches that limit the view of the rugged upper canyon.

Near the beginning of the clearcut there is a view of the imposing east wall of the canyon—a rampart-like ridge of cliff layers, a wild and impressive scene. Unfortunately, the tour offers only a couple such views and, depending on your skiing values and priorities, the two fleeting views may or may not be sufficient reward for the amount of uphill effort. The long return glide, however, should be a suitable consolation as you are down in what seems just a few moments.

LOLO PASS/LAST CHANCE MOUNTAIN

Intermediate to Advanced	High point 3420 feet or 3600 feet
Round trip up to 16.1 miles	USGS Bull Run Lake
Unmarked roads	
Elevation gain 1420 feet to 1600 feet	Map—page 63

Lolo Pass is 10.5 miles north of Zigzag, which is on Highway 26. From Zigzag take Road 18 to the snowline. There are two basic tours in this area: to the pass and along the nearby roads, and—snow permitting—the Last Chance Mountain tour, a 9.2-mile ski descent from the pass to Old Maid Flat. This latter tour is recommended only in good snow; otherwise, it could be demanding even for strong skiers. The pass area is open, with exciting views of deep valleys and the west face of Hood rising 8000 feet above. Springtime is a good time to ski the area because then the road is drivable to a higher elevation, thereby shortening the approach and permitting more time to explore and enjoy the high country. Because of the profusion of roads, a Forest Service map is essential.

At Lolo Pass ski north only 100 yards or so to get a view of Adams. If you ski Road 1810, dropping southeast and gently down into the north drainage, you will find open areas and a view ridge in 2 miles. The most rewarding road from the pass, however, is the Last Chance Mountain road, 1828, which has many viewpoints. You can ski 3.2 miles from the pass to a high shoulder with an exceptional view to the west and of Hood to the east. From the pass the road drops 200 feet on gentle grades, then climbs to 3700 feet at the shoulder, passing many sweeping vistas to the south, across the many large clearcuts. The first road junction comes at 2.2 miles. Take the left, uphill fork and continue climbing 1.0 mile to the shoulder.

Beyond the shoulder, the road drops to a scenic saddle in 300 yards and from there descends steadily to Old Maid Flats through corridors of fir and alder that effectively block the views for most of the tour. The first 4 miles are downhill, with the grade steadily increasing up to moderately-steep in places. The last 2.0 miles are generally level or rolling to Road 18, the end of your tour. If arranging a shuttle, drive up Road 1828 and leave one car at the snowline to eliminate having to hike when the snow runs out.

From Lolo Pass it is also possible to ski west on the Pacific Crest Trail into the Bull Run watershed, but the route does not offer good skiing and is not recommended. All other roads west are closed to all entry year around to minimize pollution and fire danger in the watershed.

Mt. Hood from the west, with Last Chance Mountain clearcuts below

PIONEER BRIDLE TRAIL

Novice
Round trip up to 8 miles
Unmarked roads and trails
Elevation gain/loss 857 feet
High point 2480 feet

Rhododendron 1623 feet
USGS Government Camp

Map—page 66

The Pioneer Bridle Trail, a little-used summer and ski trail from the village of Rhododendron eastward, offers four miles of skiing. In addition there are many miles of connecting forest roads and power line swaths in the area. Crowded between Highway 26 and Camp Creek, this long, narrow area is best explored from east to west, in a downhill direction. Numerous loops are formed by roads that parallel and cross the Bridle Trail and power line route. Portions of the Bridle Trail are thought to be segments of the historic Barlow Road.

There are numerous roadside parking spots along the four miles of highway east of Rhododendron, where it parallels the nearby Bridle Trail. Many roads leave the highway on each side, providing access to summer homes. Although the roads are not plowed, the roadheads along the highway often are for parking. Furthermore, the half mile of highway before Government Camp has wide shoulders and is always amply plowed for the installation and removal of tire chains. And while the chaining areas themselves are not suitable for parking, a number of the wider spots are. At the east end of the trail it is also possible to park at or near Roads 2639 and 2636.

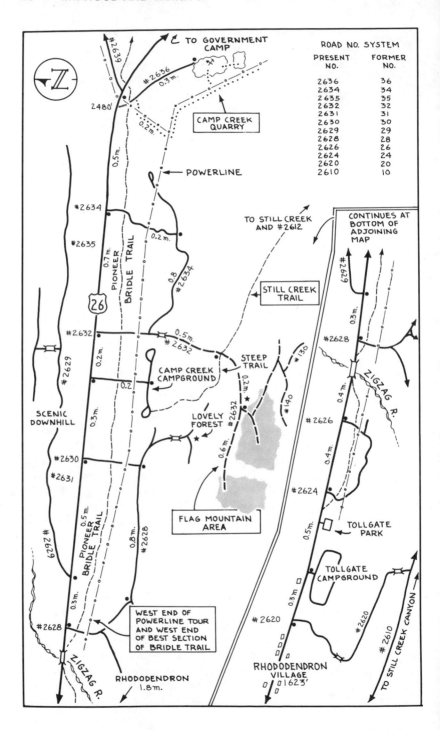

ROAD NO. SYSTEM

PRESENT NO.	FORMER NO.
2636	36
2634	34
2635	35
2632	32
2631	31
2630	30
2629	29
2628	28
2626	26
2624	24
2620	20
2610	10

Located south of Highway 26, the Bridle Trail starts just 100 yards east of Rhododendron and climbs continuously eastward at a gentle grade for 4 miles to Road 2636 opposite the Kiwanis Camp road, 2639. At Road 2636 the Bridle Trail crosses Highway 26 and starts climbing in earnest up Laurel Hill to Glacier View sno-park west of Government Camp. This section is not recommended for skiing because it is generally steep and follows sidehill routes. The last one mile of trail below Glacier View sno-park, however, is an attractive ski route, which is described under the Enid Lake Loop.

From its east end at Road 2636 the trail heads west and downhill, entering and remaining in forest the entire distance, passing first through scrubby trees, then lodgepole pines, and finally grand stands of tall firs, particularly near Camp Creek and Tollgate campgrounds. (The latter sits near where the Barlow Road pioneer toll gate once stood.) At first the trail is wide, obvious and straight, but between Roads 2628 and 2624 it is often obscure, winding and impossible to follow, and in one place, on the highway shoulder. At no time, however, is the trail farther than 80 yards from Highway 26, so getting lost is not a problem. For more solitude explore the power line swath and cross roads.

The Bridle Trail and cross roads, which provide access to many private cabins, are often marred by walkers plunging into the snow. With at least nine inches of packed base or eighteen inches of fresh snow, however, the entire area offers good skiing. Several areas in particular are to be recommended: the roads to both campgrounds—Camp Creek and Tollgate—offer deep forest tours of considerable beauty. The power line right-of-way, varying from a trail to a road in width, provides good skiing, as does the nearby road to the south. For other tours in this area see the Still Creek, Camp Creek Quarry and Flag Mountain tours.

STILL CREEK/FLAG MOUNTAIN TRAILS

Still Creek Trail Intermediate, Flag Mountain Novice	Elevation gain 150 feet High point 2350 feet
Round trip Flag Mountain 2.4 miles, Still Creek Trail 4 miles	USGS Government Camp
Unmarked roads and trails	Map—page 66

Both trails utilize the same access route, but each offers quite a different experience. The Flag Mountain Trail is an easy road tour into large clearcuts with good views of the deep Still Creek valley and its imposing, forested ridges. The Still Creek Trail is an attractive forest tour suitable for novice skiers, but the last part of the trail is a steep descent to the Still Creek road.

Drive 3 miles east of Rhododendron to Road 2632 on the south side of

Highway 26. This side road is generally not plowed and parking is on the highway shoulder.

Still Creek Trail. Ski Road 2632 0.5 mile to the trailhead of the Still Creek Trail, 780, which is on the left (east) side of the road. The trail on the other side of the road descends steeply to the Camp Creek Campground. The easy-to-follow but narrow trail climbs gently to moderately through scenic woods for about a mile. Then, in the last several hundred yards, it descends steeply to Still Creek, with tight turns around stumps and trees. To negotiate this section it may be necessary to remove your skis. Novices should avoid it entirely. All skiers should be aware that less than one foot of snow will result in rock damage to ski bases.

Flag Mountain. From Highway 26 follow Road 2632 to the Still Creek trailhead. To ski the Flag Mountain clearcuts, ski Road 2632 past the trailhead to a fork just 300 yards beyond. Ski either road. The left branch descends into a large clearcut; the right climbs gently to another clearcut near the beginning of the Flag Mountain hiking trail, which is steep and not skiable. The roads and clearcuts in this area offer both variety and views.

CAMP CREEK QUARRY LOOP

Novice	High point 2480 feet
Round trip 2 miles	USGS Government Camp
Unmarked roads and powerline swath	Map—page 66
Elevation loss 50 feet	

This small area is a good one in which to develop route-finding skills as there are a number of side roads and ski routes to explore. The area is nearly level and has a variety of terrain and ski routes not often found on short tours. From Rhododendron town center drive 4.1 miles east to Road 2636 on the south side of the highway. Suitable parking can be found near the trailhead on the highway shoulders. The road passes the abandoned quarry, then branches several times. The left branch travels through alternating open areas and tree-covered lanes, eventually climbing steeply and paralleling the nearby highway before dead-ending at 1.5 miles.

From the highway ski Road 2636 about 90 yards to a power line. Continue another 40 yards to a side road. Turn right here. The side road first winds over to the power line, then follows it 300 yards to another power line. Turn left and ski along the power line to the quarry area. (If you turn right at the power line, you can follow it back to Rhododendron, with several miles of good skiing.) To close the loop turn left at the quarry on Road 2636 and ski 0.4 mile back to the highway. The loop is also easy to follow in the reverse direction.

Just beyond the flat, open area of the quarry, on its south side, a side road leads down to the nearby Camp Creek, passing first under the power line. Skiing in from the highway along the main access road, you will find a side road on the right some 340 yards from the highway. This side road branches several times. One branch parallels the access road and returns toward the highway, offering a more interesting alternative return route.

LAURANCE LAKE

Novice
Round trip from last house 6 miles
Unmarked road
Elevation gain 697 feet

High point 2924 feet
USGS Mount Hood North

Map—page 69

This is a road tour leading to a scenic lake basin with steep rock slides, open slopes and heavy forest. Beyond, there is a tour for hardy skiers to a ridge top with views. From Portland drive I-84 east to exit 64, "Mt. Hood Highway." Drive south on Highway 35 from Hood River for 16 miles to the Parkdale exit. Drive west about 2 miles to Parkdale, a small town in the Upper Hood River Valley. Then drive south on Cooper Spur road almost 3 miles to Road 2840, which leads to the lake.

Drive on Road 2840 to the last house, where snow plowing ends. From there, it is just over 2 easy miles into the steep-walled valley containing the man-made lake. South of the lake, Road 2840 climbs and forks, ultimately leading to the Pinnacle Ridge and Elk Cove trails, which enter the Mt. Hood Wilderness, but which are steep, difficult trails to ski.

The road leading to the lake continues up the valley around the lake and beyond it through logged areas for 1.7 miles, where it turns and steeply climbs the hillside to the north to fine views. The high point is about 4 miles beyond the lake and worth the effort on a good day. If you decide to explore around the lake, on either roads or trails, be sure to take both the Forest Service map, and a topographic map. Neither map, however, shows all the roads. If there is ice on the lake, stay off. Because this is a low elevation lake, the ice may be very dangerous.

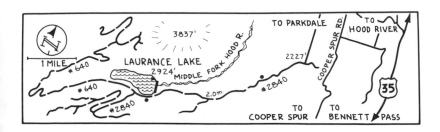

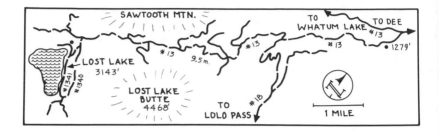

LOST LAKE

Novice to Intermediate
Round trip 12 miles or more
Unmarked road
Elevation gain up to 1800 feet

High point 3143 feet
USGS Tanner Butte, Bull Run Lake

Map—page 70

Lost Lake is the site of the classic postcard scene of Mt. Hood. Follow Laurance Lake driving directions from Hood River, but in about 5 miles exit Highway 35 for Odell, a small town to the west. There, follow signs for Dee as the road winds through orchard country. From Dee, about 7 miles from Odell, follow signs for Lolo Pass and Lost Lake. Drive southwest to Road 13 and follow it to the lake. The road from Dee is plowed to the last house (1270 feet) during low elevation snowfalls. The snow line, however, may be higher, making the tour much shorter than the 9.5 miles to the lake from the last house. Lost Lake is 15 miles from Dee.

The road tour is entirely through forest with few views. Once at the lake, however, you will be rewarded by the splendid scene of the lake nestled between high, forested hills and Mt. Hood rising 8000 feet above to the southeast. For the classic view follow a spur road that goes a short distance west around the north end of the lake. The trail around the lake begins at the road end.

With low elevation snow this could be a long, tiring tour unsuitable for novice skiers even though the road is always gentle in grade. If there is ice on the lake, stay off, for ice is usually thin at this low elevation. Take a road map on this tour as there are numerous junctions. For overnight campers there are two shelters on the east side of the lake, but there is no wood or fireplace in either shelter. The public campgrounds are on the east side of the lake.

Chapter 6
GOVERNMENT CAMP/TIMBERLINE

Government Camp is a small winter-sports-oriented village on the south side of Mt. Hood that serves as the trailhead for many ski tours. Government Camp is particularly popular with novice skiers who are unfamiliar with other parts of Mt. Hood and who find the area convenient in terms of rentals, parking, and a wide selection of trails.

The complex of touring trails at Government Camp has something for all skiers, from easy trails for the first-time novice to fast trails for advanced skiers. The trails offer scenic places to enjoy such as old-growth forest and nearby open areas to explore such as Multorpor Meadows, a peaceful place of frozen ponds, streams and level areas. Challenging trails such as the twisting Barlow Road Trail, the Race Course Loop, and the Alpine Trail Loop will lure advanced skiers. The Enid Lake Loop is one of the loveliest tours when there is adequate snow, and in combination with the Glacier View Loop offers considerable variety. Future plans by the Forest Service include circling Government Camp with a loop trail, the south half of which now exists.

Government Camp serves as the primary access point for the Timberline Lodge area. The Timberline shuttle bus from Government Camp offers a fine opportunity for Nordic skiers who are interested in cross-country downhill skiing. Government Camp also provides access to the northern end of the Trillium Basin (which see) near the Timberline road. Comprising some eight square miles, the basin has 19 miles of snow-covered roads and offers a wide variety of terrain, as well as forests and clearcuts. Since most of this large area is suitable to novice and intermediate skiers it is the prime area of Mt. Hood for future Nordic trail development. It is hoped that the future will see the basin set aside for quiet users, with the introduction of trails and huts to complete what could be a unique Nordic skiing experience.

MIRROR LAKE

Advanced
Round trip 3 miles
Unmarked trail
Elevation gain 700 feet

High point 4120 feet
USGS Government Camp

Map—page 73

Nestled in a scenic alpine basin, Mirror Lake offers a fine view of Mt. Hood and serves as a starting point for high country tours on Tom Dick and Harry Mountain. The parking area and trailhead is 0.8 mile west of the Ski Bowl and Glacier View sno-parks. Cross a foot bridge to the trail, which climbs at a moderately steep grade to the lake. The trail crosses a rock slide with views twice and has five switchbacks. Since the trail is popular with winter campers and day hikers, usually traveling on foot or on snowshoes, it is likely to be roughed up, rutted, and packed—not ideal for Nordic skiing. The trail is especially difficult to descend.

The lake lies in a shallow basin opening toward Mt. Hood, a spectacular setting. For the advanced skier the towering Tom Dick Ridge rising over 900 feet above is a challenge. It is also possible to climb and contour east to the Upper Bowl ski area, a rugged trip for experienced off-trail skiers only! This wide-open bowl is dangerous due to avalanche potential in its upper reaches.

ENID LAKE AND GLACIER VIEW LOOPS

Novice to Advanced
Round trip Enid Lake Loop 1.5 miles,
   Glacier View Loop 2.5 miles
Marked roads and trails
Elevation gain/loss 50 feet/200 feet

High point 3700 feet
USGS Government Camp

Map—page 73

There are three loops here that may be skied independently or together, as they join to form figure-eights. These loops offer something to every skier—uphill, downhill, open forest, a scenic lake and views of Mt. Hood. There is both road and trail skiing here to please any skill level. Several side tours provide some challenges and additional distance. Ski trails off the Glacier View require two feet of snow to be safely covered. Less snow and the skiing will be very rough.

Enid Lake Loop. Enid Lake affords a lovely view of Mt. Hood. The variety of skiing and the old-growth forest will delight all skiers. The Enid Lake Loop will certainly tax all the skills of novice skiers, even those who have been on skis several times. This is not a good loop for first-time skiers due to the numerous dips and irregularities in the terrain.

From the Glacier View sno-park, ski along the snow-covered road about 200 yards (just beyond the third power pole) then turn right and enter the tall timber. Just 200 yards more of skiing brings you to the lake. With some luck, evidence of beaver and other wildlife may be seen here. Wood duck nesting boxes have been placed by the Forest Service on several lake shore trees.

The trail passes along the south side of the lake, climbing gently eastward through forest and eventually turning and crossing a summer marsh. Then it heads back into the forest, descending through beautiful trees to where it meets the Pioneer Bridle Trail, from Rhododendron, which forms part of the Glacier View Loop.

To complete the Enid Lake Loop turn left at this trail junction, climb a winding, moderate, uphill grade and return to the trailhead. Because of

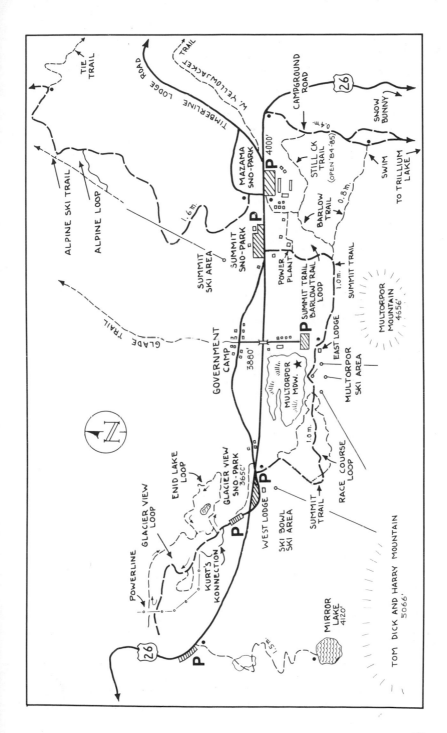

73

the hill this loop is best skied in a counter-clockwise direction.

Glacier View Loop. This is a gentle downhill road tour, with an uphill return on the Pioneer Bridle Trail through lovely forest. Three side road tours are also possible for the adventurous skier.

From the Glacier View sno-park follow the snow-covered road as it winds downhill past a good view of Mt. Hood. The end of this abandoned section of former highway eventually joins the present highway to Government Camp after a 200-foot elevation drop from the trailhead.

About 250 yards from the lower end of the road a power line crosses the ski route you are on. Fifty yards prior to the power line, an obscure trail on your right (north) enters the trees. Descend this tricky 80-yard trail to the Bridle Trail. Turn right and ski east following this lovely trail uphill. You will eventually reach the junction with the Enid Lake Loop on your left 0.7 mile from the power line crossing. To complete the loop, proceed straight and up the winding hill to the road and the trailhead. You will not see it, but at the top of the hill is the site of the pioneer Barlow Road as it headed to nearby Laurel Hill, where the wagons were lowered with ropes as they dragged tree trunks to brake their descent. If you wish to extend your skiing distance turn left at the Enid Lake Loop trailhead and ski into the lake then follow the loop trail in a counter-clockwise direction.

Kurt's Konnection. This trail forms a 1-mile loop, starting just beyond the Glacier View sno-park. It turns left off the snow-covered road, entering the forest and paralleling the present highway not far to the south. The loop is almost level and offers no real hazards, though when icy the first 100 yards are very fast and will get your adrenalin going if you are not used to sudden surprises while skiing. The only hill on the loop is a short climb back onto the Glacier View road. This scenic loop is suitable for first-time skiers.

At this time, this trail is the only example on Hood of an area that was purposefully logged to construct a skiing route. It is hoped that there will in the future be more of this foresighted timber harvest planning to provide a few well planned, safe trails to serve as interesting alternatives to road skiing and as connectors to encourage skier dispersement.

Powerline Connector. Just 500 yards down from the Glacier View trailhead the power line leaves the road and goes left. It offers an alternative route to the end of the Glacier View road, from where either the road or the Bridle Trail will complete a return loop.

Where the power line leaves the road, descend an 80-yard moderately steep road under the overhead lines and follow the poles and lines along the generally level terrain for several hundred yards to the lower end of the Glacier View road.

The last 100 yards of the power line route to the road are moderately steep and cause this otherwise easy tour to be rated advanced. This section could be difficult, depending on snow conditions, due to steepness. If difficult, walk down or return along the power line. From the junction with the road turn right for 50 yards, then turn left (north) to the Bridle Trail for the return to the trailhead.

Campground Loop. One hundred yards down the road from the Powerline Connector is a side road leading to the left. This is an abandoned campground road about 400 yards long that goes downhill then climbs back up to the main road only 100 yards from where it started down. Though not particularly interesting, it can be skied.

Historical Note. The Barlow Road of pioneer days, now only a trail in this area, crosses the Glacier View ski routes in two places. It is recommended that you visit this area in summer to explore the old road. Then it may be seen near the top of the hill on the last part of the Enid Lake Loop and can be followed to where it joins the Glacier View road. It also crosses the steep hillside portion of the Powerline Connector just above the Glacier View road. In both places it is only a trail, as it has not been cleared or maintained.

SUMMIT TRAIL/MULTORPOR MEADOWS

Novice	High point 4000 feet
Round trip 4 miles	USGS Government Camp
Marked road	
Elevation gain/loss 320 feet	Map—page 73

This is the perfect introductory tour for novices as the trail is generally level, has views, gentle hills, forest, and an opportunity to visit beautiful Multorpor Meadows.

The west end of this trail begins at the east end of the Ski Bowl sno-park, where a wide snow-covered road leads to the Multorpor Ski Area 1 mile away. The trail is a road tour all the way, and occasionally ski area snow vehicles are met along the way. At the Multorpor Ski Area the trail follows a service road at the edge of Multorpor Meadows and just behind the various ski lifts and buildings.

For a pleasant side trip ski into and explore Multorpor Meadows. Although adjacent to a major ski area the chairlift operations do not seem to intrude on the quiet of the meadows. Several streams meander through the meadows, and there are several beaver dams and ponds. About three feet of snow are necessary for stream crossings. The meadow is effectively screened on most sides by fringes of forest, and even Highway 26 at the north edge is not noticed.

From the East Lodge (Multorpor Day Lodge) the trail continues as a road into tall trees and climbs slightly, then levels out and winds toward Highway 26, ending at the Mazama sno-park just after passing the Government Camp auxilliary power plant, a square metal structure. At the plant the trail cuts off to the east and passes several Forest Service buildings and cabins to where the Barlow Trail starts into the Trillium Basin.

Both the Summit and Mazama sno-parks give access to the east end of the Summit Trail.

Barlow Trail-Summit Trail Loop. This 1-mile loop combines part of the Summit Trail with the first part of the Barlow Trail, offering an interesting variation and serving as a challenging loop on which novices can practice downhill skills. Actually, this loop should be rated intermediate, but novices have to push their ability, and this is a good place to do it. Some knowledge of edging and snowplowing is helpful here. For maximum downhill skiing, start from the trailhead for the Barlow Trail near the Forest Service buildings just west of the Mazama sno-park. That way there are a number of gentle hills, and some not so gentle, but all are short and provide excellent practice.

The forest along the Barlow Trail is beautiful old-growth timber. Where the trail turns east, starting down to the Trillium Basin, there is a short connector trail heading right and leading directly up a short hill to the Summit Trail, on which you turn right to close the loop.

The only hazard is the mixing of fast skiers with novices on the Barlow Trail. Remember, uphill skiers should always give way to downhill skiers, and faster skiers have the right of way to pass slower skiers, who should yield the trail. Be a courteous skier and yield by stepping aside and clearing the trail.

RACE COURSE LOOP

Intermediate
Round trip 1.8 miles
Unmarked trail
Elevation gain 200 feet
High point 3850 feet
USGS Government Camp

Map—page 73

This loop, formerly used by local race teams, is a challenging trail starting near the Ski Bowl Ski Area and offering every type of terrain. It extends to Multorpor Meadows, first on one side of the Summit Trail road (here called the "Transit Mall"), and then on the other side on the return leg. It is a quite demanding course.

A challenge to aggressive skiers, the loop is an excellent practice trail where intermediates can test and improve their skills. The trail has some difficult moves and is bound to thrill and challenge every skier, particularly the upper half of the loop above (south) of the Transit Mall. This half of the loop, named "Tom's Troublemaker," is well named as it has a number of difficult dips, short twisting hills, and tough turns. This part of the loop is designed for advanced intermediate or advanced skiers.

Otter tracks in Multorpor Meadows

The loop is most directly approached from the east end of the Ski Bowl sno-park, where a snow-covered road (the Summit Trail or Transit Mall) leads south to Multorpor Ski Area. At the end of the first long curve to the left you will see below you on the left an embankment and a small bridge. The Race Course Loop exits here from the trees onto the road you are skiing on, then turns left and goes uphill on your road. Do not enter this side trail as it is the wrong way (the loop is skied in a counter-clockwise direction).

Continue on the road as you are now on the west leg of the loop, which is the easiest. Follow it to where it emerges at the edge of the Ski Bowl Ski Area before turning left into the woods. The Race Course Loop leaves the road here for only a few yards then crosses it, re-entering the forest and becoming the south leg of the loop—Tom's Troublemaker. This most difficult and challenging part of the loop honors the many years that Tom Gibbons (Cascade Ski Club, Oregon Nordic Club, Mazamas) unselfishly devoted to the coaching of young cross-country ski racers. This race course was in large part built by Tom and his racers and was for years his team's training track.

The narrow forest trail then roughly parallels the Transit Mall as it climbs and drops suddenly, turns and dips, and finally again crosses the road near Multorpor Meadows. It then turns left (west) and continues in the trees with a number of short but exciting downhills and a few sharp, fast turns before crossing two bridges and climbing the embankment to the road, not far from the sno-park trailhead. This north leg of the loop is fun yet challenging to the intermediate skier. Called the "Tender Trap," it has sudden surprises that give a few thrills to even the best skier.

Inexperienced skiers often get onto the Race Course Loop, so if you are skiing fast be careful of other skiers ahead of you. If you are a slow, cautious skier, yield the right of way to faster skiers by getting out of their way to the side of the trail. The downhill skier has the right-of-way, and faster skiers should be permitted to pass. It is safer and more fun to ski the loop counter-clockwise. Be prepared for falls and be sure to fill your "sitz-marks," the holes made by your falling body.

WEST LEG ROAD

Intermediate
Round trip 10.6 miles
Marked road
Elevation gain 1950 feet

Highest point 5950 feet
USGS Mount Hood South

Map—pages 73, 79

The "West Leg" is a long uphill tour starting at Government Camp and following a former highway to Timberline. Good exercise, views at the upper end, and a long downhill run are your rewards. This is a good tour

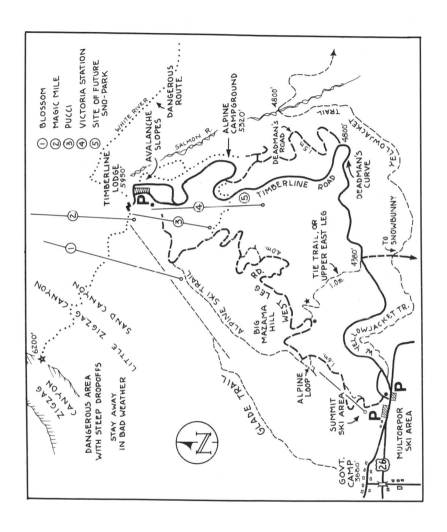

BLOSSOM
MAGIC MILE
PUCCI
VICTORIA STATION
SITE OF FUTURE SNO-PARK

AVALANCHE SLOPES
DANGEROUS ROUTE

WHITE RIVER
SALMON R.

TIMBERLINE LODGE 5950'

ALPINE CAMPGROUND 5320'

DEADMAN'S ROAD
TIMBERLINE ROAD
DEADMAN'S CURVE
4800'
4800'

YELLOWJACKET TRAIL
TO SNOWBUNNY
4580'

TIE TRAIL OR UPPER EAST LEG
1.0 m.

4.0 m.

ALPINE SKI TRAIL

RD.
WEST LEG
BIG MAZAMA HILL

YELLOWJACKET TR.

6200'
ZIGZAG CANYON
LITTLE ZIGZAG CANYON
SAND CANYON

DANGEROUS AREA WITH STEEP DROPOFFS
STAY AWAY IN BAD WEATHER

GLADE TRAIL

ALPINE LOOP
.6 m.

SUMMIT SKI AREA
P
P
MULTORPOR SKI AREA

GOVT. CAMP 3880'
26

N

79

for a car shuttle to get you uphill the easy way. Or use the Timberline shuttle bus.

Starting from the Mazama sno-park opposite the Timberline road, cross the highway to the north side and walk up a narrow plowed road 100 yards west of the Timberline junction. Follow this side road 50 yards then climb the snowbank on the left onto a snow-covered road. This is the West Leg road (Road 2645). If the Mazama sno-park is full, park at the Summit sno-park, just 200 yards west, and gain the West Leg by climbing up through the ski area.

As you ski upward the road winds and turns through the Summit Ski Area, and in one place a bypass trail off the right side of the road allows you to avoid the hardpacked ski runs that follow and cross the road in several places. At 1.6 miles from and 600 feet above the Mazama sno-park the East Leg road (here called Tie Trail) joins from the right at an obvious switchback. Just below here and a short distance out on the Tie Trail are several good viewpoints. Otherwise the West Leg tour is almost entirely enclosed by forest.

About a mile below the bottom of the Pucci chairlift there is a side road, at a powerline crossing, that leads to a short, primitive road bypassing a curve of the West Leg road. This bypass-road is moderately steep and is an interesting alternative route for intermediate skiers.

A short distance below Timberline the West Leg crosses chairlift runs so be alert to fast-moving skiers. Careless, inattentive Nordic skiers in this area can easily become involved in serious collisions. To avoid the most congested areas leave the West Leg just above the last switchback, about 0.5 mile from the lodge, and ski upward to join the upper Glade Trail, which leads to the lodge. With the Blossom chairlift operating near this area it is almost impossible, however, to avoid meeting downhill skiers streaking by. To further complicate the tour, you will find that the alpine ski runs are often hardpacked and difficult to ski, particularly downhill.

If you wish to start your tour at Timberline, you can for a fee take the Timberline Lodge shuttle bus from Government Camp. It runs on a regular schedule and loads at the Huckleberry Inn. For those interested in concentrated doses of downhill running and practicing turning skills, using this bus or a car shuttle is an excellent way to ski many downhill miles in a day, especially when the snow is good. See Alpine and Glade trails for other downhill ski routes.

If you have never skied up the West Leg you will discover that finding the snow-covered upper end of the road is not easy. There are two access points to the West Leg from Timberline. The recommended approach is to ski west from the lodge, first above Pucci Chairlift (the one nearest the lodge) then, climbing slightly, under the Magic Mile chairlift. Continue west for another 200 yards to a 100-yard wide clearing, which is the top of the Glade Trail to Government Camp. The Glade Trail, descending in a southwest direction, is steeper than the West Leg. Most Nordic skiers prefer the West Leg because the Glade Trail requires strong turning and edging skills. Descend the Glade Trail about 400 yards to a 20-foot pole. Signs in the center of the trail indicate that a connector trail to the West Leg angles left. Follow the blue trail markers to the West Leg road, just above the last switchback.

The other approach to the West Leg from Timberline Lodge is to walk or ski to the lower end of the main parking lot and then to just below the unloading ramp of the Victoria Station chairlift. Below here the snow-covered road descends under the chairlift in a southwest direction at a 45° angle to the chairlift line. After skiing 100 yards it is easy to see the road-bed, but be alert to fast-moving downhill skiers and yield the right of way to them. This is their turf. You are the intruder so be considerate. Once you have located the road, the quickest way to join it in the future is to descend the steep snow bank immediately opposite the lodge and ski down the rope tow hill.

If snow is hard packed or icy, descent of the West Leg can be frightening for a novice or even an intermediate skier. Remember that some of the downhill skiers are not in full control and may not be able to avoid you. Be careful.

ALPINE SKI TRAIL

Advanced
Distance one way 3 miles
Unmarked trail
Elevation loss 1950 feet

High point 5950 feet
USGS Mount Hood South

Map—pages 73, 79

The Alpine Ski Trail connects Timberline Lodge with the Summit Ski Area just east of Government Camp along a very direct and fast descent route formerly used by many downhill skiers. Only the most rugged Nordic skier uses this trail today, but with the growing interest in cross-country downhill it will see more use. The trail is only for skiers who have advanced turning skills and who are used to off-road skiing. It is fun only when the snow is easy to turn in.

If you are planning to ski this trail uphill follow directions for the West Leg road tour and ski 1.3 miles up the West Leg, turn left onto the Alpine Trail where a small sign points to the trail, only 50 feet to the left through a narrow opening in the trees. Follow the trail uphill to the nearby base of Big Mazama Hill (open slopes) and climb the hill to the top left corner.

Continue up the ridge along the trail, where red markers appear infrequently. Ski up Corkscrew Canyon, a tight, narrow gully, above which you curve up and right for several hundred feet to end at the bottom of the Blossom chairlift. The lower terminus of the lift is located just 100 yards west of a sharp switchback about 0.5 mile below Timberline Lodge.

If you are skiing down from Timberline, ski to this obvious switchback (see West Leg), then down and west through open areas into a wide, open clearing at the lower end of the Blossom chairlift. Below the chairlift there is an open area beside a gully. The open area is marked with a large orange-painted sign marking the start of the Alpine Trail.

ALPINE LOOP

Novice
Round trip 2.6 miles
Marked trail
Elevation gain 400 feet

High point 4400 feet
USGS Mount Hood South

Map—pages 73, 79

This short, pleasant loop has been greatly shortened by installation of the Summit Ski Area chairlift. The loop provides an interesting goal for short-distance skiers and a nice change of pace from the uniformity of the West Leg Tour. The loop itself is only 0.5 mile long.

Follow directions for the West Leg tour and Alpine Ski Trail. Once on the Alpine Ski Trail ski downhill on the west leg of the loop to a side trail heading left just above the top of the Summit chairlift. Follow the side trail as it immediately turns uphill and winds gently for 300 yards to the West Leg road. This portion of the loop is a narrow, twisting trail through the woods, passing a marshy slide alder clearing. The loop is scenic and worthy of your attention.

If you are coming down the West Leg from Timberline you may find the west portion of the loop a pleasant alternative route for your return to the Summit area or Mazama sno-park. From the top of the chairlift you may either descend the alpine ski runs to Summit or bear left to regain the West Leg.

GLADE TRAIL

Intermediate
Distance one way 4 miles
Unmarked trail
Elevation loss 1150 feet

High point 5950 feet
USGS Mount Hood South

Map—pages 73, 79

The Glade Trail descends from Timberline Lodge to Government Camp in a most direct manner. It is rarely used in the uphill direction, but will see more cross-country downhill in the future with growing interest in that sport. The Glade Trail demands good turning and edging ability, skills that many Nordic skiers do not have. The less-steep West Leg road seems to be preferred by most skiers. The Glade Trail offers many fine views on the descent. You may have the sensation on the upper Glade of being suspended far above the country below—an interesting experience.

See West Leg road tour for directions to the upper end of Glade Trail. Once on the wide swath of the trail it is hard to stray off. The terrain is irregular, and the trail drops relentlessly, demanding skill and strong legs. For a way the trail follows the wide, former route of the ill-fated Timberline Tramway of 1950. An overhead cable suspended from many towers carried a city bus body with its own cable-climbing propulsion motor. The tram failed to operate properly and was soon a financial failure.

The trail leaves the tramway swath to enter the forest on the right, following a narrower trail to Government Camp, where it comes out onto the main street opposite the road to the Multorpor sno-park. Not far away is the Huckleberry Inn, where you can catch the Timberline shuttle bus for another ride up.

The upper Glade Trail, to the bottom of the Blossom chairlift (5480 feet), is heavily used by alpine skiers, resulting in a hard-packed surface. Snow is often a problem on this trail. It is seldom smoothly packed, and is often rutted. Due to elevation differential from top to bottom, the snow is often not consistent. On those days when it is cold at Government Camp and there is a mantle of fresh snow, the Glade is a great run. If hard-packed or icy do not attempt this trail. If the upper part is bad, the lower part may not get better, so head down and to your left to West Leg road for a safer, more enjoyable descent.

TIMBERLINE LODGE AREA

Novice to Intermediate	High point 620 feet
Round trip up to 4 miles	USGS Mount Hood South
Unmarked routes	
Elevation gain up to 250 feet	Map—page 79

Timberline is a popular area to ski because of its varied terrain, its beautiful frosted and snow-sculpted trees, and its remarkable panoramic view to the south of Trillium Lake, Mt. Jefferson, and many minor Cascade peaks and ridges. Because there is almost no level skiing terrain here, Timberline is not suitable for first-time Novice skiers.

The Timberline area has a number of unique hazards. In poor weather it is easy to become disoriented as there are no landmarks in the forest below and it is easy to ski out of the area without realizing it. The ravines and canyons have great potential for danger in poor visibility, when it would be easy to ski right off the edge into one. Finally, be careful of alpine skiers. Stay off their runs if possible, and if not, cross rapidly.

Zigzag Canyon. The area west of the lodge attracts many skiers by its varied slopes and the beauty of its scattered islands of subalpine trees.

Timberline Lodge

Most of the skiing is up and down over challenging terrain. From the lodge ski west, climbing slightly through the ski area, then under the Magic Mile chairlift and past the top of Glade Trail. Then ski up open slopes into scattered trees and across rolling terrain through the Blossom chairlift ski runs. Cross Sand Canyon, hardly noticeable, then Little Zigzag Canyon, which is about fifty feet deep. Continue to the edge of Zigzag Canyon, which is over 400 feet deep. Do not enter this canyon because it is often a dangerous avalanche area.

The Blossom chairlift, the farthest from the lodge, was constructed in 1981 and has changed Nordic skiing patterns in the area. What was once exclusive Nordic terrain is now criss-crossed by packed alpine runs. Be careful of the downhill skiers and cross the runs as fast as possible. If you must climb through this area, stay to the side of the runs.

White River Canyon. The area east of the lodge is not heavily skied due to the difficulty of the terrain and should be attempted only by intermediate or advanced skiers. Climb behind the lodge then cross a very steep ravine to the east. This is the headwaters of the Salmon River, and it is often dangerous due to avalanche potential. Beware of this steep, deep ravine during or immediately after heavy snowfall. Wind-blown snow piles up in deep unstable drifts at the edge of this and other ravines, making them dangerous for two days or more after storms.

Several hundred yards east of the Salmon River ravine is the White River canyon, which has precipitous side walls and is almost always corniced with over-hanging snow. This canyon is over 400 feet deep and is always dangerous regardless of snow or weather. *Do not go near the edge!*

Above Timberline Lodge. Vast open slopes above the lodge stretch for almost two miles across the south slopes of Mt. Hood. They are particularly suitable for spring skiing, when the snow is consolidated and the weather is more stable. This south slope is cut by two long chairlifts, and the great open slopes on each side have their own unique views. If you ski there, select a warm, sunny day to best enjoy the wonderful views of the deep valleys, ridges and six major Oregon volcanoes. To the east are the deserts and high country of eastern Oregon, and to the west seemingly endless forested ridges. The descent can be made with long traverses back and forth to extend the tour and savor the experience to its fullest.

Below Timberline Lodge. Cross-country downhill skiing has enjoyed growing popularity since the late 1970s when the sport gained impetus in the Rockies, with Telemark racing and chairlift skiing in free-heel equipment. This "new" sport is taking hold on Hood, and a popular way to practice it is to ride the Summit Ski Area or Timberline chairlifts or to ride the Timberline shuttle bus and ski down the Glade Trail. The bus is often filled with Nordic skiers on days of good snow. Multorpor Ski Bowl also has suitable slopes for this type of skiing, where moderate grades are best. To enjoy this sport to the maximum, however, heavier boots, and wider, edged skis should be used.

Historical Note. Timberline Lodge, located at the upper forest limit, was dedicated by President Franklin Roosevelt in 1937. The structure of the lodge is like no other in America. Every massive beam, every stick of furniture, every rug and painting and door and doorknob was fashioned by human hands. Like Mt. Hood it is a priceless asset to all of us who enjoy the mountain sports of the area.

DEADMAN'S CURVE/ALPINE CAMPGROUND

Intermediate	**High point 5950 feet**
Round trip up to 3 miles	**USGS Mount Hood South**
Unmarked roads and off-trail	**Map—page 79**
Elevation loss up to 1150 feet	

There are several ski tours in the upper Alpine Campground–Deadman's Curve areas that offer opportunities for exploring. The area has both second-growth and old-growth forests, views, and a variety of terrain. Due to the presence of two chairlifts and the lack of convenient connecting trails at this time these tours are not neat little packages, as most tours are, and will therefore require some experimentation.

A sno-park is planned for this area, but until it is constructed this area is best reached by descending the West Leg road to the bottom of the Pucci chairlift, then skiing east across the nearby runs of the Victoria Station chairlift to the Timberline road, crossing two low ridges en route. Across the Timberline road, ski through open timber to Deadman's road or to the Alpine Campground area, depending on your skiing plans.

From either of these areas you may ski upward through open forest and meadows to the east of the Timberline road and then to the edge of the Salmon River Canyon. The edge of the canyon and the very steep slopes east of and leading up to the lodge area must be skied with care. During and after heavy snowfall, these steep slopes should be avoided due to avalanche danger. Early morning sunshine hitting these slopes on a warm day can be very dangerous.

A 1.5-mile abandoned road, the Deadman's Curve Trail, winds consistently uphill from Deadman's Curve to the Alpine Campground, passing through fine stands of old-growth timber. It is a peaceful, beautiful area. Numerous off-trail ski routes are possible, all of them uphill and downhill, in the Alpine Campground area. One runs near the lower edge of Timberline road as it curves below the campground, then along the east side of the road, climbing north through scenic, open stands of firs to the east side of Timberline Lodge. It is also possible to ski through the campground area within the curve of the road, crossing the Timberline road to either Deadman's Curve road or the spur logging road to the east. This road, the site of future logging, swings north, almost touching the campground area. You can ski short, easy loops through the old growth of this area. The possibilities are limited only by your imagination. Be aware that crossing the Timberline road requires caution due to traffic, and in winters of deep snow, the snow banks may be difficult to climb.

TIMBERLINE LODGE TO WHITE RIVER TOUR

Advanced	**High point 5950 feet**
Distance one way 3.5 miles	**USGS Mount Hood South**
Unmarked off-trail route	
Elevation loss 1727 feet	**Map—pages 79, 156**

This is an exciting, long descent to White River and Highway 35, requiring wilderness skiing skills. It is all downhill except for the first 400 yards.

Do not attempt this tour except in good weather with good visibility. If snowfall has occurred a day or two prior to your trip, avalanche potential is high. In fog or snowstorm it would be easy to become disoriented, even with map and compass. In poor visibility to use the canyon edge as a guide would be dangerous. For the first mile or more the canyon is often corniced and abrupt. Do not ski near the edge in any weather or conditions. If a cornice were to break off the drop is steep and distant. This canyon wall is a dangerous avalanche slope much of the winter. Stay clear of it.

From the northeast corner of the main parking lot at Timberline Lodge, cross the road and ski northward past the former maintenance building (usually buried under snow), climbing gently for about 300 yards to a very steep gully. Cross this potentially dangerous gully and head southeast, contouring to another similar gully which also must be crossed. Continue to near the edge of the White River canyon, which is perhaps 700 yards from your starting point.

Follow the crest of a ridge downhill, keeping the White River Canyon on your left. There are a few trees on this ridge, and you may find the upper parts quite rough-going due to the wind-formed snow convolutions on the ridge. There are fine views from here of the immense medial moraines of the White River glacier, and of the mountain rising far above.

The ridge soon broadens as it continues its gradual descent, offering wide, shallow bowls for long traverses. Continue to about 5200 feet (0.7 mile), where a descent may be made on steep, open slopes into the canyon. If snow appears unstable, continue southeast down into the trees, where the descent will be easier and safer.

Once on the flat floor of the White River canyon, follow it to the White River bridge by way of either the left side or the right side, where a bench with scattered trees descends to the bowl, then to the bridge.

EAST LEG ROAD TOURS AND LOOPS

Novice to Intermediate
Round trip up to 6.8 miles
Marked roads and trails
Elevation gain up to 750 feet,
   loss 250 feet

High point 4600 feet
USGS Mount Hood South

Map—pages 79, 88, 89

Built in the 1930s, the East Leg road was the first to Timberline Lodge. Today it is the basis for a number of interesting loops ranging from 3.2 miles to 7.9 miles in length. In addition, there are two trails that can be skied out and back. This compact area offers considerable variety for novice skiers, and for experienced skiers there are a number of interesting loops. Several clearcuts offer views and off-road skiing.

Snow Bunny Trail-Tie Trail. From the Snow Bunny sno-park the East Leg road, called the Snow Bunny Trail, starts near Snow Bunny Lodge and climbs gently through the forest for 1.6 miles to the Timberline road. Crossing the road, it continues gently upward along an abandoned roadbed, here named the Tie Trail, through second-growth firs and lodgepole pines for 1.0 mile to a prominent switchback at 4600 feet on the West Leg road. This switchback is 1.6 mile above the Mazama sno-park. The scenic high point of this tour is near Still Creek, just 200 yards before reaching the switchback turn, where there are partially obstructed views

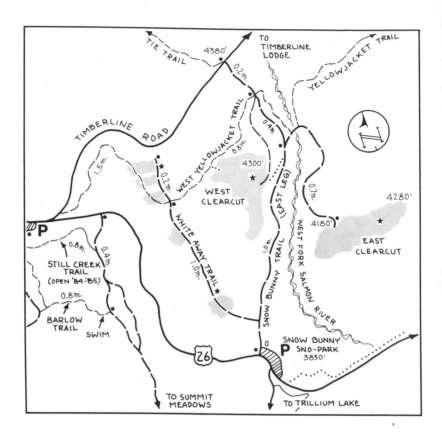

of Hood and to the south of lesser peaks—Multorpor, Eureka, Veda, and Tom Dick and Harry. Novice.

White Away Trail. Just 0.1 mile beyond Snow Bunny trailhead, near the lodge, you may notice a side road to the left, near the snow play hill. This road is the White Away Trail, which ends 1.2 mile from the trailhead. A short way up the road, there is a clearcut with a view of Mt. Jefferson, and near its upper end several clearcuts have great views to the west. This road climbs through forest to a junction with the West Yellowjacket Trail, where by turning right you can form a loop to the East Leg road (the Snow Bunny Trail), then back to the trailhead, a total loop distance of 3.2 miles. Intermediate.

West Yellowjacket Trail. This rugged forest trail starts near the Timberline road–Highway 26 junction, then travels through big timber 2.3 miles to where it joins the Snow Bunny Trail at a point 1.4 miles above Snow Bunny sno-park. Several loops are formed by using this trail.

The trail enters dense forest. It climbs steadily, with several bridged creek crossings, sidehills, and steep pitches before it reaches the White

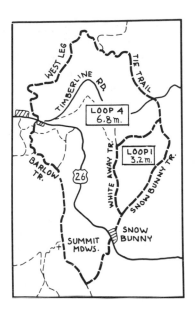

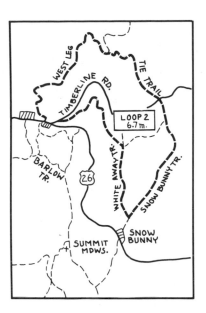

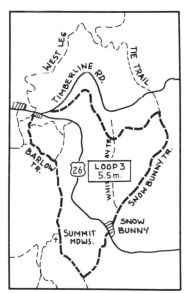

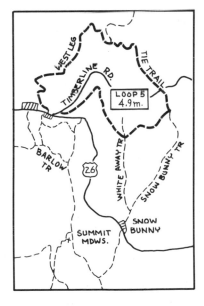

LOOP 1: SNOW BUNNY, W. YELLOWJACKET, WHITE AWAY
LOOP 2: SNOW BUNNY, TIE, WEST LEG, W. YELLOWJACKET, WHITE AWAY
LOOP 3: SNOW BUNNY, W. YELLOWJACKET, BARLOW, SUMMIT MEADOWS
LOOP 4: SNOW BUNNY, TIE, WEST LEG, BARLOW, SUMMIT MEADOWS
LOOP 5: W. YELLOWJACKET, SNOW BUNNY, TIE, WEST LEG

Away Trail, a road. From there it continues through the trees above the west clearcut to the East Leg road (Snow Bunny Trail). The trail has many challenging ups, downs, and turns. From west to east it is generally uphill to the White Away Trail, and rolling from there to the Snow Bunny Trail. Several clearcuts on and just off the trail provide views. In low snow years, minor stream crossings may be tricky, but with caution are quite safe. For details see Yellowjacket Trail.

If the upper end of the White Away Trail is icy for the return trip, take the West Yellowjacket east to the Snow Bunny Trail and descend that trail to the sno-park. Even if exploring clearcuts, you are not likely to get lost in this area, as all roads lead down to Snow Bunny sno-park.

Loop Skiing Suggestions. The three trails just described, in conjunction with others, offer many loop skiing opportunities, some of which will challenge even the hardiest novice skier. In all there are five loop combinations, which may be skied from either the Mazama or Snow Bunny sno-parks. Loop 1 is the only one for novice skiers; the rest are for intermediate skiers.

SNOW BUNNY CLEARCUT TOURS

Novice	High point 4340 feet
Round trip 4 miles	USGS Mount Hood South
Marked road	
Elevation gain 510 feet	Map—page 88

There are two large clearcuts above Snow Bunny Lodge that offer views of Mt. Hood, Mt. Jefferson, and the Trillium Basin peaks. Both are undemanding tours following the Snow Bunny Trail.

From the sno-park at Snow Bunny walk to the nearby lodge then to the trailhead near the snow play hills. Continue past the snow play hills on the East Leg road (the Snow Bunny Trail), then put your skis on and start up the road.

It is 1.0 mile to a junction, where a side road goes right. From there it is 0.7 mile to the east clearcut, which should be skied to its top for the best views: Mt. Hood through a screen of trees, all the nearby peaks of the Trillium Basin and Still Creek canyon areas—Veda, Eureka, Multorpor—and Devils Peak in the distance.

Back at the road junction, to reach the west clearcut, either climb the steep bank to the left or continue uphill 0.4 mile to where signs mark the crossing of the Yellowjacket Trail. Immediately back, at a sharp reverse angle to the left is a road that leads 0.4 mile to the west clearcut and good views. Ski into the clearcut to see Mt. Hood, Mt. Jefferson and other familiar peaks. This large clearcut is a good place to sharpen skiing skills. By skiing along the top of the clearcut to the White Away Trail, you can use this clearcut as an alternative to the West Yellowjacket Trail.

YELLOWJACKET TRAIL

Advanced
Distance one way 6.3 miles
Marked trail
Elevation gain 800 feet

High point 4800 feet
USGS Mount Hood South

Map—pages 88, 156, 221

Following a route cut through the forest from the Timberline road to the White River, the Yellowjacket Trail is an achievement against which to judge your skiing skills, for most of them will surely be required before the tour is ended. If you can ski this trail with aplomb, you may consider yourself an advanced skier. It is a physically demanding trail and while marked along its entire length, some route-finding skills will be needed. This trail is a "classic" tour that every experienced skier wants to ski for the notoriety it has acquired.

The Yellowjacket is a long, tiring tour for which a car shuttle is recommended. To make a 16-mile loop tour, however, you may return via Boy Scout Ridge or the Barlow Saddle connector trails to Barlow Pass, then through the Salmon River area to Snow Bunny, where off-trail skiing would be required. From Snow Bunny the full loop is 14 miles and slightly less demanding. This first leg of the Yellowjacket Trail, herein called the West Yellowjacket Trail (see East Leg Road Loops and Tours), heads east through big timber 2.3 miles to East Leg road (Snow Bunny Trail).

The Yellowjacket then crosses the East Leg road, turns south and goes downhill, paralleling the East Leg road, then popping out onto the east clearcut road to cross the West Fork of the Salmon River. It then continues uphill along the east side of the creek before turning east.

If you are skiing the Yellowjacket from Snow Bunny, ski up the East Leg road for 1 mile to the first side road on the right. Turn here and ski 200 yards to the first creek crossing. Look carefully for the orange markers—five-inch square, painted metal plates—which extend the length of the trail. They are losing their coat of paint with the years and are becoming increasingly harder to see.

Follow the markers uphill on the east side of the creek until the trail turns right and continues winding through the forest. The trail climbs and eventually reaches a ridge shoulder, then follows uphill along the west edge of the Salmon River canyon, far above the creek itself. The Salmon River, little more than a creek here and farther up, usually offers little if any problem at the crossing.

Along the west edge of the canyon, the trail climbs steeply and seemingly without end, but finally descends (markers not easy to see) to the river, at 4800 feet, which is crossed on snow. The trail then doubles back and continues descending through open forest. At the 4500-foot level it turns left (north) and contours toward the White River, reaching a meadow in about 600 yards.

Hoarfrost crystals on ice

The trail crosses the meadow and enters beautiful open forest. Continuing with more gentle ups and downs, it finally switchbacks sharply to the right and descends a moderately-steep slope into and out of a deep gully. Crossing gentle terrain, the trail contours just below The Bowl at White River, soon reaching the highway. An eventful, tiring, but rewarding tour has ended, unless you are skiing a loop back to your starting point!

Skiing from west to east, the only steep downhill sections are near the White River end of the trail. Much of the Yellowjacket is uphill; the remainder is moderate downhill: not a difficult tour, but long and tiring. If skied in the reverse direction, however, steep sections on the west side of the Salmon River would be difficult to descend. The pleasure of this tour depends on selecting the right snow conditions. New, heavy snow would be very tiring. Late spring conditions may mean tree wells, dirty snow, and icy surfaces in the shade.

As with most advanced tours carry appropriate gear and an emergency repair kit. And be prepared to do some route finding as some markers are hard to see. The trail, however, is well-defined overall, and there should be few problems. Select a safe crossing for the Salmon River at the high point of the tour.

Historical Note. This trail was conceived by Homer Blackburn, who was instrumental in laying it out and in effecting its ultimate completion, after four years and 2540 volunteer worker-hours. The Mazamas, Trails Club of Oregon, and the Skinny Ski Club, which was Blackburn's club, were the primary forces in the trail construction. The trail received its name from the many stings suffered by the trail workers. As originally constructed, it extended from the Timberline road. The first part of the trail has been called West Yellowjacket in this guidebook to minimize confusion in loop descriptions.

Chapter 7
TRILLIUM BASIN

The Trillium Basin is unique on Mt. Hood: no other area on the slopes of Hood has Nordic skiing terrain of comparable extent, quality, and variety. Furthermore, the basin is convenient, being accessible directly from Government Camp, with its parking, ski rentals, public facilities, and other amenities.

Trillium Basin lies just southeast of Government Camp, extending six miles from north to south and covering about eight square miles. It is an area of gentle, rolling hills and flats enclosed by two high ridges: the Eureka-Veda-Sherar Ridge on the west, and Mud Creek Ridge on the east. The two principal drainages are the upper Still Creek in the far northwest and Mud Creek, which flows south from the Trillium Lake dam. The skiing limits of the basin are defined on the east and south by the Salmon River as it flows south along the east base of Mud Creek Ridge and then curves westward in the extreme south to encircle the basin on two sides.

The many clearcuts in the central and southern portions of the basin are a considerable advantage to skiers as they offer splendid views and off-road skiing, and serve as connector routes for several of the loops. Meadows, frozen ponds, and historical sites add both beauty and interest to the tours. Most tours are on gentle terrain. Safe skiing and the open nature of most of the basin inspires a sense of security that brings the average skier back time after time.

Beautiful Trillium Lake also draws large numbers of skiers, and the lake loop is usually crowded. The lake area and those to the north are heavily used by novice and intermediate skiers seeking the safety of numbers, easy terrain, and comfortable skiing distances.

Aside from the lake and Summit Meadows the basin is only lightly used by skiers. Yet away from the crowded and popular half-day tours lies an area of considerable beauty, fine views, and a variety of skiing experiences. There are nineteen miles of snow-covered roads in the basin, providing tours of up to fourteen miles. And by using clearcuts and connector routes, it is possible to ski long distances without retracing your tracks. The ever-changing scenery, numerous views of Mt. Hood, Mt. Jefferson, the high peaks of the Clackamas, and the Salmon River valley are ample rewards for those who ski the longer tours.

If there is a problem with the basin, other than crowding on the popular tours, it is that all ski routes into the basin are downhill, and while short, they are somewhat steep for the novice. The large numbers of novices using the basin, however, suggest that the rewards are worth the exertion and adrenalin demanded by the initial hills.

The Forest Service, which controls the marking of ski routes in the

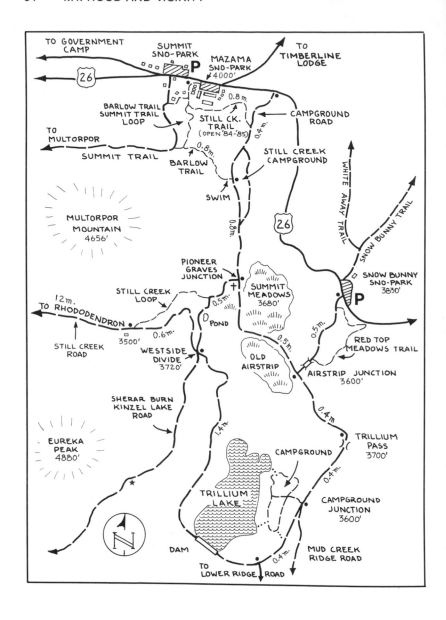

area, has unfortunately overlooked the potential of the southern basin, with one consequence being the overuse of the lake loop. So if you are looking for solitude, ski beyond the limits of the half-day tours.

Trillium Basin's natural attributes, its location near Government Camp, and good parking at the trailheads are all factors that will enable this area eventually to become the major touring center of Mt. Hood. Future years will see the Forest Service recognize the full potential of the basin for heavy, dispersed skier use. It is reasonable to foresee many more miles of marked trails, construction of forest trails, easier access routes to the basin, day-use huts and skiing loops for all skill levels.

TRILLIUM BASIN ACCESS ROUTES

Map—page 94

The Forest Service recognizes three routes leading into the basin—all downhill. These three—the Barlow, Snow Bunny Hill, and Red Top Meadows trails—are difficult for novice skiers, who seldom have downhill skiing skills. Under packed snow or icy conditions some skiers even remove their skis and walk down the steeper sections. An easier route, the Still Creek Trail, probably will not be completed before the 1984–1985 season. A fifth route, the campground road, is possibly the easiest of all the access routes, but it is not recognized by the Forest Service as it requires walking on the highway to reach its trailhead, a possibly dangerous additional hazard for skiers.

Snow Bunny Hill. This route follows a wide road down gentle to moderate grades. It is the shortest route to the Trillium Basin and the most popular for skiers of all skill levels. This route is recommended to novice skiers as the least difficult of the access routes.

Park at the Snow Bunny sno-park, which is located on Highway 26 1.6 miles east of the Timberline road. The trailhead is across the highway, where you have a choice of two routes into the basin: the Snow Bunny Hill road (by far the most used) and the Red Top Meadows Trail (see below). The Snow Bunny Hill road descends several hundred yards, flattens out, crosses a creek, then reaches the Airstrip Junction in a few yards. Total distance: 0.5 mile. By turning right at the junction, you can go to Summit Meadows. By turning left (staying on the main road), you are headed for Trillium Lake. Snow Bunny Hill is generally packed hard, requiring use of the snowplow to control speed. If the snow is deep, the descent is slower and safer for novices.

The Airstrip Junction is located at the south end of a former emergency airstrip for small planes. Near here was located a CCC camp for the many workers and artisans who built Timberline Lodge in the 1930s.

Red Top Meadows Trail. Misnamed, this trail is never close to Red

Top Meadows and is the least used trail into Trillium Basin. To find the trail ski down the Snow Bunny Hill road 50 yards then turn left (signs) and enter the trees. The first half of this half-mile route is on forest trail. Then it follows a primitive road, crosses a small meadow, and soon joins the Snow Bunny Hill route at the creek just before the Airstrip Junction.

Well marked, the route goes through scenic second-growth. There are only two moderately-steep sections on the trail portion. The road portion is of moderate grade. This route is less direct but has scenic charm that the Snow Bunny Hill road lacks. It is also less crowded and serves as an interesting alternative for your return trip.

Barlow Trail. Following the route of the historic Barlow Road, this beautiful forest trail travels through scenic old-growth. Because of several short, steep sections it is recommended only to skiers with downhill experience.

From the Mazama sno-park at the Highway Department area, opposite the Timberline road the Barlow Trail winds 0.8 mile to the campground road, then another 0.8 mile—all of it downhill—to the Pioneer Graves Junction at the north end of Summit Meadows.

The trailhead is at the west end of the sno-park. Ski down and around several Forest Service cabins and watch for trail signs. At the south edge of the cabin area is a trail entering the forest, climbing a slight incline. This is the start of the Barlow Trail. The trail twists and descends quickly at first, with an abrupt turn and several dips and tricky pitches and turns, then soon joins a trail coming down from the right. The Summit Trail is just up the hill west of this junction. The Barlow Trail now turns left and continues descending gently, then moderately through tall trees, twisting along the sunken, historic roadbed. So many skiers pass this way that the run is often packed smooth, resembling a wide tobbogan run with rounded walls: for the good skier an exciting run!

There is one final steep pitch of about fifty yards before the abrupt creek crossing near the site of the former Swim Resort. Operating in the early 1900s, the hotel and cabins were open year-round. Nothing remains except the concrete walls of the old swimming pool. Interestingly, this area is protected for the study of a rare species of dragonfly. There is a final, steep, narrow pitch to the creek crossing, but this may be avoided by taking a short side trail to the right.

The last few turns before the creek crossing are challenging to the best skier. If you ski fast, be alert for skiers below you around the bends, for many skiers fall on these turns. Once across the creek at Swim, proceed about fifty yards to a small bridge leading to the campground road, where you turn right (south) for the final leg to Summit Meadows and the Pioneer Graves Junction.

If you park at the Summit sno-park, reach the Barlow Trail by crossing Highway 26 and taking a short spur road just a little east of the sno-park exit. This leads to the Government Camp auxilliary power station (a square metal structure), where you turn left to the nearby Forest Service cabins and the trailhead.

Campground Road. To avoid the steepness of the other access routes some skiers elect to ski the campground road. Walk east from the Mazama sno-park for 300 yards along Highway 26, then leave the highway at a large open area on the south (right) side. Enter the trees and ski the campground road down a gentle hill, eventually passing the junction with the Barlow Trail on the right. It is 1.2 miles to Summit Meadows along this road. The Forest Service discourages use of this road because it requires walking along the highway. Highway relocation is planned for this section in the future and it may change the access to this approach considerably.

Still Creek Trail. This route, providing new and gentler access to the northern Trillium Basin, is scheduled to be ready by the 1984–1985 skiing season. Park at either the Mazama or Summit sno-parks. Less demanding than other access routes into the basin, this is a forest trail, at first following the initial short hill of the Barlow Trail. Then it turns left into old growth and winds downhill, eventually crossing Still Creek and connecting with the lower part of the campground road.

TRILLIUM LAKE LOOP

Novice
Round trip from Mazama sno-park
   6.8 miles, from Sno Bunny sno-park
   4.6 miles, Loop only 3.6 miles
Marked roads

Elevation loss 250 to 400 feet
High point 3830 to 4000 feet
USGS Mount Hood South

Map—pages 94, 103

This is the most popular and crowded of all the trails of the basin. Proximity to sno-parks and constantly changing scenery and points of interest make this loop the first tour for many beginning skiers. This loop, however, is a bit long for some novices, so exploring the Summit Meadows area is recommended to less aggressive skiers.

From the Airstrip Junction (see Access Routes) ski south down a wide, gentle road, before climbing up and over Trillium Pass, 3700 feet. After descending a long, gentle hill, ski along a flat to the Trillium Lake Campground entrance. Continue straight along the flat as it eventually curves right to a gentle descent to the dam at the foot of the lake (3600 feet), a popular lunch and rest spot with a good view of Mt. Hood.

Although the lake ice may appear solid, be careful. The best idea is to explore the lake by skiing along the east shoreline. Continuing the loop tour from the dam, climb a long, gentle hill past a view of the lake and a hill that is a popular practice area for downhill runs. Farther along, reach the Westside Divide, the junction of the Sherar Burn and Still Creek roads. From the divide a moderate downhill run leads past a frozen pond and along the level, winding road across a flat leading to the Pioneer Graves Junction, at the north end of Summit Meadows.

The white picket fence surrounding the three graves is a scant fifty yards south of the junction. The small headstones date to 1882. Just 50 yards north of the junction is the site of the former Summit House, where the historic Barlow Road crossed the meadows, marked now by a line of small alders growing eastward.

If you are returning to the Summit or Mazama sno-parks, head north on the campground road. If your destination is the Snow Bunny sno-park, follow the road or meadow south to the Airstrip Junction.

There are few hazards along this route. Under icy conditions the hills, though gentle, will be fast and dangerous for novices. If the weather is bad or the novice is not in good shape, it is possible the tour may be too long. If so, turn around at the dam and retrace your route, foregoing the longer loop. The lake ice is not always safe, so it's best to stay off the lake.

STILL CREEK LOOP

Novice	High point 3830 feet
Round trip from Snow Bunny 3.6 miles	USGS Mount Hood South
Marked road, but loop not marked	Map—page 94
Elevation gain 440 feet cumulative	

This short loop offers good exercise and a change of pace from the usual spin around Trillium Lake. A good viewpoint warrants a short side trip from the Westside Divide even if you are not skiing the complete loop.

From Snow Bunny sno-park ski to the Pioneer Graves in Summit Meadow (see "Access Routes"). From there ski west on the Trillium Lake Loop toward the Westside Divide. Where the lake loop road curves southward, the north leg of the Still Creek Loop goes straight west onto an obscure side road. Do not take this road, however, because the loop is best skied in a clockwise direction so that you can benefit from the downhill section. So continue to the Westside Divide and turn sharply right onto the Still Creek road. Ski a short distance to the viewpoint. In fair weather you can enjoy a view of Mt. Hood, Barlow Butte, Panorama Dome, Mud Creek Ridge, and Ghost Ridge, although roadside trees seem to be increasingly obstructing the view.

Continue the tour by descending moderate grades to an abandoned house, a former Forest Service building. At the house leave the Still Creek road by doubling back sharply onto an abandoned road that leads back along the north leg of this loop. The entrance to this road is quite overgrown with alder and it is not obvious. A number of places on the north leg road bed are slowly growing over with slide alder, and at least three feet of snow are required to easily get through this area. Within a year or two this leg will be cleared of brush for skiers.

STILL CREEK CANYON TOUR

Advanced
One way to Hwy 26/Road 32 10.5 miles, to Hwy 26/Road 2620 13.5 miles
Unmarked road
Elevation loss 2370 feet
High point 3900 feet
USGS Mount Hood South, Government Camp

Map—pages 66, 94

This long road tour, mostly downhill, requires an unusual combination of conditions for success. Once out of the Trillium Basin the road follows the deep and impressive Still Creek canyon.

Start from the Mazama sno-park and ski down the Barlow Trail to Summit Meadows (see "Access Routes"). Turn right onto the Trillium Lake Loop and ski to Westside Divide. There, turn sharply right onto the Still Creek road. (Or take the north leg of the Still Creek Loop to avoid this short climb.) This is the beginning of Still Creek canyon. In 0.6 mile pass an abandoned house. Continue down the 1500-foot deep canyon, which is quite wide at this point. As you descend the narrow, winding road, however, the canyon narrows and the scene changes constantly—forest, clearcuts, rushing stream, and snow-covered rock slides.

Cross the first of four bridges at 4.5 miles from Westside Divide. The second is 1.0 mile farther and the third 0.8 mile beyond that. You will reach the Still Creek Trail, 780, (2100 feet) 1.2 miles after the third bridge. If you cross a fourth bridge and have not seen the trail, it is 300 yards back. It begins in a clearcut directly opposite a short spur road leading down to the creek. From the road the trail, hidden by brush, angles sharply twenty feet east of the trail sign. Exit there to Highway 26 for a 10.5-mile tour.

Another exit route to Highway 26 is via Road 2620 which is reached 1.5 miles from Highway 26. The unmarked intersection with Road 2620 is the first obvious right angle intersection, and as you turn right (north) make a short descent to a bridge. Road 2620 then winds through the cabin area for 1.1 miles to Highway 26, 200 yards east of the center of the town of Rhododendron. If you miss the Road 2620 junction or elect to end the tour at Road 10, you will end up 0.6 mile west of the town center.

Do not undertake this tour unless you are a competent skier in good condition who fully understands how different snow conditions affect your skiing. You must have all the conditions in your favor. Verify how low (or high) the snow line is and the snow conditions for your day, knowing that they may change. The road is not steep enough to offer a

Summit Meadows near the Pioneer Graves plot (fence) in Trillium Basin, Ghost Ridge in distance

good glide except in exceptional conditions. If you cannot glide, you will have to diagonal stride the distance. You may want to leave a car at the lower end, particularly if the snowline is far up the canyon. Scout the lower end of the tour, then make your decision. As this is an extended tour, carry the ten essentials and a good supply of energy food.

MUD CREEK RIDGE/PORCUPINE TRAIL

Intermediate
Round trip from Snow Bunny 8.2 miles
Marked and unmarked roads and off-trail
Elevation gain 1200 feet cumulative

High point 4150 feet
USGS Mount Hood South,
** Mount Wilson**
Map—pages 102, 103

Enjoy views of the basin, Mt. Jefferson, Mt. Hood, the Salmon River ridges, and the Clackamas high country on this popular tour. The last mile is along a lovely, primitive road where signs of elk are sometimes seen.

From the Campground Junction east of Trillium Lake (see Trillium Lake Loop) take the road angling uphill for a long, gentle climb to the Jefferson Viewpoint, 1.8 miles from the junction. Several prior clearcuts offer good views across the Basin to Veda Butte and Eureka Peak. The road makes a sweeping curve at the Jefferson Viewpoint, where—as you might suspect—there is a fine view of Mt. Jefferson, 40 miles to the south. Follow the road as it curves eastward; then, where it starts to curve south, leave the road and enter a large clearcut to the north (following a primitive road if the snow is shallow, but with normal snow depth this road is not visible).

The Porcupine Trail begins at this clearcut. To find where it leaves the clearcut and enters the forest, closely examine the map on page 102. The Porcupine Trail follows the narrow road for just about one mile. First, the trail angles uphill, northeast across the clearcut, then it follows along the north side of a prominent tongue of forest that penetrates the clearcut from the east. After entering the forest, the trail climbs northerly along the east side of Mud Creek Ridge, soon passing good views of Mt. Hood and Ghost Ridge before descending to its end in another clearcut. The Forest Service may eventually continue this trail around Mud Creek Ridge to Trillium Pass to form a long loop. For the time being, however, retrace your tracks, passing views to the southeast of the Salmon River valley and to Blue Box and Wapinitia passes between Frog Lake Buttes and Wapinitia Ridge.

The Jefferson Viewpoint is a popular lunch spot, and the large clearcut below, Telemark Hill, offers good skiing and serves as the connector route for the Mt. Jefferson and High Divide loops (which see). At the bottom of Telemark Hill is the Lower Ridge road, which forms part of these loops, and which eventually leads you back past the quarry and on to Trillium Lake.

Mud Creek Ridge Overlook. You can reach the overlook by a short off-trail climb to the ridge crest, where there is a striking view, one of the best in the basin. From the Jefferson Viewpoint climb open slopes northward through scattered, small trees, contouring around the west side of the ridge to avoid dog-hair growth. The climb up moderate slopes is easy, taking only ten minutes or so, depending on snow conditions.

A different approach is to ski to the back of the large clearcut to the east of the Mud Creek Ridge and pick up a primitive road on the hillside, which leads to the ridge crest. A short steep section will require sidestepping.

The high point is an open shoulder of the ridge with a splendid view of the basin and its surrounding ridges and peaks. The Clackamas, Mt. Jefferson, Olallie Butte, Ghost Ridge and Frog Lake Buttes are the principal landmarks.

There are several possible descents from the overlook to the road. Head straight down to the west over open slopes to a small quarry and

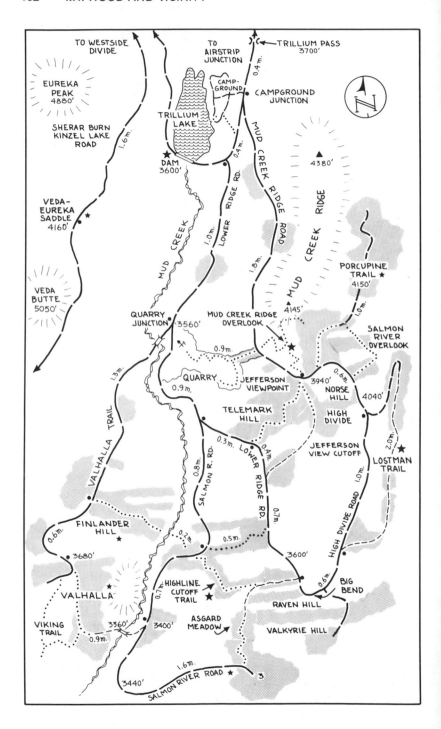

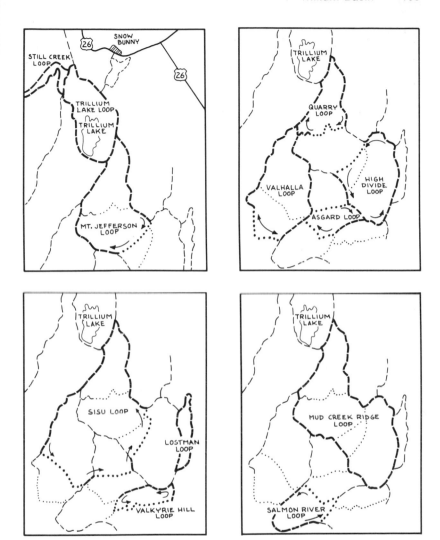

the road. Or ski back to Jefferson Viewpoint by reversing either of the ascents described above. If you follow the obscure, primitive road (about 80 yards northeast of the high point) that leads to the large clearcut to the east, you can ski on to the Porcupine Trail, if you wish, or just swing south to the road and back to the Jefferson Viewpoint.

Salmon River Overlook. Barely 300 yards off the main trail is an un-expected vantage point from which you can see the Salmon River valley and meadows. From the Jefferson Viewpoint follow the road east for about 200 yards to the bottom of a prominent clearcut. This rectangular patch extends east to the ridge top and the overlook. Ski to the northeast corner of the clearcut and follow openings 80 yards to the fine viewpoint. The beautiful Salmon River Meadows are spread out at your feet in their full length, with Ghost Ridge above and Frog Lake Buttes beyond. The highway leading to Wapinitia Pass is seen just above the meadows.

From the overlook backtrack about 80 yards to the small openings before the clearcut. Look north and you will see other openings (actually a skid road) which lead to another clearcut. The final few yards are through a narrow band of dense forest. This clearcut leads gently downhill to the cut-over basin behind the Jefferson Viewpoint, where the Porcupine Trail passes through.

By skiing a loop, first to the Salmon River Overlook, then via the connector to the north and back to the Jefferson Viewpoint you will travel about 1.5 miles. The distance from Snow Bunny to the Jefferson Viewpoint is 3.1 miles.

Return to the Campground Junction along your uphill route. This long, gentle descent, which can be fun if tracks and snow are good, is another of the tour's rewards for the 340-foot climb.

QUARRY LOOP

Intermediate
Round trip from Snow Bunny 6.4 miles
Marked road and off-trail
Elevation gain 850 feet cumulative

High point 3900 feet
USGS Mount Hood South

Map—pages 102, 103

This short loop is one of the most interesting in the basin. Follow Mud Creek Ridge road to a long, narrow clearcut, about 250 yards northwest of the Jefferson Viewpoint (see Mud Creek Ridge/Porcupine Trail). Descend the clearcut to its lower end, where you will pass by an unusual, isolated small cedar tree that appears to belong to an oriental landscape. Here you turn right and follow a moderately steep road as it zigzags downward into the quarry area, where open slopes and views abound. You will no doubt find a number of interesting slopes in the quarry on which to practice downhill techniques.

The road then continues down into another open area just before reaching the Lower Ridge road, which leads back to the Trillium Lake area. An alternative descent through the quarry is to ski northwestward along the top of the large, open area (there are no cliffs or dropoffs). Eventually you will find a series of easy, connected benches to descend. This is the easiest descent route from the top of the quarry. Do not ski into the upper quarry if visibility is restricted as there is a chance of skiing onto steep slopes that are normally easily avoided. From the Lower Ridge road, ski northward back to Campground Junction.

MT. JEFFERSON LOOP

Advanced
Round trip 7.7 miles
Marked roads and unmarked clearcut
Elevation gain 830 feet cumulative
High point 3940 feet

USGS Mount Hood South,
   Mount Wilson

Map—pages 102, 103

There are opportunities on this loop to try both off-road skiing and some good downhill skiing. Ski the loop in a clockwise direction so the clearcut may be skied downhill. The road portions of the loop are often combined with those of the High Divide Loop to form a longer, combined loop. There is a good view of Mt. Jefferson at the high point.

Follow the Mud Creek Ridge road (see Mud Creek Ridge/Porcupine Trail) to the Jefferson Viewpoint. There, leave the road and ski down into the Telemark Hill clearcut to the Lower Ridge road below. Only three feet of snow are necessary to cover most of the obstacles in the clearcut. With a few turns you will ski about 0.7 mile before encountering the lower road. Once on the road, ski north through forest, then in open areas past the quarry. A long, gradual ascent through forest finally takes you to the Trillium Lake Loop road, from which it is only a short distance to the Campground Junction.

In bad weather the high point is exposed to wind and storm. If snow is shallow beware of stumps, limbs, and brush on Telemark Hill. Ski this loop only when the clearcut hill is well covered.

HIGH DIVIDE LOOP

Advanced Intermediate
Round trip 10.2 miles
Marked roads and unmarked clearcuts
Elevation gain 1040 feet
High point 4040 feet

USGS Mount Hood South,
   Mount Wilson

Map—pages 102, 103

Interesting views, a sense of isolation, and gentle terrain make this road tour a good one for miles of exercise. Ski the Mud Creek Ridge road (see Mud Creek Ridge/Porcupine Trail) to the Jefferson Viewpoint, where this loop begins. As this is one of the longer tours in the basin, you should be better equipped than for shorter tours. Carry extra clothing, map and compass. Be careful for buried stumps and limbs in the clearcuts, where three feet of snow should be the minimum before downhill skiing is considered safe.

This loop is perhaps best skied counter-clockwise. There is a choice of how to ski the initial mile: either directly down Telemark Hill to the

Lower Ridge road (then southward), or partway down Telemark Hill then across to the Jefferson Viewpoint Cutoff Trail, which is slightly more direct but at the price of losing some good downhill skiing. From the Jefferson Viewpoint to the Lower Ridge road is a 350-foot loss of elevation.

Once on the lower road, ski south up a gentle grade past clearcuts to the Big Bend, where the road swings northward toward the High Divide. Near this bend a side road leads west to clearcuts (Highline Cutoff connector area), providing a shortcut route to the end of the Salmon River road (see Highline Cutoff Trail and Salmon River Loop).

Back on the main road, beyond the Big Bend, another side road heads south to the Valkyrie Hill Loop. Continue along the main road as it climbs gently through forest and past a clearcut to the high point of the loop, the High Divide, 4040 feet, where the Lostman Trail starts. That side road leads east to nearby clearcuts and offers a good view of Mt. Hood and the Salmon River valley.

From the High Divide the main road descends gently to the Jefferson Viewpoint. Along the way a narrow clearcut on the left (Norse Hill) provides a fine view of the Clackamas peaks, including High Rock and Signal Buttes. At the Jefferson Viewpoint another descent of Telemark Hill gives you two loops for the day, as you ski back to the Trillium Lake area on the lower road.

If the High Divide Loop is skied clockwise, you may wonder which clearcut is Telemark Hill. They all seem to look alike. The top of Telemark Hill is recognized by the ragged, scattered forest giants on the skyline. The climb up the hill is not as long or tiring as it may appear from below. A more direct but less scenic route to the top is to take the Jefferson Viewpoint Cutoff Trail.

LOSTMAN TRAIL AND LOOP

Intermediate	USGS Mount Hood South,
Round trip 10.4 miles	Mount Wilson
Marked road and unmarked trail	
Elevation gain 990 feet cumulative	Map—pages 102, 103
High point 4040 feet	

Some of the loveliest meadow-like skiing in the entire Trillium Basin is on this tour, along with fine views of Mt. Hood, Ghost Ridge, the Salmon River valley, Frog Lake Buttes, and Wapinitia Pass. You experience an unusual sense of isolation on this superb tour.

Follow the Mud Creek Ridge road (See Mud Creek Ridge/Porcupine Trail) for 0.6 mile beyond the Jefferson Viewpoint to the High Divide, the highest point on this part of the ridge. Here, the Lostman Trail is the obvious, short side road to the left (east). The trail shortly curves north for almost 0.5 mile as it drops into a large, level clearcut overlooking the Salmon River valley. Turn right and ski south, following an old logging road on the west side of the clearcut. Continue south on this road as it travels through partially regrown logged areas on mostly level terrain. In periods of limited visibility it may be difficult to follow a precise trail through the open areas of the Lostman Trail, but in reality this is a minor problem because the forest on either side of the route will channel your course in the right direction.

If the snow is deep the road bed is not visible, but the tour is easy to follow because one open area naturally leads to the next as you ski south to a junction with the High Divide road. When you reach this road turn right and ski uphill, northward, to the High Divide and Jefferson Viewpoint. For several interesting, short side tours near Jefferson Viewpoint see Mud Creek Ridge/Pioneer Trail.

HIGHLINE CUTOFF TRAIL

Advanced
Round trip from Snow Bunny
  10.6 miles
Marked roads and unmarked trail
High point 4040 feet

Elevation gain 1050 feet cumulative
USGS Mount Hood South,
  Mount Wilson

Map—pages 102, 103

This is one of the most scenic and interesting off-road trails in the basin. It is particularly suited to those who want to experience exploratory skiing, although it is easy to follow and never exceeds moderate grades. A beautiful meadow occupies a bench halfway along the trail.

The Highline Cutoff Trail links the High Divide and Valhalla loops and is part of the Valkyrie Hill and Salmon River loops. It is best skied from top to bottom (east to west). The east or top end of the trail is near the bottom of the High Divide Loop, just west of the Big Bend. To reach this point ski south on the Mud Creek Ridge road and High Divide road (see High Divide Loop). The Lower Ridge road also offers access to Big Bend but is not as scenic or interesting for skiing as the higher route.

Just west of the Big Bend look for a side road leading west into a clearcut. This is the start of the Highline Cutoff. Follow the side road down a gentle slope along the south edge of a long and narrow clearcut. This side road eventually curves left (south) to Asgard Meadow at the foot of Valkyrie Hill. At the point where it starts curving south, you angle right and ski through small trees into another long, narrow clearcut corridor (actually the same one you started on).

Ski west down this corridor. Within about 300 yards you will encounter a small, level meadow (a summer marsh) with a beautiful surrounding fringe of forest. After exploring this lovely place, ski north on the level to the top of an open slope that leads to the Salmon River road below. This clearcut slope, with a good view of Mt. Hood, is studded with small evergreens and provides good downhill skiing on moderate grades.

At the road turn right (north) to return to the Trillium Lake Loop or turn left for the Valhalla Loop, which adds only about 1.8 miles to your return trip and about 300 feet of additional climbing, a small price to pay for the scenic rewards. If not too tired by this time, this is an interesting return route.

In times of shallow snow watch for buried limbs and stumps and melt-water streams along the cutoff. Off-road skiing can baffle the most experienced skiers at times, particularly when landmarks are not visible. Trust your compass. Forest Service maps will be of some use here, but the Mount Wilson USGS quad is of little value because of its small scale and because the road at the Big Bend is shown inaccurately. Forest Service maps have perpetuated this inaccuracy. The map in this guidebook is your most accurate reference.

SALMON RIVER ROAD AND LOOP

Advanced
Round trip from Snow Bunny
   13.4 miles
Unmarked road
Elevation gain 730 feet
   cumulative

High point 3850 feet
USGS Mount Hood South,
   Mount Wilson

Map—pages 102, 103

The most remote tours in Trillium basin, offering solitude along a dead-end road leading to the Salmon River valley, with its impressive scale and massive south ridge. This is an exciting area to explore in good weather. Do not attempt this tour, or any of the long loops in the basin, unless snow conditions and weather are favorable. Off-road skiing experience is necessary before you try this loop.

Leave the Trillium Lake Loop (which see) at a point just east of the dam, where an obvious side road—Lower Ridge road—heads south. Follow the Lower Ridge road 1.9 miles to its continuation, the Salmon River road. Continue south, reaching the Highline Cutoff Trail in 0.8 mile and the lower end of the Valhalla Loop in 1.5 miles. From the Valhalla Loop climb over a low divide (3440 feet) and then swing east, with ups and downs, 1.6 miles to the end of the tour in a huge clearcut (3400 feet) on the north side of the Salmon River.

The Salmon River road forms a loop with the Highline Cutoff Trail (which see), involving off-road exploratory skiing. Ski the Highline Cutoff Trail into Asgard Meadow, then southward down to the end of the Salmon River road, crossing a small stream and several clearcuts enroute. Ski west along the road which crosses a pass and turns northward to the bottom of the Valhalla Loop. Continue another 0.7 mile to the west end of the Highline Cutoff Trail. Head east up the hill to complete the loop. There is no particular best direction to ski this loop as the hills are about equal in either direction. Although the terrain is not steep and most of the tour is through clearcuts, only experienced skiers should attempt the loop.

Note on Maps. The southern basin unfortunately is not covered by a single USGS map. Instead, three USGS maps (*Mount Hood South*, *Mount Wilson*, and *High Rock*) are required for this area, and the scales of these maps do not match. Although Forest Service maps are not completely accurate for the road in the Big Bend area, they are adequate. Together with the maps in this guidebook—and some common sense—you should get by quite well. Except for the southern basin, the maps in this guidebook are never a suitable substitute for appropriate USGS and Forest Service maps. For serious skiing use all three.

VALHALLA LOOP

Advanced
Round trip from Snow Bunny 9.6 miles
Unmarked road and unmarked clearcuts
Elevation loss 490 feet

High point 3850 feet
USGS High Rock
Map—pages 102, 103

You will experience a sense of solitude and remoteness in skiing this loop. Some off-road route finding will be required providing a feeling of adventure as you work out the loop on your first tour. Elk often winter in this distant area and their tracks are sometimes seen. The name Valhalla was selected to commemorate the memory of the Scandinavians who brought skiing to America and skied in the basin in the early years of this century.

The Valhalla area is often skied in combination with the High Divide Loop and the Highline Cutoff Trail. Otherwise, if skied as a loop, it is best skied in a clockwise direction for the least tiring return to the trailhead.

From just east of the Trillium Lake dam (see Trillium Lake Loop) take the Lower Ridge road, which descends gradually southward for 1 mile to Quarry Junction, the northern end of the Valhalla Loop. Take the left (east) road. Ski past the hillside quarry and continue a gentle descent to the next junction. Go right here onto the Salmon River road.

From Quarry Junction it is 1.7 miles to the lower (west) end of the Highline Cutoff Trail, a hillside clearcut on your left. Continue skiing on the road 0.7 mile to the southern end of the Valhalla Loop, where you will see on your right, west of the road, a steep, round, forested hill. Shortly past the hill is a clearcut on the right that is partially grown over with small firs. Look for an indistinct, narrow road leaving the main road at an angle and heading west (right) to the bottom of the clearcut. This primitive road leads to an obvious, narrow clearcut corridor and soon crosses an old but sturdy bridge over Mud Creek. At 3360 feet, the stream marks the lowest elevation on the Valhalla Loop.

After crossing the bridge, climb west up the clearcut to the top edge of the forest, then turn right and follow the clearcut to a fine panoramic viewpoint with sweeping views of the Salmon River valley and Mt. Hood. In the right weather, as you stand in this isolated place the remote, cold beauty of the scene may in some way invoke thoughts of a Norseman's winter Valhalla.

From this viewpoint in the center of the clearcut, to the north for a mile or so elk tracks are often seen, being the wintering area of a small herd. At the north end of the clearcut enter the forest at an obvious opening and follow the road as it climbs past additional clearcuts before descending to Quarry Junction. Before reaching the junction enjoy several good views of the basin and quarry. A pleasant 1 mile through old-growth leads you to the Trillium Lake Loop.

As with many loops in the basin, distances are long and the road skiing occasionally seems a bit monotonous, but this loop offers considerable isolation and adventure. It is a rewarding, interesting tour. There are no hazards here for the advanced skier who is well-equipped and in good physical condition. Some route-finding is required at the southern end of the loop.

VALKYRIE HILL LOOP

Advanced
Round trip from Snow Bunny
  12.4 miles
Marked roads and unmarked
  clearcuts
Elevation gain 1400 feet cumulative

High point 4040 feet
USGS Mount Hood South,
  Mount Wilson

Map—pages 102, 103

This is an interesting loop worthy of a side trip from the High Divide Loop. Ski this loop by itself, or link it with the Highline Cutoff Trail or the Salmon River Loop. The hill offers a fine view and some good downhill skiing. Ski to the Big Bend (see High Divide Loop). From just east of the lowest part of the Big Bend take a side road leading south. Ski about 150 yards, then climb into the first clearcut on the right (west) and follow this long, narrow opening upward to the top of Valkyrie Hill and views south of the Clackamas high country. The west slope of this hill drops about 200 feet at a moderately steep angle to Asgard Meadow, a flat open area about 100 yards south of the Highline Cutoff Trail. To complete the loop, descend to the meadow and ski north and turn east

Valhalla clearcut with Wapinitia Ridge in background

onto the Cutoff Trail. Follow it uphill to the High Divide road near your starting point on the loop. From there return to the trailhead by way of the High Divide road or the Lower Ridge road.

VIKING TRAIL AND LOOP

Advanced
Round trip from Snow Bunny 10.4 miles
Unmarked road and trail
Elevation gain 670 feet cumulative

High point 3850 feet
USGS High Rock, Mount Hood South

Map—pages 102, 103

For the intermediate skier this loop—half through forest and half through the Valhalla clearcut—will be challenging, requiring some route finding. It is best to ski the loop in a counterclockwise direction to avoid climbing in the southern end of the loop.

From the road entering the north end of the Valhalla clearcut (see Valhalla Loop), cross the open area to the corner of forest and follow a road through trees to the right (west) for about 250 yards, where you should turn left onto an obscure side road. This skid road becomes obvious as it winds around, and in 200 yards it enters an open area, where you turn right and ski along the road as it climbs and turns left to the high point of the loop.

The road then twists downhill on a moderate grade to another side road. This leads to a small open area, where a narrow, obscure skid road enters the trees to the left. Follow it downward to the south end of the Valhalla clearcut, where the road is lost. Contour to the left in the open area, climb to the flat plateau of the clearcut for great views, and finally return to the nearby start of the loop.

Three feet of snow are required to make the last part of the forest section safe and enjoyable due to brush and windfalls. Route finding and some perseverance are needed to find your way in several places. If confused, all routes downhill from the loop lead to the Valhalla clearcut.

SISU LOOP

Advanced
Round trip from Snow Bunny 10.6 miles
Marked roads and unmarked roads and
  clearcuts
Elevation gain 1100 feet cumulative

High point 3940 feet
USGS Mount Hood South,
  Mount Wilson

Map—pages 102, 103

The Sisu Loop is a demanding tour that suits its name well. *Sisu* is a Finnish word that is difficult to translate but that means something akin to perseverance and fortitude. The tour is somewhat demanding but not

Ice on Trillium Lake

really difficult, requiring some modest route finding, clearcut skiing, a
stream crossing on logs, and hill climbing—all in all a most interesting
tour requiring determination to complete, but offering ample rewards in
the form of fine views and sense of adventure.

The loop starts at Campground Junction (see Trillium Lake Loop).
From there ski 0.4 mile south to the Lower Ridge road and follow that
road south to Quarry Junction. Keep right at the junction, ski downhill to
the crossing of Mud Creek. Beyond, the Valhalla Trail continues as a
wide road, passing several clearcuts and views. From the Quarry Junction it is 1.3 miles to the top of Finlander Hill (easily recognized as the
longest clearcut in view), descending gently all the way to the edge of
Mud Creek, 0.5 mile below the Valhalla Trail. At the bottom of the hill is
a round, level meadow—in reality a summer marsh—an interesting place
to explore.

Numerous logs provide safe but exciting crossings of the narrow,
shallow creek. Always show respect for log crossings, particularly if the
weather is cold and the logs are snow-covered or icy. Wet feet and boots

are always a hazard of creek crossings, but putting on dry socks or wringing out wet ones permits the tour to continue with little time lost and little danger of frostbite, except in bitter temperatures.

Once across, ski uphill to the Salmon River road and turn left (east) to the nearby foot of the Highline Cutoff hill. Leave the road here and follow a narrow clearcut upward from the lower east corner of the Highline Cutoff clearcut, climbing 0.5 mile to the Lower Ridge road. Here, turn left and ski to the Jefferson View Cutoff route, following a logging road upward to upper Telemark Hill. Or ski on to the foot of Telemark Hill, then climb 350 feet to the Jefferson Viewpoint. This gives you a well-earned downhill return to the Campground Junction for a total loop distance of 7.2 miles.

An area as complex as the Trillium Basin, with its many roads and clearcuts, lends itself naturally to many loop tours, providing skiers with variety and challenge to satisfy their natural proclivity to exploration. The presence of numerous loop possibilities in the basin, many not mentioned in this guidebook, encourages the imagination to seek new ski routes and experiences. The Valhalla–Sisu loop area offers the basis for more than five worthwhile loops. Eventually, names such as Outer Valhalla and Inner Valhalla will be heard as skiers seek to define other loops.

VEDA BUTTE

Advanced
Round trip from Snow Bunny 10 miles
Unmarked road
Elevation gain 1700 feet cumulative
High point 5050 feet

USGS Mount Hood South,
    Government Camp

Map—pages 94, 115

The summit of Veda Butte, with its outstanding view, is reached after a long, gentle road tour followed by off-road travel on moderately-steep slopes through scattered trees. This tour is within the capability of strong intermediate skiers who are looking for an interesting test of their skills. The less adventurous can obtain a fine view by just climbing a short distance above the road toward the summit. There is a 3-mile downhill run on the return trip along the Sherar Burn road.

West of the Trillium Basin is a massive high ridge extending from the Still Creek canyon to Kinzel Lake, miles to the west. As seen from the basin, Eureka Peak (north) and Veda Butte (south) are the most prominent features on the ridge. Just to the north of these two peaks is Multorpor Mountain, near Government Camp. Veda (pronounced *Vee-dah*) is a compound word formed from two abbreviated first names.

From Summit Meadows and Pioneer Graves Junction (see Trillium Lake Loop) ski to the Westside Divide then up the Sherar Burn road. Although the road is mostly enclosed in forest, you pass several view-

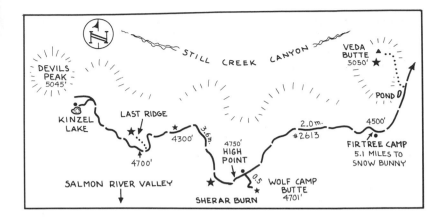

points on this upward journey—down to Trillium Lake and the quarry, across to Mud Creek Ridge, and beyond, to Ghost Ridge and the massive Frog Lake Buttes. About 1.6 miles from the divide you pass the Veda-Eureka saddle, 4160 feet. From the saddle ski 1.4 miles to where the road finally eases off, becoming almost level, and where the immature trees on the uphill side are far apart enough to enter easily. Beyond here the road finally goes downhill slightly for about 100 yards, passing a small pond (off the road) shown on the USGS map.

Anywhere along this section of road (4470 feet) is a good place to head uphill. Heading northward, climb 580 feet in 0.5 mile on a moderately steep ascending traverse to the summit, where a breathtaking view is your reward.

The entire Trillium Basin lies far below in a crazy quilt pattern of clear-cuts. It is fascinating to try to pick out familiar areas. In the distance the rolling massive summit of Mt. Wilson spreads out beyond the Clear Lake Basin. Frog Lake Buttes, Ghost Ridge, and Barlow Butte are prominent features to the east and northeast. Still farther, behind blue ridges, rise the long, flat summit of Bonney Butte and the rounded hump of Lookout Mountain—a remarkable sea of valleys, ridges, and distant peaks.

To the north Mt. Hood is splendid, and the impressive Still Creek canyon winds westward for miles, with interesting patterns formed by tree plantations. Tom Dick and Harry Mountain, a long ridge, is prominent across the canyon. To the southeast a screen of nearby trees allows only a glimpse of the Clackamas high country.

From the summit ski southeast along the generally flat ridge crest for an excellent view of the Salmon River valley and more views of the basin, almost as if seen from an airplane. From here select your descent route, traversing easily down to the road. The open slopes above the pond are the steepest, whereas the open slopes northward are less steep.

After heavy snowfall or during warm spring days some of the steeper slopes could offer avalanche danger, while the slopes nearer the summit are less steep and more protected by trees. Do not leave the road for the summit unless visibility and weather are good.

SHERAR BURN/KINZEL LAKE

Advanced
Round trip from Snow Bunny to Kinzel Lake 23.4 miles
Unmarked road
Elevation gain 2920 feet cumulative
High point 4750 feet
USGS Mount Hood South, Government Camp, High Rock

Map—pages 94, 115

This long road tour requires several elusive ingredients for success: good snow, good weather, and a good dose of determination. Many skiers turn back before reaching the lake and thereby miss the most scenic part of the tour, the last 4.5 miles. Several viewpoints are passed during the first half of the tour, but the truly noble views are kept for last, and are worth the effort. This tour offers a remarkable sense of solitude.

Ski the Sherar Burn road beyond the Veda Butte turnoff (see Veda Butte) to Fir Creek Campground, 5.1 miles from Snow Bunny. Near the campground a side trail to Veda Lake leaves the north side of the road, climbing steeply to the bench lake. This is a difficult tour and less interesting than climbing to the top of Veda Butte.

From Fir Creek Campground, not visible in deep snow, the Sherar Burn road rolls westward with long, gentle but tiring ups and downs. The route passes through forest, with no views until near the tour high point, where a side trip to Wolf Camp Butte reveals a panoramic view. This spectacular site, little more than an open sidehill, is 0.3 mile downhill from the main ski route to Kinzel Lake and 7.6 miles from Snow Bunny. This is the site of a former fire lookout. The next and possibly more impressive viewpoint of the tour is only a short distance west of and downhill from the tour high point of 4750 feet.

To reach Wolf Camp Butte take an obscure side road to the left (south) from the main ski route, which here is a distinctive, straight lane through second-growth trees. The side road to the viewpoint is about 100 yards east of the tour high point. The views from both overlooks range across the wide, deep Salmon River valley to Mt. Wilson, Wolf Peak, and High Rock, far to the south, in the Clackamas high country.

Just beyond the high point the road turns and crosses, in years of deep snow, a steep slope that requires caution if icy. From there (the 7.6-mile point) the road traverses downward, losing 400 feet in the descent, then gaining it back as it climbs to Last Ridge. A short side trip to the top of Last Ridge leads to a panoramic ridge-top view of Devil's Peak, Salmon and Signal Buttes, and Mt. Hood, a wild scene of deep canyons, peaks and ridges. A final descending traverse drops 450 feet to tiny Kinzel Lake. The traverses are always through dense or scattered trees, with little avalanche danger except under unusual conditions. The many south-facing slopes may result in hard packed or even icy stretches.

The lake is not attractive, and although it is the destination of this long tour, the primary reason skiers go the last mile or two is to enjoy the satisfaction of making a particularly long tour—one that has achieved a certain reputation among aggressive skiers.

In many places this tour is exposed to the weather and therefore demands caution. Extra clothing and safety gear are a necessary part of your pack. This tour should be attempted only in settled weather when snow conditions are good. The best time for the tour is spring, when all conditions are more stable.

Historical Note. The Sherar Burn, devastated by one of the big fires of the nineteenth century, was named after Joseph Sherar, who grazed sheep here when the area went to grass. The burn was located on the south side of the now Sherar Burn road in the area of Wolf Camp Butte. The original forest has now been replaced by second-growth. A place on the Deschutes River is also named for Sherar.

Chapter 8
SALMON RIVER BASIN

The little known Salmon River basin extends from Barlow Pass on the east to the Snow Bunny sno-park on the west. The east and west forks of the Salmon River run through the area while the main stream, a small creek, descends from near Timberline Lodge to join the two branches near the interchange of Highways 26 and 35.

The Pioneer Woman's Grave on old Highway 35, now a scenic, snow-covered road leading up to Barlow Pass, is in the eastern part of the small basin. The entire area, from the shallow basin to Snow Bunny, is characterized by generally level forests with a few gentle grades and a number of marshes and meadows hidden from view and just off the traveled trails and roads.

Accessibility to some of the tours is hampered by Highway 35, which must be crossed on foot. In years of low snowfall this is no problem, but when roadside snowbanks are high some care is required. The three principal streams of the Salmon River segment the area, but crossings are managed at the highway edge, where the streams run through culverts.

There is the potential here for miles of loop trails suitable for novices, and the future will no doubt see a sno-park and trail development. At this writing the area has limited parking and few marked trails, although there are several easily followed tours that do not appear on Forest Service winter maps.

GIANT TREES/PIONEER WOMAN'S GRAVE LOOP

Novice	High point 3800 feet
Round trip 2.5 miles	USGS Mount Hood South
Marked trail and roads	
Elevation gain 250 feet	Map—page 119

This is an exceptional loop tour, following both roads and trails, with a side tour into a group of enormous Noble firs. There is no other ski tour on Mt. Hood with such large trees. If there is sufficient snow, you can also explore a number of small meadows, open areas, and short skid roads from old logging days.

From the roadside sno-park just east of the Highway 26/35 interchange, 1.5 miles from Snow Bunny, ski along the snow-covered side road, which is a section of the former Highway 35 to Barlow Pass and is now open in summer as a scenic road alternative. Follow this road 0.4 mile to where it starts to curve right, 100 yards before the Pioneer Woman's Grave site. Leave the road here and turn left onto a marked

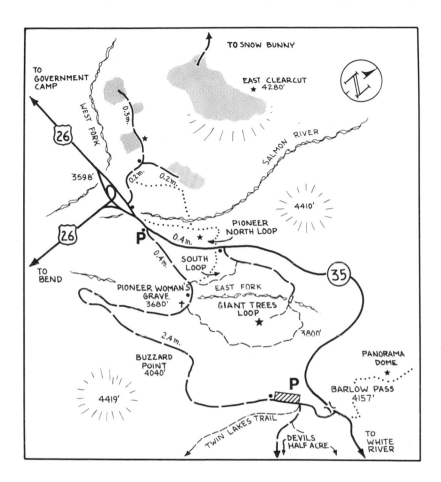

trail—the start of the Giant Trees Loop—leading into the trees. At the road this is not an obvious trail, but it soon is easy to follow.

The trail twists through the open forest, shortly passing a side road on the left, the old pioneer road, and eventually joining a logging road that heads to the right, up a gentle hill. Ski along this road for 0.8 mile to where it crosses a bridge. On the other side of the small bridge the loop trail turns left, following a primitive road uphill. Before continuing the loop, however, ski straight ahead and downhill about 100 yards into a stand of majestic trees. This is the finest stand of trees to be seen along any ski or summer trail on Mt. Hood.

Rejoin the loop at the bridge and ski uphill along the primitive road. As it levels out, the road turns south into another group of giant trees, then shortly goes downhill and crosses a creek, where it again becomes a narrow trail, paralleling closely the original Barlow Road just a few paces to the left.

From the creek crossing it is 250 yards of winding, easy downhill trail to the small meadow across the road from the Pioneer Woman's Grave site. You are now less than 100 yards from where you left the road to start the loop. In summer the grave appears as a large pile of smooth stream stones.

Historical Note. A number of forest fires have raged through this area and the Trillium Basin since the pioneer wagons passed through on the way to the Willamette Valley. Very few of the trees you now see were standing then to witness the passing of the wagons. The giant trees are some of the only witnesses left and should be preserved from logging, which threatens some sections of the area.

PIONEER ROAD LOOPS

Novice
Round trip, South Loop 0.7 mile,
   North Loop 1.1 miles
Unmarked trails
Elevation gain 20 feet

High point 3650 feet
USGS Mount Hood South

Map—page 119

Two short forest loops starting near the Pioneer Woman's Grave utilize sections of the fabled pioneer wagon route, Sam Barlow's toll road. Limited parking is available 0.2 mile east of the Highway 26/35 interchange.

South Loop. From the small sno-park ski to the beginning of the Giant Trees Loop (see preceding tour), 100 yards north of the Pioneer Woman's Grave. Enter the forest on the marked trail and ski about 50 yards. To your left is a narrow open way through the forest: this is the old Barlow Road. To your right is the East Fork Creek and the deeply carved pioneer roadbed, where it forded the stream.

Leave the marked trail here and go left (north) on the old road as it winds for 400 yards to Highway 35 and across to the other side. Small wooden signs nailed to trees at the seven-foot level mark the old road on either side of the highway. Instead of crossing, however, turn right at the edge of the highway and ski east 50 yards to a snow-covered road leading into the woods. Follow this road for about 350 yards to where blue trail markers on the right (Giant Trees Loop) indicate the return trail to your starting point near the Pioneer Grave.

North Loop. Parts of this loop offer very different scenery from that of the South Loop. Crossing the highway twice, the loop is just over 1 mile long. From the small sno-park ski to the South Loop and follow it north to Highway 35. Instead of turning right, cross the highway and follow the obscure roadway up a gentle slope through the trees. After 170 yards, the trail turns left and in one straight line angles back to the highway through scattered trees and small openings.

Pioneer North Loop, following the historic Barlow Road

You may experience some difficulty following the precise roadbed, for snow obscures it and the scattered trees do not outline the route well. On the last leg you might hear a creek clucking away out of sight on the right. Do not cross the creek, which parallels the old road for some distance. If you feel disoriented, do not fear: you cannot get lost here.

This loop eventually intersects the highway near the Salmon River culvert. Cross the highway to the sno-park, then ski the old, scenic road back to the start of the Giant Trees Loop to try the South Loop.

To expand this loop and explore this attractive area, cross the creek at the culvert or on snow bridges and ski west on the north side of the highway to a nearby primitive road loop leading north (near the culvert) or go about 300 yards to the Salmon River clearcut road (see following tour). In addition to these suggestions for expanding your horizons, there are numerous other short alternatives in this area to keep you busy for most of the day.

SALMON RIVER CLEARCUT

Novice   High point 3770 feet
Round trip 1.2 miles   USGS Mount Hood South
Unmarked road
Elevation gain 120 feet   Map—page 119

This tour offers quiet forest and a view of Ghost Ridge. If you search, there are other routes here, including a lovely primitive road that makes possible two short loops.

From the sno-park just east of the Highway 26/35 interchange ski along the north shoulder of the highway back to the interchange, where a snow-covered road leads north, curving through a former campground and then on to several small clearcuts. Ski 350 yards from the highway to a junction where roads go both east and west. The west branch goes to three clearcuts, the first with a good view of Ghost Ridge. This road ends only 0.5 mile from the highway. The other branch goes east to a nearby clearcut, from where you can ski south into the forest, connecting up with a primitive road to form an interesting loop.

For an alternative route ski north from the interchange on the snow-covered road for about 200 yards to a primitive road on the right. Go east on this obscure road as it turns south joining the highway near the culvert of the Salmon River. If you miss the leg that heads south to the highway, you may find another that stops at the Salmon River, which may or may not be crossable. If not, follow the creek to the highway where you can cross the stream above the culvert. Just a few yards east of this culvert is the old Barlow Road and the north loop of the Pioneer Road Loops.

If you enjoy off-road skiing it is possible to ski to this area from the Snow Bunny sno-park, although the forest is a bit tight in places. Most of

Snow-drifted bridge on the Giant Trees Loop. (Photo by Steve Recken)

this unmarked route is through open forest, but if you get too far from the highway you will find marshes and slide alder thickets. From Snow Bunny your best bet is to ski through the forest close to the highway to avoid streams and wet areas. You will find two abandoned highway sections here, both heavily overgrown with alders. When you reach the West Fork, it can be crossed at the highway culvert. This route is not for novice skiers, although it is not difficult nor steep.

SALMON RIVER MEADOWS

Novice
Round trip 2 miles
Unmarked road
Elevation loss 100 feet

Elevation of meadows 3374 feet
USGS Mount Wilson

Map—page 124

Located only a short distance off the highway, this large meadow offers solitude in a deep basin surrounded by high, forested ridges.

The meadow is not visible from the highway and consequently is seldom visited. From the Highway 26/35 interchange drive south on Highway 26 for 2.3 miles to a gas station, then another 0.4 mile to where the highway starts uphill. Park near the end of the west guard rail, where the obscure access road is located. Follow this road 0.5 mile down a gen-

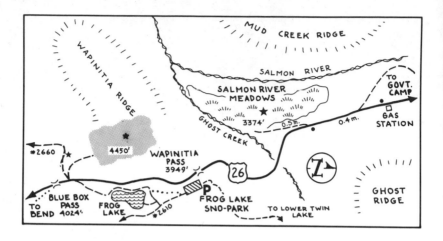

tle grade to the meadows.

Your success in exploring the meadow depends on snow depth. The meadow is at a low elevation and in some winters has a minimum of snow. The beauty of the large meadow, however, is worth exploring the possibilities. Over a mile long from north to south, the meadow is squeezed at both ends between the impressive, steep ridge to the south, extending out from Wapinitia Pass, and Mud Creek Ridge on the west.

The winding banks of Ghost Creek, the gurgling stream on the east edge of the meadow, just south of the access road, offer an interesting and scenic tour. Alder thickets and screens of firs break the flatness of the area. To the north the Eternal White Guardian is splendid in its white winter robe.

The Salmon River is separated from the west edge of the meadow by an almost impenetrable band of forest. Near the meadow's north end, however, you can penetrate this narrow band and cross the river on logs to gain access to a prominent old clearcut, now rapidly growing over, on the side of Mud Creek Ridge. This clearcut is just south of two prominent rounded bluffs.

The climb to the top of Mud Creek Ridge, offering access to Trillium Basin, is for experienced off-road skiers only. It requires deep snow and entails some brush busting and difficult going in dense, small trees. But if you are a pioneer, it is worth the effort. After climbing some vertical 400 feet you will come out near the ridge top at the Lostman Trail.

Snow pinwheel

Chapter 9
FROG LAKE

The Frog Lake area is 4.3 miles due south on Highway 26 from the Salmon River area. Frog Lake and the surrounding country offer a surprising variety of tours, most suitable for less experienced skiers. Most tours are along generally level roads and provide extensive views over clearcuts. This area is open to snowmobiles, but mid-week skiers see few of them. All the tours in this area start at the Frog Lake sno-park at Wapinitia Pass, 4.3 miles south of the Highway 26/35 interchange.

Since this is snowmobile country, the roads are likely to be hard packed and icy. Keep to the sides of the roads to avoid the speeding machines. This is their turf so respect their presence.

FROG LAKE LOOP

Novice
Round trip to Frog Lake 1.4 miles
Unmarked roads
Elevation mostly level

High point 3950 feet
USGS Mount Wilson

Map—page 126

The north end of Frog Lake is wide and meadowed, while the massive bulk of Frog Lake Buttes dominates the east shore. The lake's south end offers a view of Mt. Hood in fair weather.

From the sno-park the lake is only 0.7 mile to the south. You have a

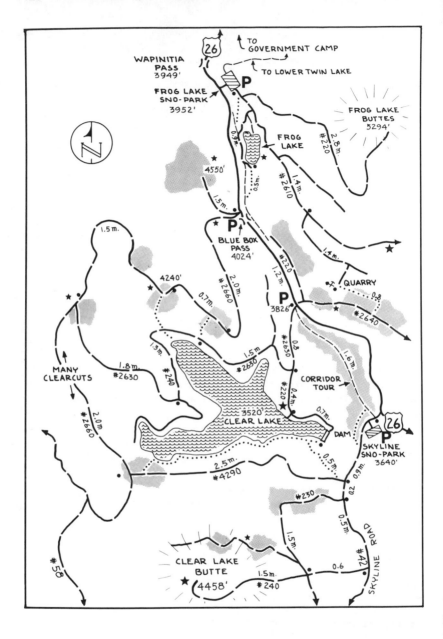

choice of two routes. The first and least interesting is to follow Road 2610 south from the sno-park for 0.4 mile. Then turn right onto a side road and descend a gentle hill. Here the road branches. The left branch goes directly to the campground at the near end of the lake. The right branch goes straight ahead to the west side of the lake and then on to the far end. Either way it is a short distance to the north end of the lake.

For the most scenic approach to the lake, however, ski south from the sno-park and in only 100 yards angle right onto a primitive road blocked by a snow mound. Follow this lovely route for 0.4 mile to where it joins an abandoned former highway section that leads gently downhill to the west shore of the lake. Link this route with the previous one to form a loop.

ROAD 2610 CLEARCUTS

Novice
Round trip 3 miles to 6 miles
Unmarked roads
Elevation mostly level

High point 3950 feet
USGS Mount Wilson

Map—page 126

From the south end of the Frog Lake sno-park ski south on Road 2610 past side-roads leading to the buttes and to Frog Lake. Continue south through forest for 1.4 miles, where a side road on the right leads to a small quarry. Do not take this road, but continue straight, traveling along the top edges of almost continuous, large shelterwood cuts that offer good views to the west. The finest view, however, is 3 miles from the sno-park, just after passing through a band of old-growth forest. Here, there are grand views south to Mt. Wilson and Crater Lake Butte (lookout tower) and across miles of forest and low ridges. The road to this point is quite level, but beyond here it starts descending, and there is little of interest to the Nordic skier.

QUARRY LOOP

Intermediate
Round trip 6.9 miles
Unmarked roads and clearcuts
Elevation gain/loss about 120 feet

High point 3950 feet
USGS Mount Wilson

Map—page 126

From the Frog Lake sno-park ski south on Road 2610 for 1.4 mile and take the side road on the right, which descends to and shortly parallels 2610. Follow this road through cutover areas for 1.0 mile to another side road. Turn right and descend a gentle grade, crossing a creek to a small quarry at the valley bottom. Ski into the quarry, heading southeast (left) along the bottom of a large shelterwood area, then climbing to Road 2640, at the top of the hill to the west. Follow the road west through cutover areas then along the edge of the forest to where a side-road (220) enters the trees on the right. Follow that primitive road north, not far from and parallel to Highway 26, to Blue Box Pass. From Blue Box Pass ski down a straight, wide snow-covered road to the west shore of Frog Lake. For a recommended alternative to this uninteresting stretch of road, just north of the pass ski through the trees on the right into a shallow draw. Follow this old roadbed to the south end of Frog Lake. This route is actually the historic Oak Grove-Wapinitia road, a long-abandoned wagon road from Government Camp to eastern Oregon. Formerly, this road left the Barlow Road at the north end of Summit Meadows (Trillium Basin) and skirted both Red Top and Salmon River Meadows, along the east foot of Mud Creek Ridge, to its course over Wapinitia and Blue Box Passes.

Do not attempt the loop in bad weather, when it is easy to become disoriented in the large clearcuts. Carry a Forest Service map showing roads, regardless of weather. The side roads to the quarry are not shown on some Forest Service maps although they are shown in this guidebook. If you are not comfortable with exploratory skiing do not ski the Quarry Loop, but stick to Road 2610, where the views are rewarding.

FROG LAKE BUTTES

Intermediate
Round trip 6 miles
Unmarked road
Elevation gain 1342 feet

High point 5294 feet
USGS Mount Wilson

Map—page 126

The unrelenting climb of more than 1300 feet to the summit and the dashing, speedy descent convince some skiers that there is truth to the old adage that once is often enough. From the Frog Lake sno-park ski south on Road 2610 for 0.2 mile to the first road on the left. This is Road 220; follow it to the summit, climbing up moderately steep grades with no letup.

There are few views on the way up, so the view of Mt. Hood from the summit snow plateau is well earned. The descent is often fast and difficult due to steepness, especially if hardpacked or if snowmobile washboards are present. This is not a particularly outstanding tour as better views are available elsewhere for considerably less effort. However, for hardy skiers the speedy descent is almost unmatched. This road to the summit is closed to snowmobiles during the month of February.

The descent is more than most skiers can comfortably control, and many falls are possible. If the road is hard packed, ski elsewhere; otherwise you will be hard pressed to control your speed and enjoy the run. If the snow is light, however, this is a great run.

LOWER TWIN LAKE

Intermediate
Round trip 5 miles
Unmarked trail
Elevation gain 608 feet cumulative

High point 4360 feet
USGS Mount Wilson

Map—page 144

Ski through impressive stands of hemlock trees to reach the lake in its scenic, forested basin. This is a good tour for advanced novice or intermediate skiers to test their ability against a variety of moderate terrain challenges. Some route-finding is also required. The heavy forest provides shelter from stormy weather. The Forest Service, however, plans a future timber sale that will result in relocation of the Pacific Crest National Scenic Trail (PCNST), thereby affecting the future route to the lower lake, and the loop tour.

Park at the Frog Lake sno-park. At its north end locate the PCNST,

Upper Twin Lake

which goes 30 yards north, then abruptly turns right near a giant tree. Wind gently upward through old-growth forest, then make a sharp left turn and continue climbing gentle to moderate grades into second-growth forest along the west side of the hill. At 1.5 miles a side trail to Lower Twin Lake leaves the PCNST at a right angle, climbing gently eastward for 100 yards to a pass at 4460 feet.

From the pass make a long, gentle traverse leading downhill, then turn sharply right and ski 150 yards to a point near the north shore of the lake. From there, the trail climbs to Upper Twin Lake (see Twin Lakes Trail). Leave the trail and descend an easy, short, steep slope to the edge of the lake. If the lake is not solidly frozen, the west shore provides easy terrain for skiing around the south end to the opposite shore. The lake is nestled in a lovely, forested basin that offers ample scenic reward. From the south shore a poorly defined and hard to locate trail leads to the summit of Frog Lake Buttes. It is possible to ski to Upper Twin Lake by trail and to ski a loop linking both lakes (see Twin Lakes Trail and Loop).

In years of deep snow tree blazes will be covered and the trail may be difficult to follow. The junction 100 yards west of the pass is easy to miss when the summer trail sign is under snow. Always beware of lake ice.

West shore of Clear Lake

Chapter 10
CLEAR LAKE BASIN

Nordic skiers have generally overlooked the Clear Lake Basin. New clearcuts and logging roads, however, now offer an increasing variety of tours. There been two main reasons for the lack of skiing interest in this area. First, its relatively low elevation means inconsistent snow depth and quality. At the same time, since the basin is situated slightly east of the heavier Cascade snowfall zone, it at times enjoys somewhat better weather than the often wet and stormy Government Camp area. The second reason skiers have avoided the area is that it is one of two centers of snowmobile activity on Mt. Hood (the other is Frog Lake). The Clear Lake area offers long, interesting tours on gentle terrain and the exceptional experience of skiing the lake's long, wide shoreline.

To reach the Clear Lake Basin follow Highway 26 only 10 miles south of Government Camp, crossing Wapinitia and Blue Box passes on the way. Clear Lake itself, with its scenic vistas and wide-open, skiable shoreline, is the star attraction of the area. The region surrounding the lake also offers variety and scenic beauty. Even if you must bite the proverbial bullet, because of snowmobile use here, you will still probably find your touring experiences rewarding.

Parking is limited but adequate. The only large sno-park is located at Skyline Road, which leads south to Timothy Lake. Off-road parking is also available just north of Blue Box Pass (Road 2660) and at Road 2630—the Clear Lake road—where there are small plowed-out roadheads. If parking on the highway, however, remember to do so outside the fog line and to use common sense. Roadside parking on or near curves is often not tolerated during snow plowing. If these small sno-parks are filled, use the Skyline sno-park and ski a different route. The Forest Service plans another sno-park in the area, but it may be several years before funds are available for construction.

Recommended tours in the Clear Lake Basin are the Lake Shore Tour, Clear Lake Dam Loop, Clear Lake Butte, and at least the first three miles of the Blue Box Pass-Clear Lake Loops. Another scenic route just across the highway, the Mountain View Tour, is for skiers who want a shorter tour on level terrain.

LAKE SHORE TOUR

Novice
Round trip to lake 2.4 miles, to dam
   3.8 miles, around lake 7 miles
Unmarked roads
Elevation loss 306 feet

High point 3826 feet
USGS Mount Wilson

Map—page 126

In summer Clear Lake is unattractive, with dirt- and stump-covered shorelines. But in winter it is transformed into a snowy expanse of shorelines—truly a scenic gem in its shallow lake basin surrounded by rolling forested hills.

The best approach to the lake is from Road 2630 (future sno-park site), 2.5 miles south of the Frog Lake sno-park. From there follow Road 2630 south for 1.2 miles to the lake shore boat ramp and campground, a gentle descent most of the way. The shore is wide and free of trees, offering a scenic tour regardless of direction. You can ski 0.7 mile by road or by shoreline to the dam or ski the other direction, following the north arm of the lake. The north arm is especially lovely, and the tour around the entire lake is long but rewarding. Crossing inlet streams may offer small, but surmountable problems, depending on snow depth.

Because of a low elevation, lake ice is often not as solid as it may appear, particularly along the shorelines. Even if the ice appears safe, it is best to stay off the lake.

CORRIDOR TOUR

Novice
Round trip 3.2 miles
Unmarked clearcut
Elevation loss 186 feet

High point 3826 feet
USGS Mount Wilson

Map—page 126

Tour through a narrow, winding clearcut connecting Road 2630 with Road 42, the Skyline Road. This attractive area, with a variety of terrain for novices, parallels Highway 26, usually within hearing distance.

From the Road 2630 sno-park, ski 50 yards down Road 2630. There, turn left, entering the trees onto a primitive road that leads to the long, narrow clearcut in 100 yards. The clearcut route drops gently from north to south, and many gentle slopes offer good practice areas for novice skiers.

If you want your downhill treat last rather than first, you can also ski the Corridor Tour from the Skyline Road sno-park. From the sno-park, enter a narrow road on the left between the sno-park and Highway 26. This area is open to snowmobiles.

CLEAR LAKE DAM LOOP

Intermediate
Round trip 5 miles
Unmarked roads
Elevation loss 330 feet

High point 3850 feet
USGS Mount Wilson

Map—page 126

The Dam Loop is one of the finest tours in the area, offering considerable variety in skiing and scenery. There is skiing through clearcuts, beautiful forest, and along roads, and shoreline, where great vistas open up to distant hills and forested ridges that surround the ice-covered vastness of Clear Lake.

Follow the Corridor Tour (which see) south and downhill to its end near the Skyline sno-park. From there ski downhill on the lower section of the clearcut, paralleling Road 42 and eventually joining it by skiing through trees. Then follow Road 42 for 0.5 mile to its junction with Road 4290. Turn right (west) onto Road 4290 and in about 80 yards a small, winding road to the dam angles off to the right into the woods.

This side road, a snowmobile trail, is not obvious and may take a moment to locate. It winds around and then climbs a low ridge, traveling through old-growth hemlock, then entering a dense stand of small, immature firs. It descends through this dog-hair growth, and in just over 0.5 mile comes out at the lake's edge, just west of the dam. (In the reverse direction, from the dam, this narrow road may be difficult to find because it is becoming overgrown. From the dam follow the obvious road (see map) and make a sharp left turn onto the obscure ridge road.) As snowmobiles frequent this area, their tracks may help you find this road or perhaps confuse you with the many erratic directions they travel. Cross the dam and follow the lakeshore road to the boat ramp. Then ski uphill along Road 2630 to the sno-park.

WEST SIDE TOUR

Intermediate
Round trip 10 miles
Unmarked road
Elevation loss 306 feet

High point 3826 feet
USGS Mount Wilson

Map—page 126

This road tour through heavy forest has no views to commend it, but it is protected from the weather and does serve as a shortcut exit from other tours in the area.

From the Road 2630 sno-park take the road south for 0.8 mile. Turn right (west) at a junction and follow the rolling road (still 2630) as it circles the north end of the lake, eventually meeting Road 240 in 2.8 miles. Road 240 passes around the west arm of the lake, providing a sheltered route in adverse weather and access to the end of the lake. It is possible to ski to the lake shore from several points along Roads 2630 and 240.

BLUE BOX PASS-CLEAR LAKE LOOPS

Skill level Intermediate, loops are Advanced
Round trip to second clearcut 5.4 miles, Short Loop 7 to 9.2 miles,
   Long Loop 11.5 miles
Unmarked roads and clearcuts
Elevation gain 970 feet cumulative, loss 504 feet cumulative
High point 4240 feet
USGS Mount Wilson

Map—page 126

Several loops starting from Blue Box Pass provide impressive views of the Clear Lake basin and scenic lake shore touring. The first 2.7 miles along Road 2660 offer a good out and back tour for intermediate skiers. The longer loops, requiring long distance skiing and some route-finding, are definitely for advanced skiers only.

Blue Box Pass is 1.4 miles south of the Frog Lake sno-park and 5.7 miles south of the Highway 26/35 interchange. The trailhead for the loop tours is a small roadhead sno-park located on the west side of the highway at Road 2660.

From the sno-park follow the lower of two roads. In the first mile lose 250 feet elevation along moderate grades through hemlock stands and past logged areas. There is a fine view of massive Mt. Wilson some ten miles to the southeast. The road briefly levels out, then climbs 350 feet around a ridge shoulder to a clearcut with large second-growth trees. This clearcut, 2.0 miles from the trailhead, offers views to the south and west. Another 0.7 mile of up and down skiing brings you to a second clearcut with a splendid view of Clear Lake, Mt. Jefferson, and Timothy Lake. This is the end of the scenic tour for intermediate skiers.

Short Loop. The route for this loop leaves Road 2660 at the first clearcut for a 7.0-mile tour or from the second clearcut for the longer 9.2-mile tour. When snow is deep enough, ski the first clearcut down into old-growth timber to Road 2630 (the West Side Tour) and the nearby lakeshore. In poor snow a steep logging road at the very west edge of the clearcut may be descended on foot. These off-road descents should be attempted only by advanced skiers with experience in route finding. The wide lakeshore can be followed easily southeast to the campground and boat landing, where Roads 220 and 2630 lead north for 1.2 miles to Highway 26.

To complete the loop, cross Highway 26 and take Road 2640 a short distance to a clearcut, where you turn left and ski north along the clearcut edge on Road 220. Follow this road as it closely parallels Highway 26 for 1.2 miles. Keep left and it eventually comes out opposite your parking spot at Blue Box Pass.

Long Loop. Follow the Short Loop route beyond the second clearcut. Mt. Hood appears as the road descends 250 feet to the 3.5-mile mark. The lake comes into view as you ski through alternating forest and clearings. The junction with Road 2630 is in a clearcut at 4.2 miles. Road 2660, your main route, goes right, while the road to your left (2630) goes out onto the peninsula between the two arms of Clear Lake.

Continue on Road 2660, proceeding through forest and in one place between high roadside embankments. Two miles of skiing brings you to a large clearcut, where you have a choice of two routes to complete the loop.

Alternative One: From the west end of the lake stay on the road, crossing the large clearcut to its eastern edge. Follow Road 4290 east for 2.5 miles to the Skyline Road (Road 42), then turn left and ski 0.9 mile to the Skyline sno-park. From there take the Corridor Tour (which see) to the Road 2630 sno-park. Then follow the Short Loop route north to the Blue Box Pass sno-park for a 12.2-mile loop.

Alternative Two: From the clearcut at the west end of Clear Lake, ski only 100 yards through a band of forest to the west arm of the lake. Then ski along the lake shore (or follow a primitive road through the second growth at the edge of the lakeside forest) to the east end of the lake. Cross the dam, then follow either the lake shore or the parallel road to the Road 220/2630 junction, then uphill to Highway 26 and on to Blue Box Pass, as described in the Short Loop. This loop totals 11.5 miles.

The Skyline Road (Road 42) and even Road 4290 are sometimes plowed out in winter and spring for logging. Depending on your loop plans, road plowing may affect route selection or plans for car shuttling. The Bear Springs Ranger Station will supply road plowing information.

Depending on snow depth, or visibility, several clearcuts may cause delays in route selection, particularly at road intersections. Be sure to use your maps constantly on this tour, even in clear weather. The road may "disappear" in some clearcuts. Always have a good idea of your location in relation to the maps. The loops demand serious skiing, survival gear, repair kit, map, and compass.

BLUE BOX PASS TOUR

Intermediate	**High point 4450 feet**
Round trip 3 miles	**USGS Mount Wilson**
Unmarked road and clearcut	**Map—page 126**
Elevation gain 426 feet	

A short, moderately steep road leads past an outstanding view into mixed rolling and level terrain on Wapinitia Ridge, where selective harvesting has left many large, beautiful trees. In fast snow conditions the descent from the large clearcut above Blue Box Pass along the steep access road demands skill.

From Blue Box Pass sno-park (see Blue Box Pass-Clear Lake Loops), take the road to the right, which climbs past a fine view of miles of valley and Mt. Wilson in the distance. The road ends in 1.5 miles in the selected-harvest area. This is a vast area where you can explore at leisure the forest scene that seems to stretch endlessly northward.

MOUNTAIN VIEW TOUR

Novice	**High point 3826 feet**
Round trip up to 3 miles	**USGS Mount Wilson**
Unmarked roads	**Map—page 126**
Elevation gain negligible	

This tour is open-ended. There are extensive clearcuts and roads with outstanding views of Mt. Hood and Frog Lake Buttes. The area is generally level, and the road complex—part of the Frog Lake road system—extends north and south for miles. Though often used by snowmobiles, this is a good area for midweek skiing, and the scenic rewards are great. If you are planning long tours in this area, a compass and recent Forest Service map showing roads are essential because the road system here is complex.

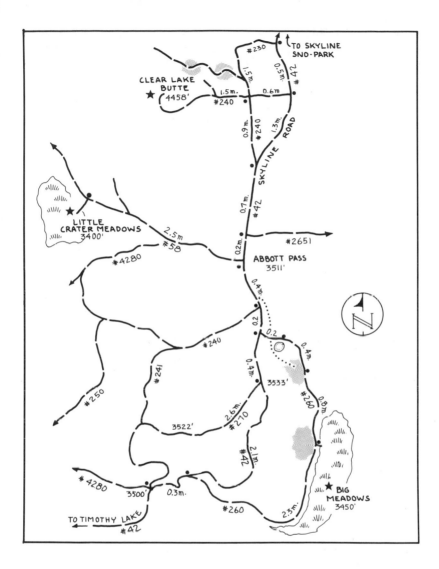

From Road 2630 sno-park (see Lake Shore Tour) cross to the east side of the highway, climb the snowbank, and follow snow-covered Road 2640 for about 100 yards. There Road 220 goes north and Road 2640 continues southeastward. An alternative approach to this area is to park at the Skyline sno-park, ski north along the Corridor Tour route to Road 2630, and cross the highway.

Road 220 goes north, following the edge of the forest, with a large clearcut on the east. It ends near the north end of the clearcut. To ski to

Blue Box Pass, ski about a mile on Road 220, then enter the forest on your left. Find a side road or ski about 80 yards through the trees to a snowmobile route. This old road, closely paralleling the highway, goes north about 300 yards to where it joins the highway just south of the Blue Box Pass sno-park.

From the clearcut edge near where you parked Road 2640 heads southeast through large, level clearcuts with splendid views, continuing for miles and connecting with other roads.

CLEAR LAKE BUTTE

Advanced   High point 4458 feet
Round trip up to 10.8 miles   USGS Mount Wilson
Unmarked road
Elevation gain 900 feet   Map—pages 126, 137

The summit of Clear Lake Butte has a sweeping view of the entire region, including Mt. Hood. The return trip offers a downhill run of about 2 miles. Pick a good day to ensure the best view.

Your driving destination is the Skyline sno-park, 9 miles south of the Highway 26/35 interchange. From the sno-park ski south on Road 42 (the Skyline Road). The first mile of gentle, downhill grade is followed by a brief climb for 0.2 mile to Road 230 (just past Road 4290 on the right). Road 230, a logging road, is not obvious, but if you are alert you will have no problem spotting it. It offers the most direct route to the top of Clear Lake Butte.

Road 230 climbs gently westward through forest, soon passing a shelterwood harvest area on the left, where many trees have been left standing. This cut-over area soon merges with a clearcut where immature trees are establishing themselves. At this point the road seems to disappear and a large shelterwood area appears on the right. Climb along the edge of the immature trees to a flat area where the edge of dense, mature forest to the south meets the shelterwood area.

Ski along the level, following the edge of the forest to the far end of the shelterwood area on your right. There make a left turn onto an obscure forest road and follow it south to its junction with the road descending from the lookout. The gentle climb from Road 42 to this point covers 1.5 miles, with a similar distance remaining to the summit. Turn right onto the lookout road (Road 240) and begin to ascend more steeply. Road 230 is the most interesting and scenic of the routes leading to the lookout road.

There are, however, two alternatives to Road 230. First, continue south on Road 42 past Road 230 for 0.5 mile, turning right onto a wide side road and climbing a relentless, monotonous road 0.6 mile to the Road 230/240 junction. Second, take the original route to the summit.

Little Crater Lake and Meadows

Ski 1.8 miles on Road 42 from Road 230 to Road 240, where you turn back sharply to the right. This junction, marked by three tall, prominent conifers, is just past a slight curve to the left. The side road climbs gently for a mile, past a clearcut, then joins the lookout road descending from the summit.

In winters of little snow Road 42 is often plowed for logging, thus shortening the approach from Highway 26. If so, drive the road as far as you can and allow ample passing room when you park.

Be prepared for cold winds on the exposed summit. Carry a Forest Service map for road skiing decisions, but remember that some of these roads may not be shown. If there are no ski tracks to follow in the shelterwood areas, you will have to be careful of the route. Future timber sales are planned for this area and will eventually alter route finding.

LITTLE CRATER MEADOWS AND LAKE

Advanced
Round trip 13.2 miles
Unmarked roads
Elevation loss 240 feet

High point at sno-park 3640 feet
USGS Mount Wilson

Map—page 137

Almost entirely along forest roads without views, with very little climbing or descending, the beauty of the meadow will more than make up for the distance traveled. On the return trip you can climb Clear Lake Butte for an outstanding view of the entire Clear Lake basin. Although this tour is entirely on major roads, carry a Forest Service map, for there are numerous confusing side roads.

From Skyline sno-park (see Clear Lake Butte) ski south on Road 42 for 3.8 miles to a broad, major junction with Road 58, which gently descends to the west. Turn right on Road 58 and ski 2.5 miles to a side road on the left (Road 230), which leads the last short distance to the campground and road end at the edge of Little Crater Meadow.

Small, deep, crystal-clear Crater Lake is quite unusual. Located 300 yards from the end of the campground road, it is surrounded by rail fences to keep cattle out as they wander about the vast, beautiful meadow in the summer. The meadow, fringed by an undulating tree border, is inspiring. Mt. Hood rises above the forest to the north.

If you climb Clear Lake Butte on the return trip via Roads 240 and 230 (see Clear Lake Butte), you will add only 3.6 miles to the day's total. In the spring and in some winters the Skyline Road (Road 42) is plowed for logging, thereby greatly shortening this tour.

BIG MEADOWS

Intermediate
Round trip 14 miles
Unmarked roads
Elevation loss 190 feet

High point 3640 feet
USGS Mount Wilson

Map—page 137

Big Meadows are the largest below timberline on Mt. Hood and certainly the most perfect in several respects: wide, two miles long, curving out of view, and dominated by the majestic bulk of the heavily forested Mt. Wilson. The meadow enjoys a spectacular natural setting, surrounded by rolling, forested hills.

From the Skyline sno-park, ski Road 42 to the Little Crater Meadows junction. But instead of turning west on Road 58, continue south. Ski 0.6 mile on Road 42 and turn left onto a prominent side road, Road 260. Opposite the first clearcut is a dense screen of trees concealing a lovely, circular pond that is worth visiting. The road then curves and goes south past several clearcuts and over a low pass.

Big Meadows is 1.4 miles from the Skyline Road (Road 42) and hidden from view by a narrow band of trees. A short side road through this band suddenly opens onto a magnificent scene—the wide, long meadow extending to the foot of Mt. Wilson, which rises 2000 feet above in a smooth sweep of forest. As you ski along the edge of the meadow, the scene changes, providing a variety of impressions.

Although the meadow is 5.8 miles south of the sno-park, the tour may be much shorter if Road 42 is plowed for logging. Call the Bear Springs Ranger Station to verify plowing.

Big Meadows Loop. A challenging alternative to just skiing into the meadow and back to your car, this 7-mile loop tour offers scenic variety and several miles of interesting skiing along primitive roads. The loop starts at Road 42, 4.4 miles from the Skyline sno-park, and follows the usual 1.4-mile approach to the meadow. From the side road, ski into the meadow and head first south and then west as it curves and eventually narrows, squeezing you either into dense pine thickets or old-growth, depending on your choice. Ski north to a nearby primitive road and turn left. Follow this winding road to Road 42. Turn south or left for 0.3 mile, then pick up a road on the right. This forest road climbs gently to a large cut-over area, eventually leading back to the Skyline Road at the point where you started. Skiing the loop adds 4.2 miles to the trip.

Snowmobiles may be seen in this area, and may even have broken a track for you. There are no physical hazards as the roads are gentle for the full distance. Carry and use a Forest Service map as there are many side roads. All maps are not current, and some roads will not be shown. If snow is not deep, road signs will be visible.

Chapter 11
BARLOW PASS

Barlow Pass, at 4157 feet elevation, was the highest point reached by the first wagon road across the Oregon Cascades, portions of which remain to this day to be hiked and skied. This pass, located on Highway 35 between Snow Bunny and White River, is a great attraction for those seeking forest trail skiing and areas that are not heavily used.

Trails radiate from Barlow Pass in all directions, offering a variety of scenery and two outstanding viewpoints not far from the trailhead. Several of the trails provide fine forest skiing experiences.

The principal trails are the Twin Lakes and Devils Half Acre trails on the south and the Panorama Dome-Boy Scout Ridge, and Yellowjacket trails on the north. In addition, connector trails join Barlow Pass with Barlow Ridge and White River. A downhill run along the old snow-covered highway starting at the far end of the sno-park leads to the Giant Trees Loop and Pioneer Woman's Grave.

The future existence of the Barlow Pass sno-park as we know it today depends on the Department of Highways' evaluations of snow-removal problems and on the development of other sno-parks in the area. In heavy snow years this sno-park is difficult to plow because it is narrow and has a winding access road.

A sno-park planned for Barlow Saddle, at the foot of Barlow Ridge, will be constructed when funds are available. It will be named Alps sno-

Trailhead at Barlow Pass sno-park

park and will be located one mile north of Barlow Pass on Highway 35. It will improve access to several fine, seldom-used trails and eliminate the problem of access to the Barlow Ridge area and Boy Scout Ridge.

The skiing area around the proposed Alps sno-park is contiguous with Barlow Pass and will be included in this same section of the guidebook. Several trails connect the two areas by running through the forest and paralleling the highway. Other trails that are suitable to novice skiers but that are now accessible only from Barlow Pass will be easily reached from the Alps sno-park. The result will be to disperse growing numbers of skiers onto lesser-known but suitable trails.

To appreciate fully the fine skiing opportunities of these areas, study the maps for this section. Interesting loops, both short and long, are possible by using connector trails that link the principal trails.

TWIN LAKES TRAIL AND LOOP

Intermediate to Advanced
Round trip to upper lake 7.6 miles, lake loop 9.7 miles
Marked trails
Elevation gain 975 feet cumulative
High point 4550 feet
USGS Mount Hood South, Mount Wilson

Map—page 144

This very popular tour starts out along the Pacific Crest Trail, travels through a variety of scenic areas, and offers some long, moderate downhill runs. The complete loop, however, is rated advanced because of the moderately steep slope between the lakes.

Be alert for trail junctions, particularly after new snowfall and before the trail has been broken. The trail is quite obvious in most places but may require some care between the lakes and after leaving the lower lake for the pass to the west. Beware of thin lake ice.

From the northeast corner of the inner sno-park, enter the forest a few paces, then turn south and follow the Pacific Crest Trail through old-growth. The trail twists and turns, climbing gently then moderately to "The Shoulder" and then on to the nearby high point (4550 feet) which is 1.3 miles from the trailhead.

At The Shoulder there is a brief view of Mt. Hood, and just a few paces off the trail to the east there are semi-open slopes for views down to Devils Half Acre meadow and across to Barlow Ridge. The trail then descends gently along the east side of Ghost Ridge.

From the high point descend more than 0.5 mile to a section of trail that is more or less level for several hundred yards. Near the end of this level section, 2.3 miles from the trailhead, turn left (east) at the Twin Lakes Trail junction.

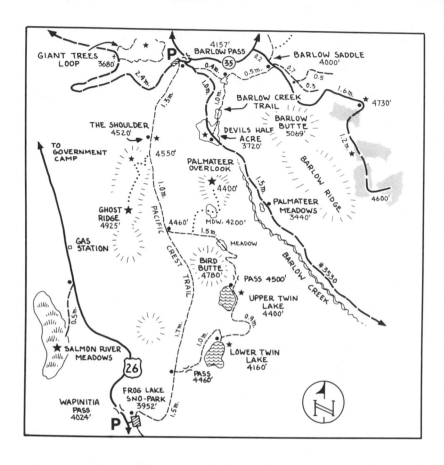

If no one has preceded you here, it is possible to miss the junction, which is not well marked. If you do miss it, you will remain on the Pacific Crest Trail and will soon begin climbing, ultimately ending at the Frog Lake sno-park and passing en route the junction with the trail to Lower Twin Lake.

Back at the junction, descend the Twin Lakes Trail through second-growth, then into old-growth, where the trail levels out. The trail then climbs gently through second-growth, with only a few fleeting views to the north, reaching a small meadow, then climbing in two switchbacks to a pass at 4500 feet. The trail then descends moderately through open forest for several hundred yards to the upper lake at 4400 feet. The trail continues around the east shore to a view of Mt. Hood, seen from the south end of the lake.

For many skiers the most exciting part of this tour is the return trip: the descent first from the pass and then from The Shoulder. From the high point on the Pacific Crest Trail it is a short, restful descent to The

Shoulder, from which there is almost a mile of downhill skiing to the trailhead. In good snow this is an exhilarating dash, with some fairly fast and exciting sections.

The descent is well balanced for speed, for as you start to feel you are going too fast a flat section always seems to appear in the nick of time. Strong stemming of the lower ski in many places helps to control speed, as does an occasional turn uphill into the deep snow to stop and rest. Be alert for slower skiers ahead, as well as for skiers headed uphill. There are many easy turns to negotiate on the descent, and it is difficult to see skiers around the bends.

Advanced skiers can make a loop by skiing to Lower Twin Lake and returning north along the Pacific Crest Trail. From Upper Twin Lake ski across the lake or along the east shore trail and descend to Lower Twin Lake, 4160 feet, on moderately steep grades through open forest, following the trail as well as possible. From the lower lake climb a short draw then turn left and ascend a long traverse to the pass at 4360 feet, just west of the lake (see Lower Twin Lake for more details).

From the pass descend 100 yards west to the Pacific Crest Trail and turn right (north, uphill). Ski north along the west side of Bird Butte through dense timber without views. When you are finally back on the Twin Lakes Trail, you will start to recognize the area as you climb to the high point for the exhilarating downhill run to the trailhead.

An alternative to these tours is to ski from the Barlow Pass trailhead along the Pacific Crest Trail to the Frog Lake sno-park. If you can set up a car shuttle, this is a nice one-way tour for less-experienced skiers who want to avoid the fast ski run down from The Shoulder to Barlow Pass.

PALMATEER OVERLOOK

Advanced	**High point 4550 feet**
Round trip 5.4 miles	**USGS Mount Hood South**
Unmarked off-trail route	**Map—page 144**
Elevation gain 600 feet	

This exceptional viewpoint near Barlow Pass is only reached with some effort, as off-trail skiing is required. The short off-trail stretch is interesting, easy, and leads into a lovely meadow from where you can reach the overlook by climbing along an open ridge. Two summer trails lead from the Twin Lakes Trail to Palmateer Camp Meadow. Not shown on the guidebook map, these trails are difficult to ski and not recommended.

From Barlow Pass ski the Pacific Crest Trail to the Twin Lakes Trail junction. Take the left fork and descend about 300 yards to old-growth forest. After skiing for about 150 yards through the old-growth, the trail starts gently uphill through second-growth. This is where the off-trail skiing begins.

Here at the edge of the old-growth (and the 2-mile marker) turn left off the trail and, keeping left, traverse on an almost level course through beautiful open timber. If you drop too far to the right, you will end up in difficult slide alder thickets. If so, bear left to keep above the alder.

The route through the timber is almost a side-hill traverse but hardly a hill as it is so gentle. After 300 yards, enter second-growth pines and firs. Keep bearing left if there are any problems. Contour where necessary to avoid dense areas, but if you start going slightly downhill where possible you will ski right into Palmateer Camp Meadow. This off-trail section is easy and there is almost no way to get lost, for all downhill directions lead into the meadow, which lies in a shallow basin.

From the upper end of the meadow ski eastward to the adjacent low ridge for a view of the Barlow Creek valley. Continue up the narrow, tree-covered ridge and it soon widens and opens up. A moderately steep slope climbing 200 feet from the meadow leads to the ultimate viewpoint at 4400 feet. Several picturesque snags reign over this remarkable ridgecrest and viewpoint.

The view, to say the least, is spectacular. Devils Half Acre is far below, and the U-shaped Barlow Creek valley extends away for miles. The view of Mt. Hood is especially striking due to the foreground ridges and hills that sweep grandly up to its vast snowfields. To stand on this high point with the snow dropping away on all sides is exciting.

Although the tour description sounds complicated, the tour is really quite direct, gentle and easy to follow. Nevertheless, carry a compass and map and ski this tour only if you can leave a good track for your return.

Ghost Ridge Overlook. This viewpoint is just off the Twin Lakes Trail route and a large open slope provides a wide view. From Barlow Pass ski south on the Pacific Crest Trail to The Shoulder, from where you can see an open slope ahead on Ghost Ridge, just above the high point of the trail. Leave the trail at the high point and make your way southwestward through dense, small trees, quickly reaching the open slope (4800 feet). A singularly beautiful view greets you if you ski to the upper western part of the slope. The view sweeps from the Trillium Basin to the west past Mt. Hood and on to Barlow Ridge, Elk Mountain, Lookout Mountain, and Bonney Butte to the northeast.

For those wanting an even more expansive view, continue climbing moderately upward through alternating dense stands of trees and open areas, making your way where resistance is least. From the 4925-foot summit of Ghost Ridge the view also includes to the south Mt. Wilson, Timothy Lake, Broken Top and Mt. Jefferson. Because you are on the very top of the ridge, the looking is unobstructed and panoramic.

The descent is not difficult, with only a couple of short, moderate slopes, depending on your upward route. It is only 0.5 mile from the trail to the highest point. The lower overlook slope is for intermediate skiers; the summit, for strong intermediates. Continuing to the summit requires persistence and favorable snow conditions for an enjoyable descent.

DEVILS HALF ACRE LOOP

Intermediate
Round trip 2.5 miles
Marked road and trail
Elevation loss 407 feet

High point 4157 feet
USGS Mount Hood South

Map—page 144

This loop starts with a road descent to a delightful meadow in the deep Barlow Creek valley and returns along a lovely forest trail, following the route of the historic Barlow Road.

From the northeast corner of the Barlow Pass sno-park descend Road 3530 in a southeast direction for 1 mile to Devils Half Acre. The road descends at a moderate grade, losing 400 feet as it winds its way through heavy timber to the meadow, where Mt. Hood can be seen.

About 250 yards down the road from the sno-park a trail sign marks a trail branching off to the left, which in summer is seen to be the heavily worn pioneer Barlow Road, descending to Devils Half Acre. This, the Barlow Creek Trail, descends a difficult, narrow, moderately steep road bed for 0.4 mile to a small meadow. The trail forks in the meadow: the left branch goes uphill to Barlow Saddle, 0.5 mile east; right goes downhill for 1 mile to Devils Half Acre. There are three very short, moderately steep sections on this trail. To complete the loop, turn right on Road 3530 and ski uphill to the trailhead.

If this is your first trip to the area, you may have difficulty finding where the Barlow Creek Trail leaves the meadow. From where the road enters the meadow ski 200 yards straight ahead, crossing Barlow Creek, a small stream. Turn left and ski uphill into an arm of the meadow and then into another meadow, where you will see trail markers.

When returning via the Barlow Creek Trail, a variation on the loop is possible. Turn right at the small meadow and ski uphill to Barlow Saddle on the connector trail and then to Highway 35. Cross the highway onto the Boy Scout Ridge road to Panorama Dome and from there down to Barlow Pass to complete an eventful tour of only 4.0 miles (it may seem longer).

Palmateer Meadows. From Devils Half Acre ski down the valley to Palmateer Meadows 1.5 miles along Road 3530. Ski to the southeast corner of Devils Half Acre, cross a bridge, and follow the road along Barlow Creek. The road goes through second-growth in an area the pioneers called the "Big Deadening" after a forest fire in 1849 totally burned the area. The road drops 280 feet to an obscure side road that leads to the meadows. Palmateer Meadows, only 200 feet in diameter, are not attractive and hardly worth the effort. Some skiers enjoy the road tour, however, and the meadows are a good turnaround point.

If you miss the obscure side road to Palmateer Meadows, you will soon reach a series of short S-turns where trees crowd the narrow road. Retrace your tracks about 200 yards to the side road.

The road descent to Devils Half Acre can be fast and difficult if the

Devils Half Acre meadow, with Barlow Creek valley and Palmateer Overlook on right

snow is icy. The initial descent from Road 3530 to the small meadow on the Barlow Ridge Connector Trail is always difficult, even for the best skiers, and can be dangerous if it is melted out or if tree wells exist. Walk down if difficult.

PIONEER WOMAN TRAIL

Novice	High point 4157 feet
Round trip from 0.8 to 4.8 miles	USGS Mount Hood South
Unmarked road	
Elevation loss 526 feet	Map—pages 119, 144

This is a road tour on *old* Highway 35, now a scenic summer side trip, and snow-covered in winter. From Barlow Pass it offers a long downhill run on a gentle grade for almost the full 2.4 miles to the grave site. In summer the grave is a large pile of stream stones; in winter, a rounded hump of snow.

From Barlow Pass climb the snowbank at the far end of the sno-park and start down the road, which is a fine, uninterrupted downhill glide if the snow is favorable. The grave site is opposite a small meadow, the only one on the tour, near the last bend of the road. From there it is a short, level tour to the Highway 26/35 interchange (see Pioneer Road Loops). If you are looking for a trail skiing experience, take the Giant Trees Loop (which see), which takes off from near the grave site.

Historical Note. The original Barlow Road, a toll road and the first across the Oregon Cascades, descends from the center of the west side of the Barlow Pass sno-park. At this end it is not skiable, but at the lower end, near the grave site, the Giant Trees Loop uses part of the old road.

BARLOW RIDGE TOUR

Novice to Intermediate
Round trip 5.6 miles
Unmarked road
Elevation gain 730 feet

High point 4730 feet
USGS Mount Hood South

Map—pages 144, 151

This tour goes up the north side of Barlow Ridge along a gently climbing road to a fine viewpoint of the White River valley, then continues on the level through several clearcuts to a dead end.

Roadside parking is sometimes possible near Barlow Saddle on Highway 35, but the tour is often done from Barlow Pass for a round trip of 7.4 miles. Just east of Barlow Saddle the snow-covered road heading south from Highway 35 forks: take the right fork to the Barlow Ridge. (The left fork is of no interest to skiers.) The road climbs gently and steadily through the old-growth hemlock and noble fir forest for 1.6 miles to the high point, 4730 feet, where the road makes a sharp turn, levels out, and passes the first clearcut.

At the high point on the shoulder of the curve there is an inspiring view of Mt. Hood and the sprawling White River valley more than 1000 feet below. You can see up the valley all the way to its head at the White River glacier and from there down along its deep, twisting course as it widens and flattens out. Covered with winter snow, the sand and gravel flats far below form interesting finger patterns groping downvalley.

Beyond the high point curve the road descends gently across a clearcut and re-enters forest. Just beyond, a high, steep clearcut leads directly to the ridge crest (5100 feet) for views. Continuing along the road, you come to a second clearcut, which offers a second view of Bennett Ridge and the long, snowy-sided Bonney Butte, just across the valley. Farther along the road a third clearcut provides another route to the ridge top for more views. The tour ends in the last clearcut.

Barlow Ridge Connector Trails

Map—page 151

At this time, parking at Barlow Saddle is limited. Skiers wishing to ski the Barlow Ridge Trail must often park at either the Barlow Pass or White River sno-parks and ski to the saddle. Five routes lead from sno-parks at Barlow Pass or White River to Barlow Saddle, at the west foot of Barlow Ridge. Only one of these trails is now marked. Two others are off-trail routes, and two follow the road system from Panorama Dome and Boy Scout Ridge. Barlow Saddle is the site of a future Alps sno-park. When that sno-park is constructed, these four connector routes will become even more important as alternative routes for challenging loops in the area. Before too long, marking and bridge building also will improve these interesting routes. Note: these connector trails are marked A through D on the map.

Barlow Saddle Connector Trail. This marked connector travels through forest parallel to but at some distance south of the highway. From the Barlow Pass sno-park follow the Devils Half Acre road for 250 yards to a trail sign, turn left and ski several hundred yards down a difficult, often nasty section of trail to a small meadow. From this meadow take the trail to the left past a large tree with a sign. Enter forest and climb to a right turn then uphill along a narrow sidehill trail, usually a demanding section on the descent. The trail soon eases off, passes a clearcut, and joins the Barlow Ridge Trail just east of the saddle. Intermediate; 0.9 mile one way. (Route A)

Panorama Dome and Boy Scout Ridge. From Barlow Pass climb to Panorama Dome (see Panorama Dome/Boy Scout Ridge). Ski north along the Boy Scout Ridge road 0.3 mile to a junction. Turn right and ski downhill on Road 134 for 0.7 mile to Highway 35 across from Barlow Saddle and the Barlow Ridge Trail. The road system on Boy Scout Ridge also provides a route from White River to Barlow Saddle. Intermediate; 2.5 miles one way. (Route B)

White River Connector. There are two unmarked connector routes leading downhill to Barlow Saddle from White River. The White River Connector leads down the south side of the river. From the bridge near the White River sno-park, ski down wide, smooth snowfields for almost a mile. Going downhill, the distance is deceiving and it is easy to ski too far.

Descend to the first stand of dead trees on your right. Enter this ghost forest and ski to the lower rear corner, then cross through a band of live trees into a larger stand of ghost trees. Ski to the far (right) side of this stand of trees and look for a suitable crossing of the South Fork Mineral Creek.

Before reaching this creek, you may have to negotiate various small creeks, usually with no trouble. The South Fork, however, is another matter. Although shallow and narrow, it has steep banks. Logs are the

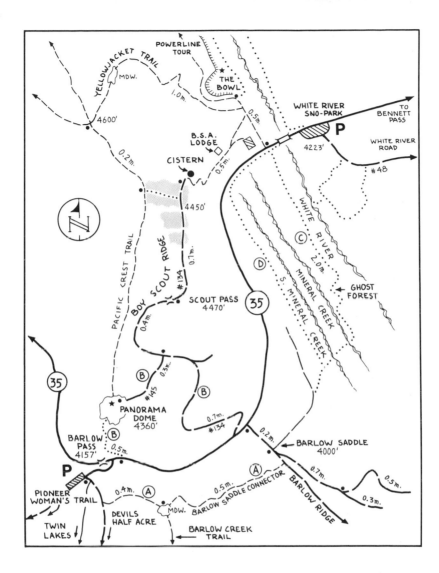

easiest way to cross. A group of fallen trees forms a good bridge, but you may have to cruise along the stream bank to find it. After crossing, ski straight away from the creek for 100 yards to a road, then turn left. You soon arrive at Barlow Saddle and the start of the Barlow Ridge Trail. Advanced; 2.0 miles one way. (Route C)

Mineral Creek Connector. This route is less interesting and scenic than the White River Connector, but it avoids all the stream crossings. From the White River bridge ski along the south shoulder of the highway until you pass the culverts carrying the two branches of Mineral Creek under the highway. Then turn south and ski downhill for 1 mile through forest to the snow-covered road leading right (west) to Barlow Saddle. It is recommended that you follow the creek bank downhill from the highway. If you do not, you may wander too far south into thick brush and downed trees. Advanced; 2.0 miles one way. (Route D)

PANORAMA DOME/BOY SCOUT RIDGE

Intermediate
Round trip up to 3.8 miles
Unmarked roads
Elevation gain 313 feet

High point 4470 feet
USGS Mount Hood South

Map—page 151

Panorama Dome, an open snow slope, has a sweeping view that captivates the eye as it ranges 270 degrees, from Timberline Lodge and Mt. Hood across the Trillium Basin and its enclosing ridges to Ghost Ridge and Barlow Butte. The gentle to moderate open slopes of Boy Scout Ridge, from Panorama Dome to White River, give you the option of skiing on a road or exploring through open forest.

From Barlow Pass sno-park. From the entrance to the sno-park walk 100 yards north along the highway. Cross the highway, climb the snow bank, and angle left up moderate slopes. Continue traversing and climbing west until you reach the smooth, rounded slope of Panorama Dome. From the inner sno-park to the top of the dome is no more than 0.5 mile.

From the dome you may follow either the Pacific Crest Trail or a snow-covered road northward toward the Boy Scout Lodge near White River. Numerous clearcuts offer good off-road skiing along the way. The road is recommended because it is more scenic and easier to follow than the trail. The road leaves from near the top of the dome and enters the trees to the east. It is about 1.9 miles along the road to the Boy Scout Lodge, en route crossing Scout Pass in the forest. See Yellowjacket Trail Loop for additional skiing in this area.

If you wish to ski the Pacific Crest Trail from the dome either to the Boy Scout Lodge area or to connect with the Yellowjacket Trail, descend slightly westward from the top of the dome. The trail's entry point into the forest is not easy to locate, nor is the trail easy to follow.

From White River sno-park. From the main sno-park cross the White River bridge and ski south along the uphill side of the road, crossing a low ridge to the Boy Scout sno-park. Ski around the sno-park to the road leading to the Boy Scout Lodge. Ski to the left of the lodge along the perimeter of the inner tube sliding hill, then uphill on a cat road heading south through the trees. The steep road leads to a round cistern located at the north end of the wide road leading along Boy Scout Ridge to Panorama Dome.

From the cistern follow the road south as it climbs gently to Scout Pass then turns right (west) and curves downhill. At the bottom of the hill the road branches. The most obvious route is straight ahead. This leads you downhill 0.7 mile to Highway 35 near Barlow Saddle. The less obvious road on the right leads south to the top of nearby Panorama Dome. The entire area offers off-road skiing at its best. This is a scenic area worth exploring. On the return to White River, to add variety to your tour, it is possible to use the Yellowjacket Trail Loop (which see).

Please respect the Boy Scout Lodge and vicinity, which is a private use area. Do not ski on their hills or tarry in the area.

From Barlow Saddle. If you have skied the connector trail from Barlow Pass to Barlow Saddle and wish to complete a loop by way of Boy Scout Ridge, then ski from the saddle a short distance up the road to Highway 35. Cross the highway and go south a few yards to locate a snow-covered road. Follow the road 0.7 mile uphill to a flat area, where you turn left to nearby Panorama Dome. Until the Alps sno-park is constructed, the only parking near Barlow Saddle (for skiing the Barlow Ridge Trail) is along Highway 35. This, however, is not a good place to park during snowfalls or when the highway is being plowed.

The road between Panorama Dome and the Boy Scout Lodge is generally easy to follow. The southern end, however, where it swings uphill to Scout Pass, is often lost in deep snow, and until you are familiar with the area you may have to do some scouting to find the way. If the weather is bad and visibility limited, it is an easy area in which to become disoriented, so carry a map and compass. There are no landmarks in the area. Note that the road location on the USGS map for Boy Scout Ridge area is incorrect on the photorevised 1980 edition. Some Forest Service maps do not show the roads in this area.

Barlow Ridge cornices. (Photo by Bill Kerr)

Chapter 12
WHITE RIVER

This immensely popular area offers six different tours and access to two nearby touring areas. White River is located seven miles east of Government Camp on Highway 35. There are two sno-parks, one at either end of the White River bridge. The main one is east of the bridge. The small one west of the bridge is primarily for visitors to the nearby Boy Scouts of America lodge.

The main attractions of the area are open, gentle slopes above the highway bridge and a gravel quarry called "The Bowl." This large amphitheater of snow entertains young and old, skilled and unskilled, and is usually crowded with skiers practicing and enjoying the slopes.

The White River is one of the most popular and congested Nordic skiing areas on Mt. Hood. Contributing to this popularity is terrain suitable to skiers of all skill levels, wide-open spaces, and well-defined trails.

Another attraction of the White River area is the physical beauty of the wide, flat valley enclosed in impressive, forested ridges. Except for the Timberline Lodge area, White River is the only Nordic sports area where you need only step from your car to behold truly breathtaking scenery.

The down-valley view is alone worth the drive, with massive, forested Bennett Ridge and snowy-sided, tent-like Bonney Butte on the left and the rugged Barlow Ridge and Butte on the right. The lower valley drops impressively into distant, hazy depths, and cloud ghosts often writhe about the ridges and through the trees, imparting an ethereal touch to the scene. On special occasions each successive tree-clad ridge is outlined by white mist, giving a powerful three-dimensional effect. Regardless of weather, even with the high ridge tops hidden in clouds, the downvalley view is ever-changing and always splendid.

The view up the valley is also one of great beauty. The mighty guardian, Mt. Hood, dominates the scene, with its intense whiteness bold against the sky. On occasion lenticular clouds move about the summit or snow banners blow from the highest point. The valley itself, with its flat bottom and steeply tilted sides, leads the eye upward along the twisting, forest-edged corridor to the Guardian. It is not surprising, then, that skiers are attracted time and again to this beautiful winter setting.

THE BOWL TOUR

Novice
Round trip 1 mile
Unmarked road
Elevation gain 100 feet

High point 4320 feet
USGS Mount Hood South

Map—page 156

The Bowl is a very crowded, popular amphitheater of snow on the south side of White River, above the highway bridge. Cross the bridge from the main sno-park and turn uphill along a road for an easy tour to The Bowl. In summer this is a dusty gravel pit, but in winter it is transformed into a large, snow-filled bowl, offering slopes and practice areas for skiers of every skill level. It is not unusual for as many as 200 skiers to be in The Bowl area at one time!

On the way up to The Bowl scattered trees and open areas to the left provide good skiing and practice. These areas, as well as The Bowl itself, are also used by ski schools under Forest Service permit. If you see a class under way, please, as a common courtesy, do not mingle or pass through the class. About 100 yards to the left of and parallel to the road is a lovely trail that also leads to The Bowl, offering a possible loop. The top of The Bowl is at 4400 feet, a 200-foot climb from the highway bridge. Rock removal from the quarry in recent years has considerably altered the shape of The Bowl.

POWERLINE TOUR

Intermediate
Round trip 3 miles
Unmarked road and trail
Elevation gain 380 feet

High point 4600 feet
USGS Mount Hood South

Map—page 156

This tour leads above The Bowl to a tree-studded bench overlooking the White River and offers a nice downhill return run through scattered trees. Ski to The Bowl (see preceding tour) and climb the moderately steep ridge on the south edge. Then proceed up gentle slopes winding through scattered lodgepole pines. There are several trails here, all leading upward, so there is no way to lose the route. The overhead power line, serving the Mt. Hood Meadows Ski Area, is about 1.0 mile above The Bowl. But continue a short distance farther to a fine off-trail view-point of the White River canyon. Most skiers turn around here and return, enjoying a fine downhill run to the top of The Bowl. Descending the south ridge of The Bowl, however, is usually unpleasant, and many falls are witnessed here.

From the high point above the power line you may continue another 0.5 mile, climbing steadily through scattered pines to where the slope

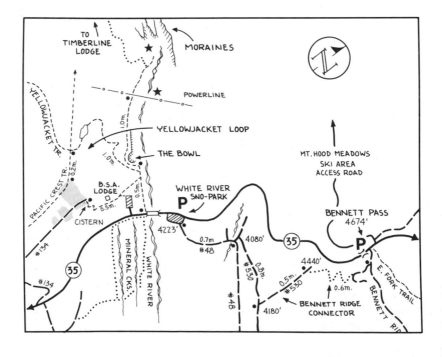

leads gently out onto the flats of the White River at 5080 feet. (Up to here a low bluff prevents easy descent to the river flats.) Cross the river on snow bridges, usually with no trouble. Return to the highway by looping back along the valley bottom on either side of the river. The north side is recommended, however, as it is wider and less used. Returning by way of the river flats avoids the south ridge of The Bowl, which is usually hard-packed and icy. Be careful near the river, and stay off the steep south-facing slopes on the north side of the valley, which may be dangerous in warm weather.

MORAINE TOUR

Intermediate　　　　　　　　　　**High point 5200 feet**
Round trip 4 miles　　　　　　　　**USGS Mount Hood South**
Unmarked valley bottom
Elevation gain 977 feet　　　　　**Map—page 156**

This superb tour takes you to the foot of giant moraines set in a wild scene of alpine solitude. The route follows the gentle snow-fields along the flat bottom of the White River valley. On the return there is a long downhill run.

From the main White River sno-park cross the highway, and ski about 100 yards west along the highway edge toward the bridge. Then turn uphill and follow gentle, open slopes upward along the north side of the river. On a clear day, as you reach the 1-mile point, the scenery is almost overwhelming, and from there it becomes even more spectacular. The steep, snowy sidewalls and forested ridges enclosing the flat valley bottom are impressive as the valley appears to turn and twist endlessly upward. You will likely feel a strong sense of adventure as you follow the gentle grade to the moraines, which resemble ridges in the bottom of the valley. The White River Glacier has been receding for years, and its present snout is about 1.5 miles above this point. This is a fine place for a spring picnic lunch in the warm sunshine. One of the moraines is flat-topped and may be climbed for even better views.

It is usually possible to cross the river on snow bridges, but it may also be crossed on foot, if necessary, by stepping on stones. Take great care, however, and use your poles for balance. Once across, you can ski back along the river or along the Powerline Tour route (see preceding tour).

Near the moraines, you will see on the south side of the valley a short, almost bowl-like side valley. This is the route leading to or from Timberline Lodge, only a mile farther on. Before attempting these steep and potentially dangerous slopes, however, read the description for Timberline Lodge to White River Tour (page 86). This ambitious tour is for advanced skiers only and should be attempted only under ideal conditions.

The lower valley is very safe, but beyond the 1-mile point the steep sidewalls on the north side offer potential avalanche danger during or after heavy snowfall and in periods of warm weather. Stay away from the bottoms of these slopes.

LOWER WHITE RIVER

Novice	High point 4223 feet
Round trip up to 4 miles	USGS Mount Hood South
Unmarked road	
Elevation loss up to 400 feet	Map—page 156

This is primarily a road tour, but there are alternative routes through the trees for a loop return. There is also a variety of terrain for practicing your skiing skills.

Climb the rear snowbank at the main White River sno-park and follow the road downhill. Although it is possible to ski down to the snowline, most skiers only go a mile or so. The greatest rewards in this area are to ski off the road, generally toward the White River, and to explore the dips and gulleys and open areas, where very good practice can be had by selecting skiing problems then attacking them systematically by repetition until you have them in hand. Set up a mini-loop and cross the many stream beds to form a pattern that is both challenging and enjoyable. Some of the stream beds and dips are sudden and demanding. Approach them at an angle that minimizes the impact. After the first go-around the track is set and becomes more fun. To add variety, reverse your skiing direction. It is also possible to ski to the edge of the White River for a peaceful short tour away from the crowds while enjoying the riparian scenery. All things considered, this is an excellent area to enjoy a variety of terrain and to sharpen skills.

YELLOWJACKET TRAIL LOOP

Intermediate	High point 4500 feet
Round trip 2.5 miles	USGS Mount Hood South
Marked and unmarked trails	
Elevation gain 380 feet	Map—page 156

This short loop takes you very quickly from one of the most crowded ski centers on Mt. Hood to a seldom traveled area of beautiful old-growth timber. This tour offers a variety of skiing and some easy route-finding exercises. This is a safe area. Even if temporarily disoriented, you are never far from the highway below.

From the main White River sno-park cross the bridge and ski up the road toward The Bowl. About 200 yards below The Bowl, look to the left for a small sign on a tree that indicates the start of the Yellowjacket Trail. If you do not see the sign, start contouring south while looking for the hard-to-see orange signs of the Yellowjacket Trail. The trail markers, orange-painted metal plates five inches across, are few and far between. Some are losing their paint and now show a gray base. However, the trail is not difficult to follow if you exercise some care because it has been brushed and cut wide for skiing.

In about 300 yards the trail leads into a gully, with a narrow, steep pitch to climb on the other side. Once across, the trail turns right, climbing steeply to a haripin turn on the left (south), about 150 yards from the gully. The turn is *not* obvious. The trail continues climbing, rounding a ridge shoulder, then traversing uphill. All climbing, except at the gully and on the following slope, is moderate.

Although the first 0.5 mile from the gully is demanding uphill travel, it is worth the effort, for the trail soon levels and enters truly fine old-growth timber at 4500 feet. Cross a meadow, the only opening in the forest, and re-enter timber as you continue across the rolling terrain.

Almost 0.5 mile beyond the meadow a double marker on a tree designates the Pacific Crest Trail, which goes from Timberline Lodge to Barlow Pass. Turn left at the double markers and ski moderately downhill along the Pacific Crest Trail for 350 yards past a meadow to the first open trees on the left. Turn left here, ski east over gentle slopes into a clearcut, and descend 150 yards to an obvious road (134). Turn left to the nearby end of Road 134, where a large, round wooden cistern serves the Boy Scout lodge, only 150 yards down the hill. Even advanced skiers will snowplow and sidestep in places on the steep, narrow cat road that descends from the cistern to the lodge.

Crossing the Terrible Traverse on Bennett Ridge

Chapter 13
BENNETT PASS

Bennett Pass is the trailhead for a number of fine tours. Because most tours in the area require you to ski long distances, often over difficult terrain, they are rated intermediate or advanced. Novice skiers are advised to ski elsewhere.

At 4674 feet elevation Bennett Pass is the highest highway pass on Mt. Hood. It is situated on Highway 35 on the southeast side of Mt. Hood 2.2 miles northeast of White River and just 200 yards south of the entrance to Mt. Hood Meadows Ski Area. Bennett Pass is 9.7 miles east of Government Camp and 32 miles south of Hood River.

The Bennett Pass, Hood River Meadows, and Pocket Creek areas are contiguous and connected by trails that form interesting and sometimes long loops. Connector trails provide short, direct access routes between the ski areas. There is an interesting assortment of trail combinations from which to select a tour suitable to your skill level and your ambitions for the day.

The most popular trail in the area is the road tour along Bennett Ridge to the Terrible Traverse, 2.6 miles from the pass. Beyond the traverse, the tours are long and often demanding, earning a rating of advanced even though the roads are seldom steep.

With more skiers on the trails each year, tracks are being pushed farther and farther. Only in recent years, for example, has it been possible to ski with reasonable ease to Bonney Butte and Camp Windy. In the past, tracks seldom extended far on the long tours, and few skiers had the strength or desire to break trail to such distant points. Today, it is not uncommon to see tracks going far beyond even these interesting places, pushing on to even more distant destinations.

The popularity of the Bennett Pass region has created a problem at the road parking area. There is simply a lack of adequate space for the growing numbers of skiers. Be sure to park legally, on the east side of the highway off the traffic lanes, outside the fog line.

An off-road sno-park is planned for this area, subject to available highway funds. Until then, however, if parking at the pass is filled, the only alternative is to ski elsewhere. Hood River Meadows is only 1 mile north and Pocket Creek only 3.3 miles north of Bennett Pass. From Hood River Meadows sno-park it is a 1.6-mile uphill tour past Sahalie Falls to Bennett Pass, a considerable inconvenience to skiers intent on Bennett Ridge.

Plans for logging the south side of Bennett Ridge above lower White River will eventually provide better access to Bennett Pass from White River and will offer miles of roads and clearcuts for exploration. The Forest Service has assured concerned groups that the logging will not affect the quality of the skiing experience on Bennett Ridge and that clearcuts will not affect the scenic values of the views from White River. Cutting on or near the top of Bennett Ridge would create snow-drift problems and affect the wind and weather protection the trail now enjoys.

BENNETT RIDGE TRAIL

Novice to Intermediate
Round trip to Terrible Traverse 5.2 miles, to Bonney Junction 8 miles
Unmarked road
Elevation gain 380 feet to Terrible Traverse, 840 feet to Bonney Junction
High point 5360 feet
USGS Mount Hood South, Badger Lake

Map—pages 162, 168

This is a splendid tour on a rolling, forest ridge. Its main attractions are the beautiful stands of open, old-growth timber, the occasional splendid views, and the interesting and changing terrain along the trail. The high elevation of the ridge often ensures deeper and better snow conditions than in other areas. The Bennett Ridge Trail also provides access to upper Pocket Creek, Bonney Butte, and Camp Windy.

The Bennett Ridge Trail enters the trees 100 yards from the highway at

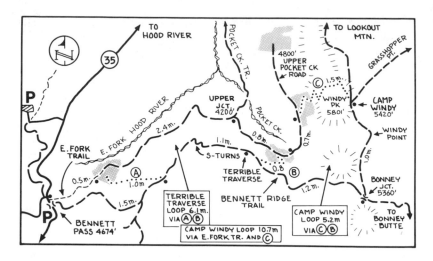

the upper end of a clearing east of the parking area. Following a narrow, old-style forest road, the trail winds gently through the woods, generally of old-growth mountain hemlock.

The trail first climbs on the north side of the ridge, where the snow is often colder and drier. After a mile, it crosses over to the other side for a gentle, long descent to the foot of the S-turns, which are on a moderate uphill grade leading to fine views to the south and west. The open slope here is a favorite lunch and sunning spot on clear days.

Within 200 yards the trail descends to Windy Saddle at the west foot of the Terrible Traverse, which is a steep sidehill traverse on the northeast side of the ridge immediately under a snow-covered cliff. This "notorious" place turns many novice skiers back, not wishing to cross what appears to be a dangerous slope. In summer, the Terrible Traverse is a narrow roadbed carved out of a rock face; in winter it appears as a steep, inclined snow shelf with intimidating slopes below.

In years of deep snowpack the Terrible Traverse is steeper than usual. It is always impressive, however, due to the steep slopes below and the rock cliffs above. Although a few skiers have slipped here, there is no record of an injury, no doubt because of extra caution used on the 200-foot crossing. At times of deep, fresh snowfall, especially during or immediately after storms, or during very warm weather, this slope could avalanche. An icy or crusty surface also increases the difficulty. In fact, caution is in order here at all times. Once the decision is made to cross on skis or on foot, proceed across rapidly.

At the east end of the Terrible Traverse there is a safe, level spot on which to rest. The platform offers grand views down the length of the East Fork Hood River valley, into upper Pocket Creek, and across to Gunsight Ridge and to Lookout Mountain, miles away to the northeast. You can also see Elk Mountain and Mt. Hood.

The trail quickly passes through the prominent rock towers of Gunsight Notch, then descends to a small saddle before once again gaining the south side of the ridge for the rest of the way to Bonney Junction. On the way up the long grade to the junction two openings in the forest permit views of Mt. Jefferson, as well as of the White River valley and both Barlow Ridge and Butte across the way. At the second viewpoint you can also see Barlow Pass, Frog Lake Buttes, and the Trillium Basin peaks, including Veda, Eureka, Multorpor, and Tom Dick and Harry Mountain.

At Bonney Junction (5360 feet), a forested saddle, roads lead to Camp Windy and Bonney Butte. From this junction, 1.4 miles from the Terrible Traverse, you can ski south to Bonney Butte or Bonney Meadows or north to Camp Windy, Gunsight Ridge, Badger Butte, Badger Lake, and Grasshopper Point. You can even ski to Lookout Mountain, but the conventional northern approach is shorter and recommended.

White River Overlook. One mile from Bennett Pass, at a high point on Bennett Ridge, a logging road goes south, curving and remaining generally level, for over 1 mile, ending on a steep hill. Follow the road to its end. Then ski through the trees to a natural hillside meadow with a fine view down the White River valley. Bonney Butte is on the left and Barlow Ridge is on the right. This is a view worth skiing to.

BONNEY BUTTE AND MEADOWS

Intermediate to Advanced	High point 5560 feet
Round trip 12 miles	USGS Mount Hood South, Badger Lake
Unmarked road	Map—pages 164, 168
Elevation gain 1500 feet	

The view from the summit of Bonney Butte on a clear day is almost unrivaled in the Mt. Hood area. You can see not only the eastern desert, but also eight Cascade volcanoes. The view 2500 feet down into the depths of the White River valley is also notable. Although rated as advanced due to distance, the trail never exceeds moderate grades.

Follow the Bennett Ridge Trail (see preceding tour) to Bonney Junction, 4.0 miles from the trailhead. Keep right and make a level traverse across the top of a large clearing. The trail, a forest road, re-enters trees, traveling through old-growth on a winding uphill course. At 0.5 mile from the junction the trail reaches the flat shoulder of a ridge, where it leaves the big trees and enters a beautiful forest of slender, pointed firs that is unique to the area.

The trail descends gently through the postcard scene of firs to Bonney Meadows, 1 mile south of the flat shoulder on a side road to the left. If you are headed for the top of Bonney Butte, leave the trail before reaching the meadows. Turn off to the right and either follow an old road to the foot of the butte or just ski through small, widely set firs.

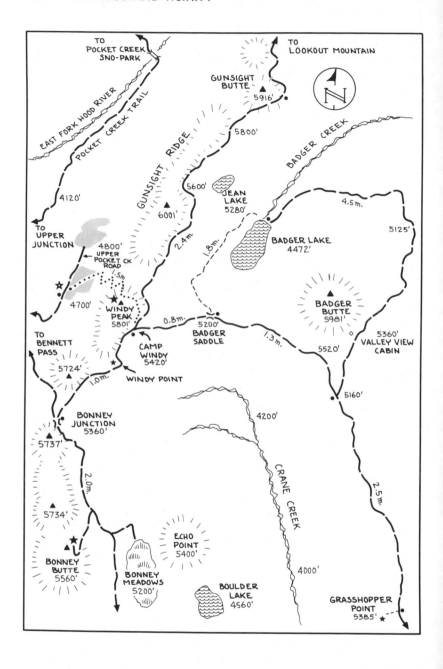

It is a short 240-foot climb to the summit of the butte, where the un-obstructed view is overwhelming, including as it does Broken Top, the Three Sisters, the tip of Three-Fingered Jack, Mt. Jefferson, Mt. Hood, and Mt. Adams. Be sure to pick a good day for this tour.

The return trip is delightful with diagonal striding up the first gentle mile, followed by seemingly endless downhill for much of the way to the trailhead. Many skiers consider this downhill run the most rewarding of all the Mt. Hood tours. There is a lot of variety and a few thrills below Bonney Junction, yet the trail is never fast enough to be intimidating.

CAMP WINDY

Advanced
Round trip 10 miles
Unmarked road
Elevation gain 726 feet

High point 5400 feet
USGS Mount Hood South, Badger Lake

Map—pages 164, 168

Camp Windy is located 1 mile northeast of Bonney Junction. It is a sloping snow slope with scattered trees in the wide, gentle upper basin of Crane Creek, which flows east to the Oregon desert. From Camp Windy one road leads south to Bonney Junction, one north to Gunsight Ridge and Lookout Mountain, and one northeast to Badger Butte, Badger Lake, and Grasshopper Point.

Ski to Bonney Junction (see Bennett Ridge Trail). From there ski northward through forest along a scenic route, traversing to Windy Point, 0.6 mile from Bonney Junction. Above Windy Point are several unusual rock formations offering fine views of the valley below, Badger Butte, Lookout Mountain, and long, flat Grasshopper Ridge. The rocks are a good place for a rest or lunch. The road, usually hidden by drifting snow, climbs gently around the point, then gently descends into trees, curving 0.4 mile to the Camp Windy area.

The "camp" site is a large, dense group of trees beside an open slope. Just above is the obscure junction of the Gunsight Ridge and Badger Lake roads. You may have to do some scouting to locate the two roads in the scattered trees; they are not well-defined. The road to Gunsight Ridge ascends gently from the junction, while the road to Badger Lake descends gently. The camp is well named, for exposed as it is to both the south and the east, it is often windy and cold.

Windy Peak (Point 5801). As you ski past the gargoyle-like rocks at Windy Point, just south of Camp Windy, Gunsight Ridge rises above you to the west, and Windy Peak is the obvious high point on the ridge above Camp Windy. The breathtaking view is well worth the short 400-foot ascent on the generally open, moderate slopes from Camp Windy. Mt. Hood, rising some 7000 feet above the East Fork Hood River valley, immediately below you to the west, is the feature attraction. To the north,

Mt. Hood from Bennett Ridge

you can see Mt. Adams, along with the gentle, forested mass of Lookout Mountain; to the south, Bonney Butte, Mt. Jefferson, and many minor ridges and forested peaks; and to the east, the wide, forested Crane Creek valley and the desert high country of central Oregon.

In periods of poor visibility, route finding may be difficult at Camp Windy. There may also be some avalanche potential at Windy Point, though skiers who have been through there many times report never having experienced any problem. Nevertheless, exercise caution there in periods of recent heavy snowfall.

CAMP WINDY TO POCKET CREEK

Advanced
Distance one way 1 mile
Unmarked off-trail route
Elevation gain 400 feet, loss 1080 feet

High point 5780 feet
USGS Badger Lake

Map—pages 164, 168

This off-trail tour adds a new dimension to skiing the Camp Windy area and offers an alternative return route to Bennett Pass, if snow conditions are favorable. It is a rugged descent through forest from the top of Gunsight Ridge to the Upper Pocket Creek road. From Camp Windy climb generally open slopes to the broad saddle just north of Windy Peak (Point 5801), then descend the west side of the ridge in zigzags to Upper Pocket Creek. If you miss the Mt. Adams clearcut, which is directly below Windy Peak, you will not miss the Upper Pocket Creek road. For further details see Pocket Creek Connector Trails.

BADGER LAKE/GRASSHOPPER POINT

Advanced
Round trip distance from Camp Windy to Badger Lake by trail 5 miles, to
    Badger Lake by road 13.6 miles, to Grasshopper Point 9.2 miles
Unmarked roads
Elevation loss to Badger Lake 948 feet cumulative, to Grasshopper Point
    580 feet cumulative
High point 5520
USGS Badger Lake

Map—pages 164, 168

All three tours start at Camp Windy, which is 5.0 miles from Bennett Pass. These tours offer distance skiing and a high degree of solitude, despite the occasional snowmobiles.

From Bennett Pass ski to Camp Windy (see Bennett Ridge Trail and Camp Windy). From Camp Windy descend gently along an obscure road (see Camp Windy) 0.8 mile to Badger Saddle, 5200 feet. The shortest distance to the lake is to follow the summer hiking trail. From the saddle the trail descends 700 feet in 1.8 miles, skirting the west side of the lake to its north end. Descending at a moderate grade, the first part of the trail is difficult to follow because of scattered trees and open areas. The lake lies in a deep forested bowl between Badger Butte and Gunsight Ridge.

From Badger Saddle the road to Badger Lake and Grasshopper Point climbs moderately along the south side of Badger Butte to a high point of 5520 feet, crossing several steep slopes that could be dangerous in heavy, new snow or very warm weather. When you see this hillside, you will appreciate the potential avalanche danger, although skiers who have passed this way many times report never having had a problem.

Enjoy views of Mt. Jefferson and the full sweep of the Crane Creek valley below from the scattered timber and many open slopes of Badger Butte. From the high point the road descends gently into dense forest. For the next 3 miles ski through rolling, forested terrain to Grasshopper Point. At the end of the tour you suddenly leave the dense forest and enter an area of smaller trees. Here, about 2.5 miles south of the Badger Lake road junction a sign indicates the Rocky Butte Trail to the east. Turn right and go through the smaller trees for about 100 yards to the view of Crane valley and to the south and west. The viewpoint is easy to miss

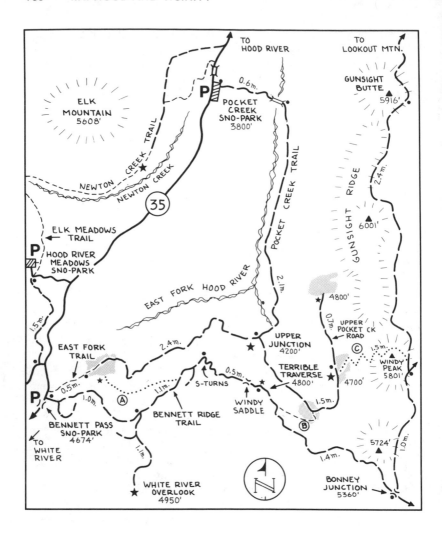

because the ridge is broad, and trees obscure the bluff-top overlook.

An alternative but longer route to Badger Lake is to take the road that circles around the east side of Badger Butte. From the high point on the south side of the butte descend 0.5 mile to the road junction. Follow the side road north as it contours to the Valley View Cabin 0.5 mile from the junction. This is a summer cabin maintained for use by Forest Service fire crews. The road continues to descend gently around the north side of the butte to the lake, 4.5 miles from the road to Grasshopper Point and 6.8 miles from Camp Windy.

These tours, all far from the trailhead at Bonney Pass, require stamina and confidence in skiing to destinations that extend one's resources, particularly in unfavorable weather or snow conditions. Carry maps, compass, survival gear and repair kit. Of course, the most valuable tools you possess are the common sense and strength to make the difficult decision to turn back short of your goal if conditions warrant such action.

GUNSIGHT BUTTE

Advanced   **High point 5916 feet**
Round trip from Camp Windy 4.8 miles   **USGS Badger Lake**
Unmarked road
Elevation gain 516 feet   **Map—pages 164, 168**

Gunsight Butte is a prominent point on the long ridge extending from Bonney Junction to Lookout Mountain. This ridge forms the eastern wall of the upper East Fork Hood River valley and dominates the Pocket Creek touring area.

From Bennett Pass ski to Camp Windy (see Bennett Ridge Trail and Camp Windy). From Camp Windy ski up the obscure Gunsight Ridge road as it climbs moderately through scattered trees into the forest, where the route becomes obvious. (For directions to this obscure road see the Camp Windy tour.) The road follows the east side of Gunsight Ridge past Jean Lake, which is out of sight below in the forest. Leave the road to climb the short distance to the top of Gunsight Butte, which is 0.6 mile beyond Jean Lake. The views here are similar to those seen from Windy Peak (Point 5801). The return to Camp Windy is a pleasant downhill run on moderate to gentle grades.

POCKET CREEK CONNECTOR TRAILS

Map—pages 162, 168

Four off-road connector routes in the Upper Pocket Creek-East Fork basins provide interesting alternative trips and loops for the aggressive skier. Although the Trillium Basin offers more off-road loop skiing, for scenery the Upper Pocket Creek and Bennett Ridge areas have few rivals on Mt. Hood.

These connectors enable a skier to go from the upper basin to Bennett Ridge, or vice versa and to form loops of various lengths. The most interesting loop, the Terrible Traverse Loop, is 6.1 miles, not including approach distance from the trailhead to the loop. Considering elevation gain and loss and distance, it is rated advanced although terrain exceeds moderate difficulty in only several places. Another connector goes over Gunsight Ridge to Camp Windy, and in combination with one or the other of the connectors forms adventurous loops of 5.2 or 10.7 miles. Among the possible loops are the following:

Trails	Miles
Terrible Traverse Loop via Connector Routes A and B	6.1 miles
Camp Windy Loop via Connector Routes B and C	5.2 miles
Camp Windy Loop via East Fork Trail and Connector Route C	10.7 miles

These connectors provide a safe, controlled way for aggressive skiers to explore and experience wilderness skiing under somewhat tame conditions. That is, the skier is always near a road or trail, where getting lost would be difficult. Nevertheless, the loops should be skied only by those with a knowledge of survival skills and proper equipment for extended touring. Carry a Forest Service map, and the USGS *Badger Lake* and *Mount Hood South* quads. There are other connector routes in this area, but they are generally too steep, brushy, or unpleasant to be described.

All four of these connectors go through forest and in late season or periods of little snowfall there may be ice, rough snow, and tree wells. Snow falling from limbs and dripping water often make for an icy surface. In bad snow, if you must continue, remove your skis and finish on foot. If conditions are not good, do not ski these routes. Usually, however, you will find these routes in reasonably good condition for skiing. Carry survival gear, repair kit and maps and compass. These are demanding loops so be prepared. You will enjoy them all the more.

East Fork Trail. This marked trail descends from Bennett Pass 200 vertical feet to a large clearcut at the head of the East Fork basin and ties in with a road leading to the Upper Junction of the Pocket Creek Trail. The trail descends through old-growth and as it is the shortest and easiest of the connector routes to Pocket Creek it will gain more use as skiers become aware of it. The trail was planned by the Hood River Ranger District and constructed in 1980 with volunteer aid from the Oregon Nordic Club.

The trail starts just 50 yards from the highway at Bennett Pass and 100 yards downhill from the Bennett Ridge trailhead at its entry into the forest. The initial slope is the steepest of the entire trail, and for much of the way it is a relatively easy sidehill descent to the clearcut. From the clearcut, with its good view of Mt. Hood, it is 1.8 miles to the Upper Junction of Pocket Creek (4200 feet), where there are large open areas. The Terrible Traverse can be seen directly above. Intermediate; 0.5 mile.

Connector Route A. This route is an unmarked, off-road tour through beautiful old-growth connecting the Bennett Ridge Trail with a clearcut on the East Fork. From there a road leads to the Upper Junction of the Pocket Creek Trail. Connector A joins the clearcut at its top end, while the East Fork Trail joins this same clearcut about halfway down.

To reach the upper end of the connector, ski on the Bennett Ridge Trail 1.5 miles from the trailhead. After a 1.0-mile gradual ascent from the trailhead reach the flat top of the ridge, where a side road to the right leads to the White River Overlook. The trail then switches to the south side of the ridge as it descends gently. From that switch-over point ski about 300 yards to where the trail turns slightly to the right. That point is the top of the unmarked connector. Turn left (north), leaving the main trail and descend westward at a gentle angle. Near the beginning of the connector, small trees may offer a minor problem in starting a smooth, easy descent angle, but the old growth you soon enter offers widely spaced trees and good skiing. After skiing about 0.6 mile from the ridge top, you come to a gully, which becomes deeper and steeper-sided the farther downhill you go. If the gully is too difficult to cross, follow it uphill to a point where a crossing is possible. The top of the clearcut is about 200 yards beyond the gully. The connector may also be skied by leaving the Bennett Ridge Trail sooner and descending more steeply through the big trees. Intermediate; 0.8 mile one way.

Connector Route B. This unmarked off-road tour through forest links the Bennett Ridge Trail with a clearcut in Upper Pocket Creek. It requires

Afternoon shadows, Upper Pocket Creek

more skiing skill than Connector A because in one place it traverses a moderately steep hillside.

Reach the upper end of this connector by crossing the Terrible Traverse, passing through Gunsight Notch, and continuing about 200 yards to where the main trail turns slightly right after the descent from the rock towers.

Right there, in the flat saddle before the trail goes uphill to Bonney Junction, leave the main trail and go east (left) into the trees. Descending gently, traverse east in a straight line across a moderately steep slope, stepping around or down through tight trees where necessary. The traverse soon gets easier and in 0.5 mile you will see a clearcut below. Continue the traversing descent, entering the clearcut, then zigzaging down to an obvious road just below. Follow the road downhill 0.8 mile to the Upper Junction. If you turn right on the road at the bottom of the clearcut, ski uphill to the nearby clearcut from where you can see Mt. Adams. This connector is uncomplicated and requires no route finding. Except for where you have to step around the tight trees, the route is obvious. Intermediate; 0.8 mile one way.

Connector Route C. This off-road, unmarked ski route joins Upper Pocket Creek with Camp Windy by climbing directly over Gunsight Ridge, the high ridge east of Pocket Creek. This is a rugged, moderately steep tour entailing exploratory skiing through forest. One of the rewards is the fine view from Windy Peak (Point 5801), just off the route a few yards. Another is the descent over open slopes into the beautiful Camp Windy area and the return by way of Bonney Junction and the long downhill run to the Terrible Traverse.

To reach the connector from the Upper Junction, ski uphill to the lower end of Connector B, in the clearcut directly under Bennett Ridge. At the clearcut the road bends northward and heads uphill to the Mt. Adams viewpoint, which is located in the first large clearcut on the right after the bend. Climb to the top of this clearcut near the north end and continue climbing moderately steep snow through the forest. Zigzag directly up the hillside to the ridge top. Crossing the ridge will take about 1.5 hours. The elevation gain is 1100 feet to the flat, tree-covered saddle north of Windy Peak (Point 5801). It is a 400-foot drop to Camp Windy on moderate, open slopes. For the longest loop from Bennett Pass, using Connector Route C, ski the East Fork Trail to Upper Junction. From there take Connector C to the Bennett Ridge Trail and back to Bennett Pass. Advanced; 10.7 miles.

Chapter 14
HOOD RIVER MEADOWS

Hood River Meadows, not to be confused with the nearby Mt. Hood Meadows Ski Area, is on the east side of Mt. Hood, 11 miles from Government Camp. The turnoff for the sno-park is 1.1 miles north of Bennett Pass. From the sno-park, which serves both alpine and Nordic skiers, five trails are available to cross-country skiers. The first mile of the Elk Meadows Trail is one of the loveliest forest skiing trails on Mt. Hood, and being almost level it is suitable to any skill level. Of course, Hood River Meadows, a round, scenic meadow in a deep forested bowl is always beautiful and serene. The Elk Meadows and Elk Mountain tours, rugged skiing experiences for advanced skiers, are challenging and rewarding.

The Heather Canyon Trail climbs gently through some of the most beautiful meadow and canyon scenery on the mountain. The Umbrella Falls Trail, a demanding uphill trail, offers a lot for the hardy skier who also wants to be challenged on the return descent. Most of the trails in the Hood River Meadows area are "out and back" tours, but there is an outstanding 10-mile loop trail, linking the Hood River Meadows and Pocket Creek areas.

Although there has been a Nordic skiing program for many years at the Mt. Hood Meadows Ski Area, and the trails in the Umbrella Falls area have been marked with plastic tape, they are not adequately marked. It is a confusing area to ski due to the lack of marking and signs, but in the meantime the area below the main parking lot near the lodge, with many meadows near the falls, offers interesting exploration. The Nordic instruction and track program is now located at Hood River Meadows, definitely a better area for novice skiers.

HOOD RIVER MEADOWS/SAHALIE FALLS

Novice
Round trip, meadows 0.5 mile,
  falls 1.4 miles
Unmarked road
Elevation gain to falls 100 feet

High point 4580 feet
USGS Mount Hood South

Map—page 174

Hood River Meadows, situated in a beautiful, deep bowl formed by forested hills, is a scenic jewel of the region, and most of the area trails are suitable to novices.

To reach Hood River Meadows sno-park, drive toward the Mt. Hood Meadows Ski Area on the east side of the mountain. When you reach the

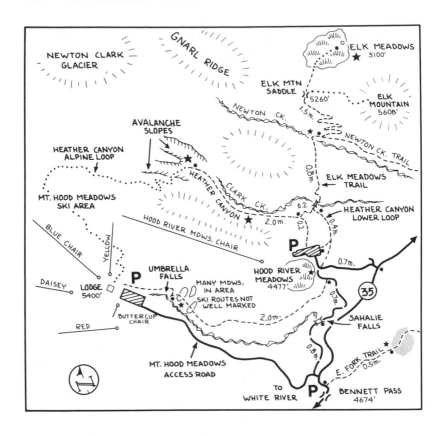

ski area access road, continue 1 mile north on the highway and turn left onto the access road leading to the Hood River Meadows sno-park. Drive 0.7 mile to the huge sno-park, which serves as the trailhead for several trails, each with a different departure point in the sno-park.

The Mt. Hood Meadows Nordic Center (lessons and rentals) is located beyond the west end of the sno-park. Just east of the center's building is a trail leading into Hood River Meadows. You can also reach the meadows and Sahalie Falls by climbing the snowbank at the sno-park entrance and skiing along the west side of the access road.

Hood River Meadows is a large, circular, level meadow surrounded on three sides by steep hillsides. Downhill ski runs and a chairlift are just off the north side but seem to intrude very little on the quiet of the meadow. The impressive east face of Hood, towering 6700 feet above, is visible from here. The meadow and the forest edge offer an opportunity for exploring and the quiet contemplation of nature.

The Sahalie Falls Trail follows a portion of old Highway 35, now a scenic summer bypass road. From the opening to the meadows off the old highway follow the road south as it climbs gently uphill past Sahalie Falls (0.7 mile), and then on to where it joins the access road to Mt. Hood Meadows Ski Area at Highway 35, 1.5 miles from the Hood River Meadows sno-park. This is an easy tour, and there is a pleasant, safe downhill run on the return trip. Sahalie Falls and Hood River Meadows may also be reached by skiing from Bennett Pass following the snow-covered scenic road.

As parking at Bennett Pass becomes less available, thanks to the growing numbers of skiers, it is possible that some people may be forced to park at Hood River Meadows sno-park and ski up the road past Sahalie Falls to reach the Bennett Ridge Trail.

HEATHER CANYON TRAIL

Novice
Round trip up to 4.4 miles
Marked trails
Elevation gain up to 800 feet

High point 5400 feet
USGS Mount Hood South

Map—page 174

The Heather Canyon Trail is a beautiful ski tour, one of the most scenic on Mt. Hood. The trail follows scenic, winding meadows along Clark Creek and offers a long downhill return run. In addition the area has a superb, demanding alpine loop, and a short, interesting loop particularly suitable for novices with some experience. All tours begin at the Hood River Meadows sno-park. (See Hood River Meadows / Sahalie Falls.) The entire uphill route is used by alpine skiers, and the lower canyon, being narrower, demands particular alertness by Nordic skiers.

At the sno-park climb the center of the north-side snowbank and enter a wide lane into the forest. There is a sign here indicating the status of avalanche conditions along the upper part of the route. The trail climbs gently, soon joining Clark Creek where a connector trail goes right (east) to the Elk Meadows Trail. Turn left, however, and ski uphill along the creek as the trail climbs gently but persistently through continuous meadows in a narrow, enchanting valley contained by steep, forested ridges. About 2.2 miles from the sno-park the meadows end and you are standing at the lower end of the upper canyon, which is wide, impressive, and immensely scenic. On the north a bare glacial moraine rises 650 feet, and on the south a massive ridge climbs steeply to the runs of the Mt. Hood Meadows Ski Area. You are standing 800 feet above your starting point at the sno-park.

Farther on, the canyon can be dangerous, so use good judgment if you wish to continue climbing and exploring. A witness to the danger of the area is an avalanche gun emplacement far up to the left on the ridge. Heed the warning sign at the sno-park as well as the sign farther along the trail. Also use your common sense. If you know little about avalanches or snow structure, *proceed no farther*, even if the sign indicates the area is open. Instead, enjoy the long, euphoric downhill run back to the trailhead.

Heather Canyon Cutoff Trail. This 0.2-mile cutoff leaves the Heather Canyon Trail at the lower end of the long, narrow meadows 0.2 mile from the sno-park. Go right, into the trees, for about 100 yards. Then follow the trail as it climbs to the right, along the abrupt edge of an old stream bank to the Elk Meadows Trail. Turn left (north) for Elk Meadows or right (south) to return to the sno-park.

To ski from the Elk Meadows Trail to the Heather Canyon Trail, ski to the Clark Creek bridge (single log with railings) and turn uphill before crossing the bridge. The Cutoff Trail parallels the creek about 100 feet to the south, eventually gaining the old stream bank edge, then joining the Heather Canyon Trail.

There are no difficulties nor steep places on the Cutoff Trail. It is a short, scenic diversion that allows you to ski an interesting 0.8-mile loop from the sno-park. See the following tour. Novice; 0.2 mile one way.

Heather Canyon Lower Loop. This pleasant 0.8-mile loop, with several exciting spots for experienced novice skiers, is also an easy, fun tour for intermediate skiers. The loop will be a challenge to even an athletic novice, with several difficult moves and abrupt dips to be mastered. Passing through beautiful forest, where tree wells may challenge even the best skier later in the season, the loop is best skied clockwise. Follow the Heather Canyon Trail and Cutoff Trail to the Elk Meadows Trail. Then return southward to the east end of the sno-park.

HEATHER CANYON ALPINE LOOP

Advanced	High point 6450 feet
Round trip 8 miles	USGS Mount Hood South
Marked and unmarked trails	
Elevation gain 1850 feet	Map—page 174

If you are a skilled off-trail skier at the upper end of the Heather Canyon Trail, you may be tempted to explore farther. Proceed, however, only if the avalanche signs indicate the area is open and if you are sure that conditions are suitable for the tour. If the avalanche sign at the trailhead says "closed," go no farther than the sign at the one mile mark. Otherwise, use a great deal of caution. If you are inexperienced in off-trail avalanche area skiing, turn around and head back to the safe confines of the lower canyon.

From the upper end of the Heather Canyon Trail (see preceding tour), climb the 700-foot ridge to your left (south) up steep, open slopes that

Upper end of Heather Canyon Trail, east side of Mt. Hood

lead to the alpine ski area. Once you are on top proceed up the broad ridge crest for 0.5 mile, gaining another 350 feet. Then cut left, locate the North Canyon alpine run, and descend it to the lodge area. Although North Canyon is the easiest of the alpine runs, it still requires strong turning and edging ability.

From the lodge ski down to Umbrella Falls and follow the Umbrella Falls Trail (not well marked at this time) for the 900-foot descent to Hood River Meadows. For details see Umbrella Falls.

The upper Heather Canyon tour offers not only the potential of avalanche danger but also the danger of collision with alpine skiers moving at fast speeds. In fact, the entire uphill cross-country ski route is used by alpine skiers, and the lower canyon, being narrower, demands particular alertness by Nordic skiers. Other off-trail, alpine loop tours for advanced skiers with route-finding skills are possible in this area, connecting with the White River and the Wy'east Trail for loops up to 11 miles in length.

ELK MEADOWS TRAIL

Novice
Round trip 2.4 miles
Marked trail
Elevation gain 130 feet

High point 4630 feet
USGS Mount Hood South

Map—page 174

This is one of the loveliest forest-trail tours on Mt. Hood. It starts at Hood River Meadows and ends at Newton Creek, at the base of Elk Mountain. The rugged Newton Creek canyon is especially scenic. The trail is almost level but has a number of dips and turns to challenge any skier.

From the east end of the Hood River Meadows sno-park (see Hood River Meadows/Sahalie Falls) take a forest trail (summer trail 645) east about 100 yards to where it turns to the left and continues its winding course through the forest. A single-log bridge crosses Clark Creek, and from there to Newton Creek the trail climbs at a grade so slight it seems level.

There are many easy turns and sudden, shallow dips that add to the fun and interest of the trail. Between Clark and Newton creeks is the "corkscrew turn," an exciting but short downhill run with two tight turns. There are many thrills and spills here. The slight downhill of the overall trail on the return trip adds to the enjoyment.

Especially worthwhile is the fine view up Newton Creek, the turn-around point for the tour. This is a rugged, cliff-lined canyon of dramatic proportions, with Hood and the Newton Clark Glacier visible far above. If snow depth and snow bridges are right, you can ski up the south side of the canyon for further views.

An alternative to turning around here is to ski to Pocket Creek on the Newton Creek Trail (described in Chapter 15).

The creek crossings may be tricky due to snow or ice on the bridges. In most places the trail forms a quite obvious corridor, but it may require care if it has not been tracked out ahead of you. The bridge across Newton Creek is difficult to maintain because of seasonal flooding. Snow bridges may be the only way to cross.

UMBRELLA FALLS

Intermediate to Advanced	High point 5240 feet
Round trip 4 miles	USGS Mount Hood South
Marked trail	Map—page 174
Elevation gain 740 feet	

This is a forest trail, with one view, climbing earnestly to the many meadows at the upper end, near Umbrella Falls. The falls are located just below the sno-park at Mt. Hood Meadows Ski Area. This trail also forms the last link of the Heather Canyon Alpine Loop.

Walk to the entrance of the Hood River Meadows sno-park (see Hood River Meadows/Sahalie Falls) and climb the west-side snow bank. Ski along the roadside to Hood River Meadows, then ski up the road 250 yards to where the Umbrella Falls Trail takes off uphill to the right. The trail may or may not be well marked. Enter the forest and climb moderately steep slopes through forest for 300 yards to a semiopen ridge, where there is a fleeting view of Mt. Hood, Hood River Meadows below, and the alpine ski runs across the way.

Once on the semiopen ridge the angle eases and the route travels through scattered then heavy timber. After traversing side hills, it goes straight up, finally arriving at the lower meadows below the falls. There are numerous meadows of all sizes scattered in every direction. Follow markers if possible, otherwise just ski uphill to the falls, a noisy cascade over slabby rocks.

Although there are several trails in the meadows near the falls, at this time the plastic tape markers appear—as they have for several years—to be temporary. The lack of directional signs also creates confusion. The downhill return to Hood River Meadows is pleasant if the snow is good: not too deep or not hard spring snow. Tree wells may create difficulties for intermediate skiers unused to rough conditions. Good downhill skiing ability is important to enjoy this return trip.

To reach the falls from the main ski lodge at Mt. Hood Meadows, ski around the left (north) side of the sno-park past a small auxilliary building. There the trail descends a moderate slope into a meadow near the falls, which are close to the sno-park. Although short, this route is difficult. Still, there is no other approach for skiers. Below the falls are many glades and openings scattered for half a mile over a gently sloping area. This is an exceptionally beautiful area for just poking about.

ELK MEADOWS AND ELK MOUNTAIN

Advanced
Round trip 6 to 8 miles
Marked and unmarked trails
Elevation gain to meadows 760 feet, to Elk Mountain 1100 feet
High point 5100 feet at meadows, 5608 feet at Elk Mountain
USGS Mount Hood South, Badger Lake

Map—page 174

The tour to the top of Elk Mountain perhaps qualifies as wilderness skiing. The tour into Elk Meadows offers considerable scenic reward. Both provide the opportunity to be adventurous and to practice rugged, route-finding skiing at minimum risk.

From the Hood River Meadows sno-park (see Hood River Meadows/ Sahalie Falls), ski the Elk Meadows Trail to Newton Creek (see Heather Canyon Trail). Cross the creek at the foot of Elk Mountain, turn right, and descend slightly for about 50 yards. Then climb east up the trail, which switchbacks up steep, forested slopes. The grade eases off about two-thirds of the way to Elk Mountain Saddle, the forested saddle at 5260 feet. The trail may not be easy to follow in places, particularly across the few steep, small open slopes. There are no notable viewpoints on the way.

From Elk Mountain Saddle descend gently through magnificent forest to Elk Meadows, where a fine view of the east face of Mt. Hood dominates the scene. Exploring the meadow on skis as you enjoy the constantly changing scenes make this tour most rewarding. Do not attempt this tour when the snow is hard or icy. Depending on conditions, it may be necessary to walk down parts of the trail.

Elk Mountain. Near the summit is the site of a former fire lookout cabin with outstanding views across the deep East Fork valley to Lookout Mountain, Gunsight Ridge, and both Bennett Ridge and Pass.

From the Elk Meadows saddle at 5260 feet, leave the trail just before the descent into the meadows, turning southeast and climbing gentle slopes through open forest. Continue to the tree-covered summit ridge and the viewpoint at the old lookout site. This viewpoint may take a while to locate due to the lack of landmarks and the dense forest.

About half way up from the saddle to the summit you will probably lose the trail in dense areas of dog-hair growth. Tree blazes are difficult to follow even in ideal conditions. It is suggested that you first visit this trail in summer to get a feel for the area and the forest. Without this experience you may not find the lookout site. The winter view is well worth the summer hike.

Both tours are best skied only by advanced skiers who are equipped with USGS map and compass and are prepared for wilderness conditions. Both also in places involve skiing without the benefit of an obvious trail. From the saddle set a compass course to the lookout site. Do not ski these tours in weather that will cover your return tracks. During avalanche conditions, the small, open slopes on the switchbacks above Newton Creek may be dangerous.

Chapter 15
POCKET CREEK

Pocket Creek, with its miles of gentle roads and many open views, is popular with novice skiers. Most skiers who visit here seek the open beauty of the upper basin, where an inspiring panorama unfolds. It is surprising, then, that few skiers explore beyond the Upper Junction at 4200 feet, for not far above several outstanding viewpoints offer even finer vistas, including a view of Mt. Adams, a peak usually seen only from the higher, more remote summits of the Mt. Hood region.

The Pocket Creek trailhead with its roadside sno-park is located 13 miles from Government Camp (3.3 miles north of Bennett Pass), and 30 miles south of the town of Hood River. The sno-park serves as the trailhead for both the Pocket Creek and the Newton Creek trails, each of which lead upward into scenic open areas.

The East Fork Trail and other connector routes from Bennett Pass and Ridge will no doubt bring more skiers into the upper Pocket Creek basin. This is an advantage to adventurers, for more skiers mean more tracks. And more tracks means it is easier to visit distant areas and to ski longer loops.

An easy but long loop trail, combining the Pocket Creek, East Fork, Sahalie Falls, Elk Mountain and Newton Creek trails, will challenge skiers who seek easier long-distance skiing opportunities than are offered by several of the Pocket Creek connectors. See Pocket Creek Connector Trails (Chapter 13) for information on the several access routes and challenging loops of the upper Pocket Creek basin.

POCKET CREEK TRAIL

Novice
Round trip 5.4 miles
Unmarked road
Elevation gain to Upper Junction
  400 feet

High point Upper Junction 4200 feet
USGS Badger Lake

Map—page 168

The easy grades, open terrain, and fine scenery of this tour make Pocket Creek one of the outstanding skiing areas of Mt. Hood. There is something here for every skier. Interestingly, the Pocket Creek touring area is in reality misnamed as the great majority of the area is the East Fork Hood River valley, while only a very small part of the upper basin is occupied by Pocket Creek itself.

A snow-covered road goes east from the sno-park, descending gently

Skiing the East Fork Trail to the Upper Junction of Pocket Creek

0.6 mile to a bridge crossing of the East Fork of the Hood River. Cross the bridge and follow the road up the east side of the valley on a gentle climb through alternating forest and clearcuts to a road junction, hereafter referred to as "Upper Junction," 2.7 miles from the trailhead.

The Upper Junction (4200 feet) is surrounded by clearcuts and has fine views of the wide valley and the enclosing forested ridges. Gunsight Ridge is to the east and Bennett Ridge and the Terrible Traverse are immediately above to the south. The Upper Junction is a remarkable place in good weather. You can clearly see the Terrible Traverse as a steep-looking, rounded knob far above you, while Elk Mountain, to the north, dominates the impressive, sweeping view of the valley below. From Upper Junction it is a long downhill run toward the trailhead. Off-road skiing is popular here, and it is a spectacular spot for a lunch break. Many skiers consider this point as the turnaround place of the tour. If so, they miss some of the best skiing and views.

At the Upper Junction there are two roads, each going in a different direction, for further touring. One road goes west along a generally level route for 1.8 miles to a clearcut, which you can ascend for the good view of Mt. Hood. From the bottom of the clearcut it is 1.1 miles to Bennett Pass along the East Fork Trail. The top of this clearcut is the bottom end of Connector A, an unmarked ski route through the forest to the Bennett Ridge Trail not far above.

The other road from the Upper Junction climbs southward beneath the Terrible Traverse (Bennett Ridge Trail) 650 feet above, then makes a long, curving U-turn, eventually going north to the road end just 2.2 miles from the Upper Junction. This road, the most scenic tour of Pocket Creek, climbs through a number of clearcuts with views of Mt. Hood and of Mt. Adams, sixty miles north.

The low elevation of the trailhead (3800 feet) results some years in shallow snow, and early melting in the spring, leaving a bare road at the lower end. If so, don't give up and drive off because it is usually worth hiking up the road to skiable snow. The upper basin normally has a deep snow pack which is protected from melting by the high ridges. As an alternative approach to the upper basin in the spring, use one of the connector trails from Bennett Pass or Bennett Ridge to descend into the basin for often excellent late season skiing. Remember, however, that in late season the snow in the forest is often rough, crusty and dirty, with tree wells offering a challenge in places. For the quality of skiing you will find in the basin, the tour is probably worth such minor inconveniences. If they are just too much for you, however, hike the connector to where the skiing improves, or hike up from the trailhead.

Although the upper Pocket Creek road is usually quite safe, the slopes below and just south of the Terrible Traverse are avalanche-prone. Stay out of the clearcut immediately below the Terrible Traverse during and after heavy snowfall or during very warm weather.

NEWTON CREEK TRAIL

Novice	High point 4640 feet
Round trip 5.6 miles	USGS Mount Hood South, Badger Lake
Marked trail	
Elevation gain 840 feet	Map—pages 168, 174

This extremely scenic and varied trail winds along primitive roads, through meadows, glades and forest, and along the lovely banks of Newton Creek. It is almost all uphill to the upper end of Newton Creek and a long, gentle downhill run back. This trail and several other routes link to form an exceptional loop (see following tour).

From the Pocket Creek sno-park (see Pocket Creek Trail) walk down the highway for 150 yards and cross the highway bridge, where you will see trail signs nearby, on the west side of the highway. From there the trail winds uphill gently along the creek, then along old skid roads through scenic forest. In about 0.5 mile you reach a wide, straight road. Follow it uphill (turn left) to its end in a large meadow.

From there a marked trail enters immature firs, crosses a small creek, and continues upward along the base of Elk Mountain. Cross many clearings, where numerous dead snags lend an interesting scenic flavor.

The trail soon reaches Newton Creek and follows it upward to the crossing at the Elk Meadows Trail. Following the edge of the creek is interesting, for the convoluted and rounded snow banks are a beautiful and changing spectacle of snow sculpture. Although the trail is marked and cleared, there are several parallel routes to select from when there is sufficient snow.

A short sidehill at the creek's edge, just before reaching the Newton Creek crossing, may be the only tricky place on the entire trail. The situation changes from year to year. If icy, you may want to walk across this fifty-foot section. So far, the skiing trail is always on the north side of the creek, and a crossing is necessary only if you are skiing the loop or wish to visit the Elk Meadows Trail leading to Hood River Meadows.

It is a pleasant surprise to find such an open, scenic trail where you might expect only forest. As you descend this trail, returning to the trailhead, the views of upper Pocket Creek expand impressively to include Lookout Mountain, which rises almost 3000 feet above the wide valley of the Hood River. The full sweep and scale of massive, forested Gunsight Ridge is also inspiring. The Eternal Guardian is ever over your shoulder as you descend this lovely trail, which provides — on a good day —possibly the finest views of any Mt. Hood tour.

NEWTON CREEK LOOP

Advanced
Round trip 11 miles
Unmarked and marked roads
Elevation gain 874 feet

High point 4674 feet
USGS Mount Hood South, Badger Lake

Map—pages 168, 174

An exciting way to ski the Newton Creek Trail is to combine it with other trails to form this interesting loop tour. From the Pocket Creek sno-park (see Pocket Creek Trail) ski to the Upper Junction. Then go west on the East Fork road to the East Fork Trail (or try Connector Route A or B for a longer loop) to Bennett Pass. Ski down the open roadside slopes to opposite the Mt. Hood Meadows Ski Area access road and cross the highway on foot. Climb the snow bank on the right side of the access road, which puts you on the abandoned former highway leading past Sahalie Falls to Hood River Meadows sno-park.

At the sno-park take the Elk Meadows Trail (which see) to and across Newton Creek (or take the Heather Canyon Trail and ski the Cutoff Trail down to the Elk Meadows Trail). You are now on the upper end of the Newton Creek Trail. Just ski down to your starting point at Pocket Creek for a respectable 11-mile loop. If you select a different connector out of Pocket Creek the loop will be even longer.

ROBINHOOD/HORSETHIEF MEADOWS

Novice to Intermediate
Round trip up to 5 miles
Unmarked roads and trails
Elevation gain up to 450 feet

High point 4000 feet
USGS Badger Lake

Map—page 186

This interesting area, just north of the Pocket Creek sno-park, offers four distinct tours: a tour along the bank of the Hood River, a forest loop, a large meadow, and a tour to a high point, with sweeping views of Gunsight Ridge and the Hood River Valley.

Robinhood is 4.3 miles north of Bennett Pass and 1 mile north of Pocket Creek. There is a plowed roadside parking spot. This little-known area will keep you busy exploring its numerous routes and hidden corners. As all routes are on mostly gentle terrain, it is a fine area for novice skiers. For skiers wanting to improve their route-finding skills, there are numerous easy problems to solve and decisions to make, adding to the overall enjoyment of the tours.

Hood River Trail. This ski route combines a narrow, primitive road and a winding trail following the very edge of the rapidly flowing, scenic river. The tour eventually ends in an old clearcut where exploratory side trips are possible. This trail requires over a foot of snow to cover minor obstacles.

From the sno-park ski several hundred yards along the campground road into the far end of the campground area. There, the road suddenly turns into a winding trail (summer trail 650) that continues along the river. A parallel primitive road to the west offers variety and less restricted skiing.

Ski 1 mile to a road crossing a bridge over the Hood River. Turn left on the road and ski a short distance to a large clearcut from which a number of skid roads go in all directions. It is possible to ski south into an adjoining clearcut, from where a route can be forced back to the river side. You will encounter marshy areas in this second clearcut and to the south. Novice; 3 miles round trip.

Forest Loop. To reach this loop ski 0.5 mile along Road 3520, just south of the sno-park. Then take a side road through attractive forest and a clearcut before returning along Road 3520 to complete the loop. Novices should ski this loop in a counter-clockwise direction to avoid a short, moderately steep, hill just north of the clearcut. The loop follows primitive roads on both the south and west sides. From the south leg of the loop several skid roads go south, inviting exploration of the gentle forest terrain. Novice; 1.3 miles round trip.

Horsethief Meadows. From the Robinhood sno-park it is about 1.5 miles along Roads 3520 and 620 to a narrow band of trees leading into the beautiful meadows west of Road 620. More direct access, however, is by

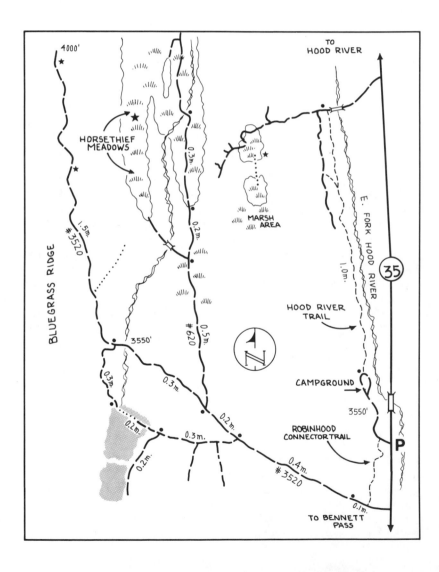

way of a primitive road that leaves Road 620 about 0.5 mile north of its junction with Road 3520. Follow the primitive road across an old dilapidated bridge only 80 yards west of Road 620. The lovely, long, narrow meadows, nestled against the base of Bluegrass Ridge, offer perhaps the most scenic tour of the entire Robinhood area. If snow is shallow, look for the old road passing through the center of the meadows and follow it as you explore the area.

Another route to the meadows is to ski Road 620 to a sharp turn, where a culvert carries Robinhood Creek under the road. Leave the road and ski through the forest band to the west to find the meadows. Novice; 4.5 miles round trip.

Bluegrass Ridge Road. From Highway 35 it is only 2.5 miles to the end of Road 3520 high on the side of Bluegrass Ridge. The last half of the tour is along the moderate grade of the steadily climbing road, where there are continuous, wide views of Lookout Mountain and Gunsight Ridge to the east.

From a point on the road a short distance uphill from the start of the climb it is possible to ski down onto open slopes, snow depth permitting, then into Horsethief Meadows. To return to the trailhead ski north around the end of the band of forest on the east side of the meadows to Road 620, or ski directly through the narrow band of forest to the road, then south along Road 620 to complete a loop. Intermediate; 5 miles round trip.

Robinhood Connector Trail. This trail is an abandoned snowmobile route connecting the Robinhood Campground access road and Road 3520. Depending on where you park, this forest trail may serve to get you from one area to the other. The north end of this trail is only about 50 yards from the parking area on Highway 35. The access to the trail is obscure, being hidden by alders. The south end of the connector starts at the edge of Road 3520 about 100 yards west of Highway 35. Near the north end, the trail twists around, climbs a short rise, and requires some simple route-finding. A downed tree or two are awkward to cross. The south end of the trail offers an obvious route. This trail is both scenic and fun to ski. Novice; 0.2 mile.

Chapter 16
COOPER SPUR

Located high on the northeastern flank of Mt. Hood, overlooking the deep, wide Hood River Valley, the Cooper Spur area offers fine views particularly of the volcano itself, but also of the rolling ridge lands to the east and of the Columbia River Gorge and other volcanoes to the north.

Cooper Spur, a prominent rock buttress extending down from the summit ice, becomes broader and gentler downslope, where there are two principal touring areas. The higher and more difficult area centers on historic Cloud Cap Inn, which is located near timberline and accessible only to skiers willing and able to undertake a long, rather tiring tour. The lower ski area is the rolling Weygandt Basin, which offers a wide range of road and clearcut skiing, almost all of it on gentle terrain.

If you are a Portland skier, you will find the distance to Cooper Spur is about 86 miles, regardless whether you drive through Hood River or Government Camp. Depending on your approach, drive Highway 35 either 23 miles south of Hood River or about 20 miles from Government Camp. Take a side road (old Highway 35) west to Cooper Spur Junction. Turn left and drive uphill to the ski area, 3.8 miles from Highway 35. Continue on the one-way road past the ski area and downhill for 150 yards to the Nordic skiers' sno-park, a wide spot in the road. The sno-park is located at the beginning of the winter road to Cloud Cap.

WEYGANDT BASIN

Intermediate	High point 4020 feet
Round trip 5 miles	USGS Dog River
Unmarked roads	Map—page 189
Elevation gain 200 feet	

Only two miles from Cooper Spur Ski Area lies the shallow, gentle Weygandt Basin, almost totally clearcut and providing a short but memorable tour. The view of Mt. Hood, towering far above, and sweeping views of the upper Hood River valley, Mill Creek Buttes, and the three major Washington volcanoes makes this tour a special experience.

Drive to Cooper Spur sno-park (see chapter introduction). Ski up the Cloud Cap road 1.4 miles to a small cliff-like quarry on the left side of the road. Before climbing to the quarry, the Cloud Cap road goes downhill and turns as it crosses Tilly Jane Creek. Opposite the quarry is a road angling off to the right. Follow this road 0.8 mile to the basin-like clearcut for fine views. The road continues over the north rim (Weygandt Summit

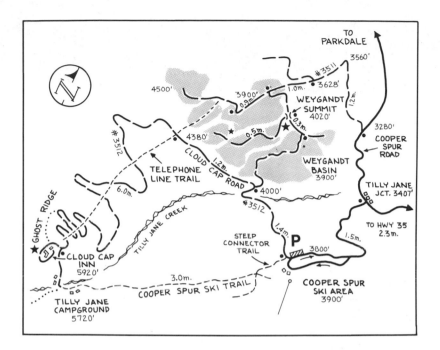

4020 feet) of the clearcut basin and descends 0.4 mile to Road 3511. This
road goes 2.2 miles east and south downhill to the Parkdale-Cooper Spur
road, the former Highway 35.

A short, interesting tour starts at Weygandt Summit and follows a logging road and continuous clearcuts west 0.5 mile up gentle grades to the
edge of the forest. There, a view to the east includes Shellrock Mountain,
Mill Creek Buttes, Dog River Butte (with snowpatch), and the partially
hidden Lookout Mountain. By penetrating the forest 50 yards west, you
can locate the old wagon road to Cloud Cap Inn. Going directly up this
old road 0.5 mile brings you to the Cloud Cap road. In the other direction, skiing downhill on the old road brings you quickly to a logging road
and a fine viewpoint, then along the road back to Weygandt Summit, a
splendid short loop.

Although Weygandt Basin has many clearcuts and shelterwoods with
views, there is a particularly good one on Road 3511 only 1.2 miles from
the Parkdale-Cooper Spur road. To reach this viewpoint ski into the
basin from the sno-park or if conditions permit, park on the Parkdale-
Cooper Spur road and ski up to the open hillside.

There should be at least three feet of snow cover for safe downhill skiing in clearcuts. If visibility is limited, be sure to orient yourself. The area
is a maze of roads and clearcuts, with no landmarks. It would be easy to
become confused.

Mill Creek Buttes (left) and Dog River Butte from Weygandt Basin

COOPER SPUR SKI TRAIL (CLOUD CAP INN)

Advanced
Round trip ski trail 6 miles, road
**   17.2 miles, loop 11.6 miles**
Unmarked trail and road
Elevation gain 2120 feet

High point 5920 feet
USGS Dog River, Mount Hood North

Map—page 189

See Weygandt Basin tour description for directions to sno-park. The trailhead for the Cooper Spur Trail, which goes to Cloud Cap Inn, was relocated in 1979 and no longer is at the ski area, where the trail originally climbed the west side of the downhill ski area. The trailhead is now on the Cloud Cap road near the sno-park, which is located 150 yards below the ski area on the one-way road.

Just west of the small sno-park, on the left side of the Cloud Cap road, a 1-mile trail climbs steeply to join the main Cooper Spur Ski Trail west of the top of the ski area. Although designed and constructed by the Forest Service for Nordic skiing, this short, steep trail is not recommended as a descent route unless you are a very competent downhill skier.

At the junction with the wide Cooper Spur Ski Trail, 1 mile from the sno-park, turn right (west) and ski uphill to Tilly Jane Campground on this wide, easy-to-follow trail. It is a remorseless climb all the way, gaining 2120 feet to Cloud Cap Inn. (Note: maps disagree on elevations in this area, and odd discrepancies occur.)

At 5720 feet, 0.6 mile below Cloud Cap Inn, the trail levels out and passes directly in front of two cabins on the left. The first is a two-story overnight shelter open to the public; the other is an old American Legion cookhouse with several wooden sleeping platforms. The first cabin is definitely the better one for overnighters. If you plan to spend the night, carry a groundsheet and foam pad. Because the cabin is heavily used, you should contact the Forest Service near Parkdale to confirm availability of space. If your name is not on the registry list, you may have to sleep out on the snow. If you sleep inside, be prepared to be crowded.

After leaving the cabins, you soon cross a small ravine, passing two green cabins just above the trail. From there follow a road bed to the main Cloud Cap road. Those wishing to continue to the vast, open slopes above timberline should follow the left side of the ravine uphill. Those going to Cloud Cap Inn should follow the roadbed for 200 yards to where it turns right. Leave the road at that point and climb left up a short, steep hillside to the inn, which is visible above.

The building just below and north of Cloud Cap Inn is the Snowshoe Club cabin, a historic, old, limited-membership social club. Both buildings are locked and not open to the public at any time, but the historic inn is well worth a close inspection. The view from the inn, eastward across distant ridges to Lookout Mountain, and southwestward to the steep, impressive north face of Mt. Hood, with its glaciers, is a superb reward for the tiring uphill trail. Eliot Glacier and Barrett Spur, a prominent buttress on Mt. Hood's north side, are just two of many alpine features to be seen. Mt. St. Helens, Mt. Rainier, and Mt. Adams are also in view far to the north, across the Columbia River Gorge.

There is off-trail skiing on Cooper Spur, above Cloud Cap Inn. In good weather this area of huge open snowfields, moraines and glaciers is the realization of the wilderness skier's wildest fantasy. You will not soon forget the wild scene of deep canyons, rugged ridges, and snowfields.

Most skiers descend to the trailhead by way of the Cloud Cap road, which offers a gentle grade all the way. If snow is favorable, however, you can bypass several long switchbacks by skiing down Ghost Ridge, a moderate descent, and joining the road at the second hairpin turn at 5240 feet. To find the top of Ghost Ridge, a wide, open snow slope, ski toward the canyon from the northwest corner of the Snowshoe Club cabin. If the skiing is good on the descent of the ridge you can easily overshoot the second hairpin, so be alert and watch for the obvious road cut on your right as you descend. Another shortcut is to descend the old Telephone Line Trail (see following tour).

The tour to Cloud Cap Inn is a tiring trip, so be sure you are in shape before attempting it. Carry survival gear, repair kit, maps, and compass. Descending the Cooper Spur Ski Trail, which was constructed during the days of heavier skis and boots, is not easy on light Nordic equipment, so most skiers select the road for the return to the sno-park.

Historical Note. Cloud Cap Inn, built in 1889 as a mountain resort, is a rustic, one story log building, which originally was held down by cables and had an observation deck on the roof. Guests arrived in Hood River by train and then rode horse coach or wagon to the inn the same day.

The Weygandts, father and son, worked as mountaineering guides here for many years. The inn closed in 1940. It was purchased by the Forest Service, and is now used by the Hood River Crag Rats alpine club as a base for mountain rescue operations.

TELEPHONE LINE TRAIL

Advanced   High point 5920 feet
One way 2 miles   USGS Dog River, Mount Hood North
Unmarked trail
Elevation loss 1540 feet   Map—page 189

The Telephone Line Trail is a shortcut route down from Cloud Cap Inn. Following the old telephone line that once served the inn, it cuts through zigzags of the Cloud Cap road. The trail descends in a generally straight line, steep near the upper end, moderating in the last two sections. It needs to be marked and cleared of brush at this time, but is relatively skiable with three feet of snow. Since the old telephone poles are no longer in place, the trail is growing over and may be difficult to find at road crossings.

The trail starts about 50 yards northeast of the Snowshoe Club cabin just below Cloud Cap Inn. The start is not obvious, but if you miss it, just ski down the road and pick the trail up where it crosses each section of road. By being particularly observant, you will spot the narrow openings along the road. Until cleared of brush and fallen trees, the trail will continue to be more challenging than it need be, particularly along the upper sections. Most skiers prefer to ski down Ghost Ridge to the second (of four) hairpin turns from the top, then follow the road until choosing to ski the Telephone Line Trail. Once on the trail it is easy to follow.

The trail, an exciting descent full of thrills and spills even for the best skier, cuts off about 4 miles from the total road distance. The upper parts of the trail are rated advanced. The lower two sections, which cut off about 1.5 miles, are intermediate.

Be prepared for sudden falls and surprises. Do not ski the trail unless the snow is favorable. If you descend too far you will cross the last section of road without knowing it and end up on a logging road in Weygandt Basin. This error would ultimately put you several miles below the Cooper Spur Ski Area and your sno-park unless you select the correct route back through Weygandt Basin to the Cloud Cap road.

Ankle deep in new snow

Chapter 17
CLINGER SPRING

East of Cooper Spur, across the Hood River Valley, lies the high, rolling, forested Clinger Spring area. Clinger Spring (4200 feet) is little more than a point on the map (the spring is not even visible in winter), but it is the departure point for a number of tours. Although the terrain is easy for intermediate skiers, the long distances of many tours earn them an advanced rating. Clinger Spring itself is 1000 feet above and 3.6 miles from Highway 35.

All tours in this area are reached by skiing (or driving) uphill on Road 44 from Highway 35. The snow line is seldom as low as the highway

(3280 feet) so it is usually possible to drive up Road 44. Unless plowed, the road is never drivable beyond a road cut at 3840 feet, 1.6 miles from the highway. There, the road makes a sharp bend on the ridge crest and enters shady north slopes where snow gathers all winter. Because snowmobiles occasionally use the area, do not block the road when you park at the snow line. Road 44 winds gently uphill from Highway 35 past several good views and Powder Spring (2.8 miles) to Clinger Spring (3.6 miles) and Road 4410, just 0.2 mile beyond.

The entire region is criss-crossed with many roads and a few trails, offering great potential for cross-country skiing. It is an area, however, where prior familiarity will ensure greater confidence and success while skiing. Therefore, you may want to explore the Clinger Spring country in summer—by car or foot—when flowering meadows and beautiful forests await you.

Road 4410 leads south to Lookout Mountain, an immense, forested volcanic peak, the highest point east of Mt. Hood and the goal of a long but rewarding tour. The summit is a spectacular viewpoint, as is High Prairie on the peak's west shoulder.

In addition to Lookout Mountain there are three other touring hubs in the area: Clinger Spring itself, Brooks Meadow, and Knebal Pass. Tours radiate from each of these centers, following either logging or primitive roads to meadows or clearcuts where there are exceptional views. The tours, however, are long, often requiring several miles of skiing from the snow line on Road 44 just to reach the touring hubs. When the snow line is low, these tours are long and could be tiring, especially in adverse snow conditions. At such times be sure to carry a repair kit along with the ten essentials.

Although round-trip distances are often given from Highway 35, they may be shorter, depending on the snow line. Very often, the tours start a considerable distance above the highway, since the snow line seldom drops that low. If you record the distance from Highway 35 to the snow line, you can adjust guidebook distances to determine the actual distances you have to ski.

Be aware that maps of the area are neither accurate nor complete. The latest USGS topographic quadrangle—the photorevised 1979 issue of *Dog River*—continues to show the old road, which was eliminated years ago, running directly through Brooks Meadow. It also shows the old guard station, which is also long since gone. Other errors also exist. For example, neither the USGS nor the Forest Service maps show the old Brooks Meadow road (a primitive road, now the Surveyor Trail) from south of the meadow to Clinger Spring. Nor do they correctly show the junctions of Road 4410 and the Clinger Ridge road with Road 44. The maps in this guidebook, however, show all principal junctions and roads accurately. It is a good idea always to carry more than one map of any area you ski in. With the construction each year of new logging roads, new side roads and junctions appear that are not on your maps.

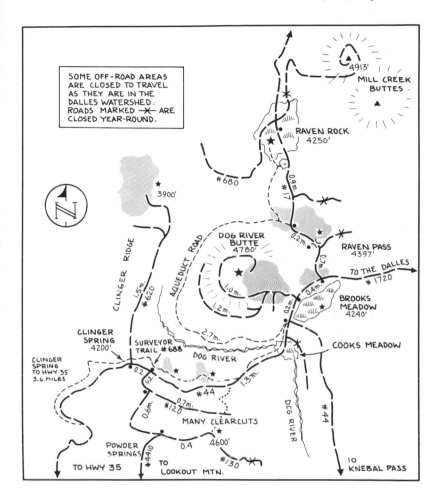

SOME OFF-ROAD AREAS
ARE CLOSED TO TRAVEL
AS THEY ARE IN THE
DALLES WATERSHED.
ROADS MARKED —✕— ARE
CLOSED YEAR-ROUND.

CLINGER RIDGE

Intermediate	High point 4200 feet
Round trip 10.2 miles from Highway 35	USGS Dog River
Unmarked roads	
Elevation gain 1200 feet cumulative	Map—page 195

From Highway 35 follow Road 44 to Clinger Spring (see chapter introduction). At Clinger Spring the first side road you encounter—Road 620, the Clinger Ridge road—heads northward to several clearcuts. The road drops gently, losing 300 feet in 1.5 miles. Along the way, several side roads to the west offer opportunities for exploring. The road ends in a clearcut (3900 feet), with a view of the Hood River Valley, Mt. St. Helens, Mt. Adams, Mt. Rainier, and the three summits of the Mill Creek Buttes. Dog River Butte is just across the steep, narrow valley to the east.

VOLCANO VIEW

Intermediate   **High point 4600 feet**
Round trip 9.6 miles from Highway 35   **USGS Dog River**
Unmarked roads
Elevation gain 1300 feet   **Map—page 195**

This short uphill side trip from Road 44 into shelterwood cuts provides views of Mt. Hood, Mt. St. Helens, Mt. Adams, Dog River Butte, and the Mill Creek Buttes. Ski past Clinger Spring on Road 44 (see chapter introduction) about 200 yards and turn right (uphill) onto Road 4410 (the Lookout Mountain road). Ski southward past the first side road at 0.2 mile. Continue along the winding road, which shortly makes an obvious turn to the left (east), arriving at a level junction at 0.8 mile. The Lookout Mountain road (see Lookout Mountain) cuts back at a reverse angle, reaching Horkelia Meadow in only 0.6 mile. For the best views, however, ski east from the level junction, following Road 130 on generally level terrain for 0.4 mile to the viewpoint. The road continues eastward but is uninteresting and closed to further travel in 0.5 mile. From the viewpoint—1.4 miles from Clinger Spring—it is possible to ski straight downhill through clearcuts to Road 44.

BROOKS MEADOW PRIMITIVE ROAD

Intermediate   **High Point 4240 feet**
Round trip from Clinger Spring to Brooks   **USGS Dog River**
** Meadow 3.0 miles**
Unmarked road   **Map—page 195**
Elevation gain negligible

From Clinger Spring this scenic old road, now called Surveyor Trail 688, goes both east and west, closely paralleling Road 44. The section going east reaches Brooks Meadow in just over 1.5 miles, offering an interesting alternative to the main road. The section heading west extends 0.8 mile to a steep, open hillside leading up to Road 44. Beyond there the route is blocked by fallen trees.

Starting at Clinger Spring (see chapter introduction), the eastern section of the old road soon reaches a small clearing with a view of Mt. Adams and in 0.5 mile or so enters a larger clearcut with a view of Mt. Hood. The road turns upward in this clearcut (see sketch map) and after another 0.5 mile, always keeping close to Road 44, joins it briefly before re-entering the forest and crossing Cooks Meadow, just 500 yards south of Brooks Meadow. Near Brooks Meadow, you ski past the obscure junction with the aqueduct road, another primitive route, which goes west around Dog River Butte.

The old Brooks Meadow road is gentle throughout, with no steep sections. The only route-finding problem might be in the second clearcut, where the road curves and re-enters the forest in the far upper corner.

Going west from Clinger Spring, the old road serves as an alternate return to your car. It very shortly makes a hairpin turn left and continues on a gentle downhill course, always close, but out of sight of Road 44. Follow the old track for 0.8 mile—or as far as you want—with the option of always being able to climb through the forest to Road 44. Logging in the near future along this route will somewhat disrupt the tour.

BROOKS MEADOW

Intermediate	**High point 4240 feet**
Round trip 10.4 miles from Highway 35	**USGS Dog River**
Unmarked road	
Elevation gain 960 feet	**Map—page 195**

The road tour into this large, beautiful meadow has a number of views, and much of the return trip is a long, gentle downhill grade. There are numerous side tours from Brooks Meadow to interesting and scenic destinations.

From Clinger Spring continue on the main road for 1.5 miles to the Road 44/1720 junction. Enter the trees straight ahead and to the right to locate nearby Brooks Meadow. For the best view of Mt. Hood ski to the far end of the meadow.

From Brooks Meadow you can take several scenic tours, ranging from a quick ascent of nearby Dog River Butte to more extended jaunts to Raven Rock and destinations beyond Knebal Pass. For details see the following tour descriptions. All offer ample scenic rewards and some the hint of adventure as well.

All the roads are easy to follow but Forest Service and USGS maps are important to the winter traveler in this area, where there are many roads and few landmarks. Most of the tours in the area are rated either intermediate or advanced, depending on distance and potential navigation difficulties.

Raven Rock and the north side of Mt. Hood from the Raven Rock tour

AQUEDUCT LOOP

Intermediate
Round trip 4.2 miles from
  Brooks Meadow
Unmarked road
Elevation gain 157 feet

High point 4397 feet
USGS Dog River

Map—page 195

Starting just south of Brooks Meadow, this 4.2-mile loop circles Dog River Butte in a clockwise direction, offering an interesting alternative route to Raven Rock. The loop follows a primitive road that once served as a maintenance route for a long abandoned aqueduct for The Dalles' watershed. Since the aqueduct was a gravity-flow underground wooden pipe, the road, which is always just above, rolls along gently, neither climbing nor descending significantly.

This route is part of the Forest Service summer Surveyor Trail 688, a combination of roads and trails. To locate the start of the loop, go to the junction of Road 44 and Road 1720, at the south end of Brooks Meadow. Ski 200 yards south on Road 44, enter the forest to the right (west) and locate the primitive road, which may take a few minutes. Follow this road as it circles the west side of the butte. At the 1 mile mark there is a short, exciting downhill run with a good runout. Continue along the road for 2.6 miles to a large clearcut. There are no views at this time from the loop, but the forest skiing on this old road is a pleasant change from the usual, wide logging roads and Road 44. Logging is planned for this area and it may change its character, which would be unfortunate. There are few of the old, primitive roads left in our woods today. Most have been widened, straightened, graded, and paved for efficient log hauling. The original character of these old roads has been lost for both the summer explorer and the skier.

If you decide to ski north to Raven Rock along the Surveyor Trail some easy route-finding may be required to find the primitive road leading out of the lower end of the clearcut on the north side of Dog River Butte. Beyond the clearcut, back on the Surveyor Trail, there is about 0.5 mile of delightful, rolling skiing along the road then it suddenly curves right. The trail to Raven Rock descends 50 yards here to the left then continues north as a summer foot trail, which is generally easy to follow, though not as obvious, wide, and free of limbs as the aqueduct road. There should be little route-finding on this tour, but you must have a compass and both the *Dog River* USGS quad and the Forest Service map to enjoy the tour and assure your safety.

DOG RIVER BUTTE

Intermediate
Round trip 2.6 miles from Brooks Meadow
Unmarked road
Elevation gain 540 feet from Brooks Meadow

High point 4780 feet
USGS Dog River

Map—page 195

Several easy roads constructed for future logging wind around Dog River Butte. By the time you visit this area, there will no doubt be several new clearcuts offering views. Until then, the most interesting route is the spiral road tour to the summit.

Ski to the Road 44/1720 junction just south of Brooks Meadow (which see). Take the first side road north of the junction, a distance of 350 yards. Enter the forest to the left and ski west into a large, old clearcut where the road divides, with branches going in several directions. Take the center road and follow its upward, spiral route through dense forest to where it exits at the top of the same old clearcut that you crossed below. The summit offers a sweeping view from Lookout Mountain to the Mill Creek Buttes, and on a clear day to the vast flat lands of eastern Oregon stretching out to the horizon. The shortest distance to this fine viewpoint is straight up the old clearcut from below, a strenuous climb.

RAVEN ROCK

Advanced	**High point 4397 feet**
Round trip 4.8 miles from	**USGS Dog River**
Brooks Meadow	
Unmarked road	**Map—page 195**
Elevation gain 350 feet cumulative	
from Brooks Meadow	

This tour offers possibly the finest views in the region, with the single exception of Lookout Moutain. Ski to Brooks Meadow (which see). From Road 1720, which parallels the west side of Brooks Meadow, take Road 17 to the left and follow it northwest into a clearcut with a view of Mt. Hood. Cross the clearcut on the road, climbing gently into the forest. Ski 0.7 mile from Road 1720 to the high point of the tour (Raven Pass, 4397 feet), where a side road closed to entry heads east. From the edge of the forest nearby there is a fine view of Mt. St. Helens, Mt. Adams, and Mt. Rainier—a view that makes the long haul from snow line worthwhile.

From that viewpoint return to Road 17 and continue north, skiing down a gentle grade into a third clearcut, then back into the forest to the final clearcut, where Raven Rock, a prominent outcrop, provides an exceptional view and lunch spot. There, near the foot of the Mill Creek Buttes,

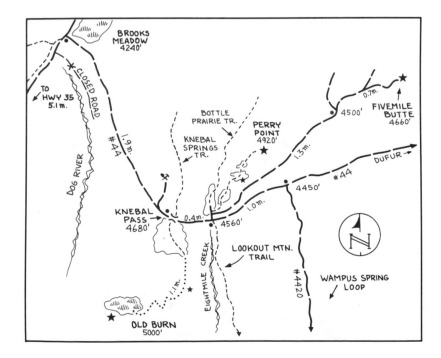

there are sweeping views of the Hood River valley and Mt. St. Helens, but the towering presence of Mt. Hood dominates the entire scene.

The prominent twin Mill Creek Buttes are just to the northeast of Raven Rock. Unfortunately the entire area east of Road 17 is closed to travel in summer and winter alike because the road is the western boundary of The Dalles' watershed. The closure reduces potential fire damage to and prevents human contamination of the watershed. Please observe the closure.

Shellrock Mountain and the scenic saddle on its north side is 2.6 miles north of Raven Rock, with an elevation drop of 160 feet. This is not a particularly rewarding tour as the road travels through dense forest with no views.

OLD BURN

Intermediate
Round trip 16.2 miles from Highway 35
Unmarked road and off-road
Elevation gain 1720 feet from
   Highway 35

High point 5000 feet
USGS Dog River, Fivemile Butte

Map—page 200

Knebal Pass (4680 feet) is 1.9 miles southeast of Brooks Meadow on Road 44, a gentle climb of 440 feet. The pass, only a road high point in the forest, is the source of three interesting destinations: the Old Burn, Perry Point, and Fivemile Butte. Each of these tours is challenging in its own way and has good views as a reward.

The Old Burn is a large, open hillside facing north and west, with remarkable views. To reach it ski a 1.1-mile off-trail route from Knebal Pass. Total elevation gain from Brooks Meadow: 760 feet.

From Brooks Meadow (which see) ski southeast up wide Road 44 1.9 miles to Knebal Pass, where a short side road to the right leads into a large cut-over area. Ski 0.4 mile to the southeast corner of the area to where an obvious open, natural corridor leads up gentle slopes. Follow this to a meadow-like hillside with scattered stands of trees. As you climb, start circling south, then southwest.

As the clearings get smaller and the lodgepole thicker, continue upward where possible through openings. (If you veer too far south, you will hit an almost impenetrable wall of doghair.) Eventually you will be climbing westward on moderate slopes. As the grade levels out at 5000 feet you arrive at the Old Burn, with grand views of the east face of Mt. Hood, Mt. St. Helens, Mt. Defiance in front, nearby Dog River Butte below Defiance, Mill Creek Buttes, Mt. Rainier, and Mt. Adams. Ski to the far west end of the Old Burn for the best views. The descent is fast and pleasant, with the opportunity to practice T-marks around the clumps of trees. The future will unfortunately see a road from Knebal Pass pushed uphill behind the Old Burn for logging to the south. That road will provide less interesting skiing than the off-road route described here.

PERRY POINT

Advanced
Round trip 17.2 miles from Highway 35
Unmarked road and trail
Elevation gain 1640 feet from Highway 35

High point 4920 feet
USGS Dog River, Fivemile Butte

Map—page 200

Only 1.2 miles from Knebal Pass, this well-hidden 4920-foot promontory offers interesting views from a unique vantage. From Knebal Pass ski east 0.4 mile downhill to an obvious road on the left (north) side of Road 44. Turn there but quickly leave the road, which goes to Fivemile Butte, and climb into a nearby opening. Then turn right (east) and climb through a meadow into the forest, following a primitive road. The route soon emerges into one clearing, then into a larger one with a view of Lookout Mountain. Keep to the upper edge of the clearing, and climb through trees at the top into a small opening, then turn east again. The route is an indistinct trail climbing eastward through forest.

The trail soon opens onto sidehill meadows with great views to the south and east. Continue to the farthest east ridge point, a craggy, snow-drifted, narrow point dominated by a most unusual group of twisted and weathered pines. From there you can see the Mill Creek Buttes and the distant Klickitat Hills, north of the Columbia River. Perry Point makes for an exciting trip and is a wild place to rest as you take in the panorama.

FIVEMILE BUTTE

Advanced
Round trip 18.8 miles from Highway 35
Unmarked roads and off-road
Elevation gain 1380 feet

High point 4660 feet
USGS Dog River, Fivemile Butte

Map—page 200

A fire lookout tower 2.4 miles from Knebal Pass is your destination. It is located on the east end of a low ridge, which is flat and wide, with views to the north, east, and south. This is a road tour. From Brooks Meadow follow Road 44 across Knebal Pass to the same trailhead as for

Perry Point—a side road to the left. This side road immediately makes a sharp right turn and almost parallels Road 44 for 2.0 miles along an almost level, sidehill route through the forest. The last 0.7 mile is first uphill, then level, as it rolls and winds to the final open area, where you can see the eastern wheatfields, the Klickitat Hills north of The Dalles, and Mt. Adams. On the last stretch to the lookout there are two side roads to the left; go straight or bear right along this section.

LOOKOUT MOUNTAIN

Advanced   **High point 6525 feet**
Round trip 18.8 miles from Highway 35   **USGS Dog River, Badger Lake**
Unmarked roads
Elevation gain 3245 feet   **Map—page 204**

Although this tour follows a road most of the way, its length and isolation nudges it toward the realm of wilderness skiing. There are few views above Clinger Spring but unsurpassed ones from the mountain shoulder at High Prairie and from the summit. Elevation gain could exceed 3000 feet, depending on how close the snow line is to Highway 35.

The roads are generally easy to follow but be alert to road junctions and meadows, where the route can be lost. Future logging will probably add more roads so carry maps and compass. Experience in extended touring is a prerequisite for this tour. This tour is best done in late winter, early spring, or after periods of stable weather, when the snow is more consolidated and weather more predictable.

Ski to Clinger Spring (see chapter introduction). From there the summit is 5.8 miles south via Road 4410, from which there are several views. This is a lovely primitive road with gentle grades its entire length.

Ski Road 4410 south from near Clinger Spring, passing a side road at 0.2 mile. Bear right, continuing south, then making a wide turn to the left (east). Three hundred yards beyond the turn the Lookout Mountain road turns off to the right (south) at a reverse angle. From this junction you can see both Mt. St. Helens and Mt. Adams in fair weather.

Continue the gentle ascent south, entering long, narrow Horkelia Meadow in 0.6 mile. The road climbs through the center of the meadow to a view of Mt. St. Helens at the upper end. A better viewpoint 1.4 miles farther on offers an exceptional look at the east side of Mt. Hood.

Continue up the road to High Prairie, a large meadow just north of and under the summit of Lookout Mountain. In entering this meadow, you will lose the road, so in less-than-perfect weather be alert for where the road enters the meadow for the return trip. As you proceed upward, passing through a maze of meadows, bear right to the open west shoulder of the summit ridge. The final moderately steep ascent involves some

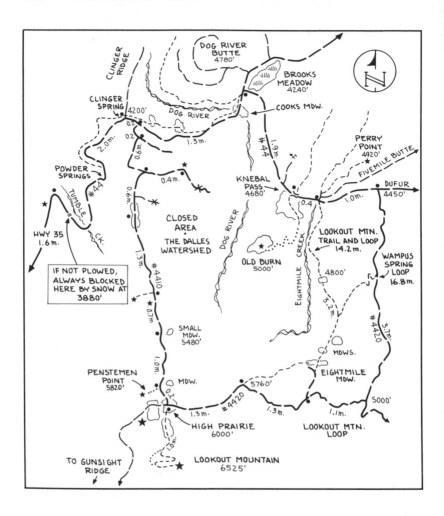

traverses if the final winding loops of the old lookout road to the very summit are obscured by the snow, as they usually are.

On a good day the summit view is a spectacular, unobstructed panorama. Five major volcanoes are visible, a big chunk of eastern Oregon, the impressive Badger Creek valley, the Pocket Creek-East Fork basin, and Bennett Pass to name just a few of the sights—a memorable experience worth the long haul.

Historical Note. In 1944, two high school boys from The Dalles, Carl Francois and Stan Davey, friends of the author, skied into Brooks Meadow from the north in an attempt to climb Lookout Mountain. Using alpine skis with cable bindings, and home-made pack boards, they reached the meadow and camped in a long since vanished cabin. They proceeded toward Lookout Mountain in heavy snowfall, camped near Horkelia Meadow, and finally realized they had bitten off too much. Retreating from their second camp, they found that a cougar had been following their tracks. These were the days before lightweight foods, so their diet included fresh pork chops and a large tin of cabbage! Campfire coals burned a series of holes through a wool sleeping bag.

LOOKOUT MOUNTAIN LOOPS

Advanced
Round trip 14.2 to 17.0 miles
   from Clinger Spring
Unmarked roads and trails
Elevation gain 2700 feet from Highway 35

High point 6000 feet
USGS Dog River, Badger Lake,
   Fivemile Butte, Flag Point

Map—page 204

Two long loops toward Lookout Mountain are possible from Brooks Meadow. The first includes the Lookout Mountain summer foot trail for part of the route and is the preferred, more interesting loop. The second loop is longer and follows roads all the way. The elevation gain, however, is the same for both loops—a respectable 1800 feet.

Lookout Mountain Loop. This route from Clinger Spring follows Road 44 to Brooks Meadow and Knebal Pass. From just beyond the pass the loop heads south on the Lookout Mountain summer foot trail to Road 4420, then west to High Prairie. From there the route follows Road 4410 back to Clinger Spring.

This is all road skiing except for the 3.2-mile summer foot trail. From Brooks Meadow ski east on Road 44 to the Perry Point/Fivemile Butte trailhead, 0.4 mile beyond Knebal Pass (which see). Directly opposite this side road, on the south side of Road 44, the Lookout Mountain summer foot trail goes south. The route at first follows a primitive road, which soon ends. There it follows a foot trail for some distance along the very edge of Eightmile Creek, where there is very dense forest. The trail then climbs moderately, winding upward in a more obvious manner past several meadows, until it joins a deadend side road that leads south to Road 4420, which goes to High Prairie. Advanced; 14.2 miles round trip from Clinger Spring.

Wampus Spring Loop. This loop follows essentially the same route except for the eastern portion. From Knebal Pass ski eastward, past the Lookout Mountain summer trail, to Road 4420, where you turn right. Follow the road south as it passes Jacket and Wampus springs then curves and climbs westward through dense forest to High Prairie. Ski downhill on Road 4410 to Clinger Spring to complete the loop. Road 4420 is a primitive road offering some of the same quality skiing as a forest trail.

Except from High Prairie, there are few views on either of these loops. Though long, they offer ample returns for long-distance skiers. After enjoying distant views from High Prairie, the long downhill descent to Clinger Spring is a bonus. If you plan to ski the Lookout Mountain Loop, it is a good idea to visit the area in summer and hike the trail to get a feel for that section of the loop, which offers route-finding problems in winter.

For the area just east of Knebal Pass the USGS quad does not show road positions accurately and does not represent road realignments and changes correctly. Locations and junctions of the Cold Springs road (Road 4420), the Dufur Mill road, and the Pebble Ford Campground roads are also not shown correctly. The present junction of Road 44 and Road 4420 is obvious, but is not shown on the USGS quad. Carry a Forest Service map to help resolve these discrepancies. Knebal Pass is a name assigned for convenience to the road high point, 0.4 mile west of Bottle Prairie on the USGS quad.

The roads are easy to follow, but under deep snow not all route changes are obvious, particularly in the High Prairie area, where you may have to scout out the downward route. Along the summer trail blazes are few and, at best, obscure. These long loops should be attempted only by experienced skiers, and then only under favorable snow conditions. Advanced; 17.0 miles round trip from Clinger Spring.

Low Rock summit

Chapter 18
CLACKAMAS HIGH COUNTRY

The Clackamas high country, just south of Mt. Hood, is characterized by high ridges—some of which are open and skiable—above deep, forested valleys. You can easily explore the area by using logging and forest roads that penetrate the valleys and follow some of the ridge tops.

Compared to the Mt. Hood area, the Clackamas is not heavily visited by winter recreationists, and a sense of isolation pervades most tours. The ski tours described in this chapter are the best in the Clackamas, although there are many other roads and areas to explore.

To reach the Clackamas high country drive to Estacada, a small town in the Cascade foothills. The town is about 40 miles from Portland via the town of Sandy on Highway 26, and about 32 miles via Highways 212 and 224. From Estacada continue on Highway 224 for 26 miles to the Ripplebrook Ranger Station, the starting point for all tour descriptions. The road is winding and scenic as it closely follows the Clackamas River through a deep, and often narrow gorge.

Highway 224 is snowplowed only as far as the Ripplebrook Ranger Station at 1420 feet elevation. How far you drive beyond there depends on the snow line, which in an average winter fluctuates between 2000 and 3000 feet. All parking is roadside, for there are no sno-parks in the Clackamas. In general, roads are well maintained, not steep, and present no unusual driving hazards under normal winter conditions.

When parking your car at the snow line do not block access to the road beyond, as other users may want by. Snowmobiles use the area but are not a significant factor to Nordic skiers. Select your parking spot with care as heavy snowfall during your tour may trap you and your car far from help.

Because trails and roads in the Clackamas are not marked for Nordic skiing, be sure to carry a Forest Service map. A USGS map, of course, is always a requirement when skiing unmarked or off-road routes. The Clackamas is an area where maps will contribute not only to your safety but also to your pleasure.

Distances given in the tour descriptions are for average winter snow levels. In mid-winter, however, when the snow line is usually low, long distances often make the high country inaccessible to day skiers. Therefore, for most skiers spring and unusual mid-winter periods of high snow lines are the best times to visit the Clackamas. When the snow line is higher, some roads may even be plowed for logging, making some trips that much shorter. Spring is especially fine because the days are longer, the snow is consolidated, and the weather is more predictable. For snow line information call the Ripplebrook Ranger Station.

HARRIET LAKE

Novice
Round trip 7 miles
Unmarked road
Elevation gain 300 feet

High point 2100 feet
USGS Fish Creek Mountain, High
Rock

Map — page 209

If you cannot drive beyond Ripplebrook due to low snow, Lake Harriet is a good consolation alternative. Nestled in a narrow, forested valley, the lake and dam provide an easy destination. Drive to Ripplebrook (see chapter introduction). Turn right on the road beside the ranger station and drive uphill 2.5 miles to the Silver Tip Work Center, the end of winter snow plowing. Park here. Ski Road 4630 into the trees and past Road 4635 along a winding route to the lake. You pass one fine view of a distant valley behind you. This is a pleasant tour through nice forest.

For an alternative tour ski to Silver Tip, but 0.4 mile beyond the work center ski instead up Road 4635. In another 1.1 miles, at a small quarry on the right, bear left at a Y-junction and follow the Cache Meadows road as far as you wish. There are some good valley views as you ski higher on the road.

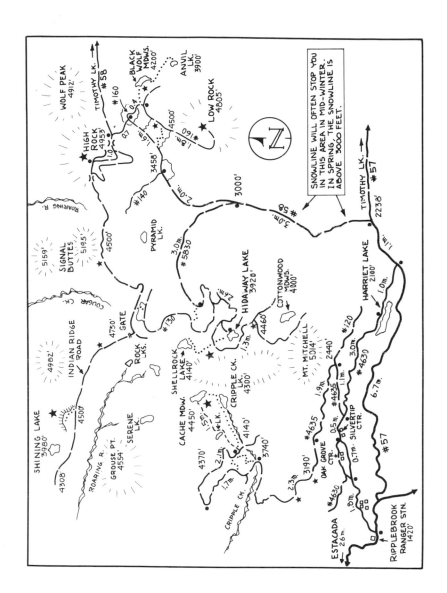

SNOWLINE WILL OFTEN STOP YOU IN THIS AREA IN MID-WINTER. IN SPRING, THE SNOWLINE IS ABOVE 3000 FEET.

CACHE MEADOW/CRIPPLE CREEK LAKE

Intermediate to Advanced
Round trip 8 to 12 miles
Unmarked road and trails
Elevation gain up to 2000 feet

High point 4450 feet
USGS High Rock, Fish Creek Mountain

Map—page 209

This tour features a road with great views and a summer trail leading through heavy timber and open areas to beautiful Cache Meadow. You can ski a loop by returning to the road by way of Cripple Creek Lake. Until this summer trail is marked, the off-road portion is rated advanced due to the route finding required.

Drive to Silver Tip Work Camp (see Harriet Lake), where winter road plowing ends. Follow the road on the left, Road 4630, for 0.5 mile to Road 4635. Turn left on 4635 and ski or drive 1.1 mile to a Y-junction at a small quarry. Take the left fork (Road 4635) and climb gently for 4.2 miles to Cripple Creek. On the way you have many views to the left, and about a mile beyond the Mt. Mitchell trailhead there is a remarkable vista of the deep Clackamas River valley and the high, imposing ridges beyond. When snow free, this road has numerous places for turning around or parking.

At Cripple Creek, in a curve of the road, you have three choices for reaching the summer trail, which begins directly above you, where the road again crosses Cripple Creek. First, you can continue on the road for 3.8 miles. Or, for your second and third choices, you can cut off about 2.5 miles by climbing either of two clearcuts. The first clearcut, just beyond the creek, has a steep cat road at its far end. Climb to the top of the clearcut, entering forest for a short distance before emerging on the upper road. For the second clearcut, ski about 200 yards beyond the first clearcut and a road on the left. Climb steep open slopes of summer rockslides and alder into the bottom of a clearcut that extends all the way to the upper road, where you turn right for a short distance to the creek. From the lower leg of the road to the upper, is only a 400-foot climb, but it represents a considerable saving in distance.

The summer trailhead is near the left or west bank of Cripple Creek. About 200 feet into the woods the summer trail forks. The right fork, marked by unblazed, orange-painted trees, goes to Cripple Creek Lake, about a mile up gentle slopes through dense trees. Take the left fork, which is marked by blazes only. It is hard to follow in winter, although sometimes orange plastic tape may also mark the route. The 1.5-mile trail is very beautiful, leading to a small lake and generally following a string of long, narrow openings and meadows above the lake. For the last few hundred yards the trail goes through old-growth forest before dropping gently into the northwest corner of Cache Meadow. There is another lovely meadow to the left and a dirty, dilapidated shelter across the main meadow on the southeast side.

From the meadow follow the creek flowing south to Cripple Creek Lake 0.5 mile away. The orange-painted trees at the southwest corner of the lake go for 1 mile to the trailhead. This route is primitive, and the close-set trees do not always offer good skiing. The trail always parallels the north bank of the outlet creek, which is easy to follow if you cannot find the orange-painted trees marking this route.

The trail is so beautiful that it is worth the trouble to locate and follow. Considering the configuration of the terrain and the location of the creek, it is hard to imagine anyone being lost for very long. Carry a map and compass.

HIGH ROCK

Intermediate to Advanced
Round trip 12 to 14 miles
Unmarked road
Elevation gain up to 2700 feet

High point, summit 4953 feet
USGS High Rock

Map—page 209

The sweeping view from the rocky summit is a fair reward even for the long trip in winter. And in spring the tour may be much shorter. Several major volcanoes are visible across the many high ridges that rise out of the deep valleys surrounding the peak.

From the Ripplebrook Ranger Station continue on the main road for 0.4 mile to a junction. Turn left onto Road 57 and follow it 7.4 miles to a junction with Road 58. At 2238 feet, this is where the snow line often stops cars in winter, 8.5 miles from the summit.

Drive Road 58 as far as possible. When you park, do not block access to the road beyond. Continue on skis. At Road 5830, the road to Hidaway Lake, you are 3.0 miles from the Road 57/58 junction. Another 2 miles brings you to Road 140, which leads to Pyramid Lake. Occasional clearcuts in this deep valley offer views, and alongside the road Shellrock Creek gurgles.

Continue up the gently ascending road past two huge clearcuts on the right. Part way up the second clearcut, there are good views. Ski all the way up for a shortcut route to Low Rock. Come to another clearcut at the junction with Road 160 on the right. The route continues along the main road as it curves to the left and enters the forest. In summer the road is paved this far. It starts climbing more steeply to the pass just southeast of the summit, where Mt. Hood first comes into view and where Wolf Peak rises nearby. At that point, Road 58 from Clear and Timothy lakes joins from the east. Continue up the main road and at a fork go right as it circles around the south and west sides of High Rock. At the saddle (4600 feet) on the west side of the peak, ski a narrow, moderately steep road to a point just under the summit. It is an easy walk to the top from there.

From the summit there is a spectacular view in all directions. To the west the open slopes of Indian Ridge and Signal Buttes are inviting — and can be reached by road skiing. The deep Roaring River valley lies just below. You can also see all the familiar skiing areas of Mt. Hood — Veda Butte, Trillium Basin, Ghost Ridge, Elk and Lookout mountains, Barlow Ridge, Bonney Butte and other old friends — as well as the volcano itself. Farther north is Mt. Adams, and prior to the big blast of May 18, 1980, just the tip of St. Helens was visible over Linney Butte.

The return to your car is all downhill and makes a splendid run in good snow, requiring almost no effort and making up for the exertion of the ascent. You are a long way from help on High Rock, so be sure to carry a full pack with extra food, emergency gear, maps, compass, and the other ten essentials. Warm clothing will be needed for the summit, which is exposed to the weather.

HIDAWAY LAKE/SHELLROCK LAKE

Intermediate to Advanced	Highpoint 4140 feet
Round trip 12 to 16 miles	USGS High Rock
Unmarked road	
Elevation gain up to 1800 feet	Map—page 209

These two forest-rimmed lakes offer serene winter beauty, and the 1-mile tour between them is very scenic. The tour up the gentle, wide valley to the lakes has many open places and numerous views. There is a long downhill run on the return trip.

Follow the road directions for High Rock, but turn left (west) on Road 5830. From Road 58 it is 5.6 miles to Hidaway Lake. The road descends gently for 0.8 mile before climbing up the valley. At 0.3 mile from the lake you come to a junction. The side road on the left goes directly to the lake. The main road continues 0.5 mile to a clearcut between Hidaway and Shellrock lakes.

From Hidaway Lake there are two routes to Shellrock Lake, a recommended side trip. Ski along the north shore of Hidaway Lake to the outlet stream on the north side. Ski into beautiful snow-covered marshes and meadows that line the outlet stream to the clearcut between the two lakes. Cross Road 5830, which passes through the clearcut and makes a good shortcut route back to Hidaway Lake junction, 0.5 mile below.

To reach Shellrock Lake, which is only 100 vertical feet above the road at the bottom of the clearcut, ski northward across the center of the open hillside. Do not climb too high, but enter the forest at the north side of the clearcut and proceed 300 yards to the lake. The east shore is flat and is the best place to appreciate the lake's steep-walled confinement and sense of isolation.

Another particularly interesting side trip near Hidaway Lake follows a scenic logging road and offers a splendid view of Mt. Jefferson and Three Fingered Jack. Ski to the clearcut between Hidaway and Shellrock lakes and follow the road as it heads west and then south around the Hidaway basin. The road climbs gently for 1.3 miles to a wide saddle (4460 feet) in a clearcut, from where the volcanoes are visible across Shellrock Creek Canyon.

From the saddle, the road going (left) south descends 500 feet and ends in 2 miles. It has no special views. The road going west from the saddle, however, circles the head of the basin, then swings south through large clearcuts with a number of views.

If the snow line is low, this is a very long tour. When it is high, however, particularly in spring, the entire area has great appeal. Winter and early spring road plowing has in the past made this area more accessible. Call the Ripplebrook Ranger Station for snow and road information. Or just drive up, check it out, and if necessary, select an alternative tour.

INDIAN RIDGE

Advanced
Round trip 20 miles from Road 58
Unmarked road
Elevation gain 1750 feet

High point 4750 feet
USGS High Rock

Map—page 209

This unusual tour follows a primitive road along a high ridge extending in an erratic westerly direction for eight miles from High Rock to Shining Lake. The road stays close to the 4700-foot level, passing a number of exceptional viewpoints from which eight Northwest volcanoes are visible. This is one of those rare tours that any serious skier will find rewarding.

Ski or drive to Road 5830 (3000 feet)—the Hidaway Lake road (see Hidaway Lake/Shellrock Lake). Follow Road 5830 for 3.0 miles to the West Fork Shellrock Creek crossing (3500 feet). Leave the road and ascend open timber east of the creek into a clearcut and to Road 130. Follow the road 1.8 miles to a long, steep, narrow, natural clearing above the road. Climb this to its south end and through a dense stand of small trees to the Indian Ridge road, a climb of 400 vertical feet from Road 130.

Turn left on this road and ski a short distance to a Y-junction. To the south you can see Mt. Jefferson, Three Fingered Jack, and the North and Middle Sisters. At the Y-junction, take the right-hand road, which seems to disappear in scattered trees. Keep skiing northward and the road immediately becomes obvious. After 0.5 mile some splendid views open

Deer tracks meet ski tracks

up to the east and north of Mt. Hood, Signal Buttes, and down Cougar Creek to the deep Roaring River valley.

Enclosed by small trees, the road soon passes to the left of a high point and reaches another saddle with more views, this time including the Rock Lakes, Mt. Jefferson, Mt. St. Helens, Mt. Rainier, Mt. Adams, and the impressive nearby ridges projecting northward.

The road continues, again passing another high point on its left, then dropping almost imperceptibly for a mile or so. It travels monotonously through dense tunnels of trees, but after a mile a small break appears in the trees on the right. Climb to this roadside opening to survey your next move.

A half mile northwest you can see a flat spur extending north from the ridge: this is your goal! Ski down the road several hundred yards and then cut north into the dense thicket of trees. (If you ski too far down the road, you will have extra doghair through which to struggle.) You soon pop out at the edge of the spur; follow the rim through beautiful, open, almost level terrain to the north end of the spur. This is the logical trip destination as the views are splendid. To continue along the road means being trapped on a rapidly descending course with no views. The High Rock ski tour route may be used to reach Indian Ridge, but would add 3 miles to the one way distance.

LOW ROCK

Intermediate to Advanced
Round trip 10 to 12 miles
Unmarked road
Elevation gain up to 2600 feet

High point 4805 feet
USGS High Rock

Map—page 209

The summit of this high, broad ridge is only 2 miles south of High Rock. In spite of its unassuming name, Low Rock offers a dramatic, panoramic view that is unequalled in the Clackamas high country. This can be a very long, tiring tour in midwinter. Do not overestimate your stamina.

Follow road directions for High Rock (which see). Turn right onto Road 160 just 2 miles from the top of High Rock and follow the road through a clearcut, into forest, and past the Black Wolf Meadows trailhead. Continue through forest as the road curves and climbs gently southward, paralleling Road 58 far below, which can be seen from the top of a huge, steep clearcut. This clearcut, covering some 650 vertical feet, offers a good shortcut route to Low Rock from Road 58. There are wide views, which include Mt. Hood, from the top of the clearcut.

The road re-enters forest and climbs to the large, plateau-like summit clearcut. For the best view climb an unusual, low rock formation, which also serves as a good wind break on cold days. The view is unexpected and contrasts with that from High Rock, which features deep valleys in every direction. On Low Rock you look across the open summit plateau to distant peaks and ridges ringing the entire horizon. Signal Buttes are prominent to the northwest and the dome of Mt. Adams is visible to one side of the buttes. To the south, Mt. Jefferson and Olallie Butte seem close, and Three Fingered Jack appears as a small spire. To the east there is a good view of Timothy Lake and of the surrounding miles of undulating forest, which extends in an unbroken carpet to the summit of massive Mt. Wilson, beyond the large lake. This is truly a scene of grand scale.

BLACK WOLF MEADOWS/ANVIL LAKE

Intermediate to Advanced
Round trip 12 to 14 miles
Unmarked road and trail
Elevation gain up to 2000 feet

High point 4200 feet
USGS High Rock

Map—page 209

This attractive meadow is two miles southeast of High Rock. From the summer trailhead a short trail goes through level forest, and although unmarked, the meadows are easily located.

Follow road directions for High Rock (which see). Turn right onto Road 160 and climb through a clearcut. About 200 yards beyond the upper end of the clearcut the road curves right and at 0.4 mile from Road 58 passes a side road on the left. The summer trailhead is about 150 feet before this side road.

The trail heads eastward through open timber. Few trees are blazed, and the summer path is not obvious. The terrain is level, however, and by going straight ahead you reach the meadow in 0.5 mile. In spring there are many melted areas and tree wells in the forest, but persevere. The half-mile-long meadow is crescent-shaped and scenic. The summer trail, marked by five-foot poles, passes along the west side.

At the south end, where the meadows narrow, the trail enters the forest to the right and parallels the small creek flowing southward to Anvil Lake. The forest is magnificent old-growth. The trail begins level but slowly starts a gentle descent, crossing the creek and continuing through tall timber. About 0.7 mile from the meadow, a side trail abruptly turns off to the small lake, only 100 yards west. If the trail is obscure, just follow the creek directly to the lake, which is rimmed by marshes and forest.

Hoarfrost

Chapter 19
OTHER TOURS

WHITE RIVER/BARLOW PASS TO HIGHWAY 26

Advanced
One way from White River 14.7 miles, from Barlow Pass 13.5 miles
Unmarked roads
Elevation loss about 1300 feet
High point 4223 feet
USGS Mount Hood South, Mount Wilson

Map—page 218

Two tours on the southeast side of Mt. Hood go one way for miles and end at Highway 26 south of Clear Lake. One follows the White River valley and the other the deep, narrow Barlow Creek valley, the more scenic and historic of the two routes. Starting at White River bridge and at Barlow Pass both tours join part way down and follow Road 43 to Highway 26, just 2.1 miles south of Skyline sno-park. A car shuttle is necessary.

Except for the initial hill below Barlow Pass, neither route has more than gentle downhill grades. Only in the best snow conditions will there be a good glide, so skiers should be prepared to diagonal stride most of the distance to Highway 26. These are long, tiring tours in most snow conditions.

With good snow each tour offers satisfying, long-distance skiing. The White River valley route offers the best views in the first four miles, after

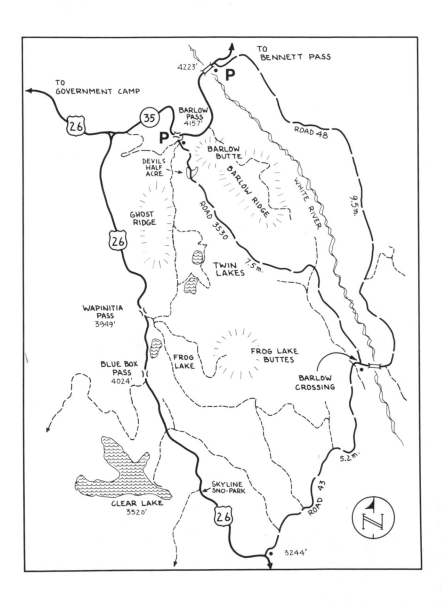

which most of the skiing is through forest. The White River road, however, is wide and monotonously uniform in grade. The Barlow Creek route offers few views but does follow a primitive, narrow road for 7.5 miles.

The White River tour starts at the main sno-park north of the bridge. At the rear of the sno-park climb the snow bank and follow wide, obvious Road 48.

The Barlow Creek route starts at the Barlow Pass sno-park. Follow the road down to Devils Half Acre (which see), then through dense forest to Barlow Crossing and Road 43. From there both routes continue through forest to Highway 26. It is 9.5 miles from the White River sno-park to Barlow Crossing and 7.5 miles from Barlow Pass to the crossing, which (at 2900 feet) is the low point on the tour. From there a gentle 2-mile climb leads to generally level to rolling terrain for the rest of the tour.

The southern terminus of the two tours is at the junction of Road 43 and Highway 26, just east of milepost 68 and 10.5 miles south of the junction of Highways 26 and 35. There is only roadside parking space here. A car shuttle allows you to examine the depth and condition of the snow at the south end of the tour, where the pack may be shallower than at the trailheads.

THE HIGH ROUTE

Advanced
One way 18 miles
Unmarked roads
Elevation gain 2050 feet cumulative, elevation loss 2400 feet cumulative
High point 6000 feet
USGS Mount Hood South, Badger Lake, Dog River

Map—pages 164, 168, 218, 221

The High Route and the Wy'east Trail are the longest ski trails on Mt. Hood—by far! While the Wy'east offers a physical challenge on a combination of trails over generally well known terrain, the High Route is the undisputed winner in the category for isolation. Each of these ski routes is a "classic" in its own right.

Starting at Bennett Pass (see Bennett Ridge Trail), the High Route crosses the Terrible Traverse and climbs to Bonney Junction. From there it heads north for many miles along isolated Gunsight Ridge to High Prairie, a shoulder of Lookout Mountain. The route then descends to Clinger Spring and on down to Highway 35, a distance of 18 miles. The last 8.5 miles are mostly downhill. There are many outstanding views from the High Route.

This tour is not for the unskilled or faint-of-heart as some sections, depending on snow depth, may require traversing steep hillsides similar to the Terrible Traverse. One must also have some knowledge of the area in the event of adverse weather, be able to make route-finding decisions with map and compass, and be thoroughly familiar with avalanches and avalanche rescue. The entire route follows a system of roads, but do not let this deceive you. Much of the territory traversed is remote, and in places the roads disappear under a concealing mantle of winter snow.

The Bennett Ridge Trail and Camp Windy sections of this guidebook cover the tour to Gunsight Butte, 7 miles from the trailhead. There the road traverses fairly steep slopes on the east side of the butte, while a short trip to the top permits an unobstructed view in all directions. From the butte the road descends a moderately-steep grade for 1.7 miles to Gumjuwac Saddle, 5200 feet, then climbs at the same angle along the western slopes of Lookout Mountain. At 0.6 mile from the saddle you will encounter Promontory Point, a steep and open ridge around which the road forces its way. There is a superb view here of Pocket Creek and of the upper Hood River valley and Mt. Hood. In winters of heavy snow this area may require steep hillside traverses.

Once around Promontory Point the road climbs steadily through forest, traversing a long sidehill. Depending on snow depth, parts of this long traverse may require a careful analysis of the potential for avalanche danger. There are two summer rock slides that in winter become exposed open-slope hillsides. Do not attempt the traverses during or after a storm nor in warm weather. Even in ideal conditions exercise extreme caution and turn back if you have any doubts whatsoever about the stability of the slopes.

At the top of the long climb on the west side of Lookout Mountain from Gumjuwac Saddle, the road suddenly turns right and levels out at a beautiful meadow just 200 yards west of High Prairie. From here Mt. Hood is just across the deep valley, and Mt. St. Helens, Mt. Rainier and Mt. Adams are prominent. A 1-mile side trip to the summit of Lookout Mountain leads to memorable views. Chapter 17, Clinger Spring, describes the remaining miles of the High Route.

From Bennett Pass it is 10.6 miles to High Prairie, of which 8.5 miles are uphill. From High Prairie it is 8.3 miles to Highway 35, almost all of which is downhill. Depending on the snow line, the actual downhill distance could be shorter as snow does not often extend down to Highway 35. This tour requires a car shuttle, for the snow line is unpredictable, and hitchhiking on Road 44 from Clinger Spring is not guaranteed.

Due to the remote nature of the country traversed by this tour, it borders on wilderness skiing, demanding careful planning, proper equipment, survival gear, repair kit, and an ability to manage difficult snow conditions. Maps and compass are essential. Plan for steep hillside traverses, although snow conditions will determine the ultimate problems, if any. This is not a tour to try after heavy snowfall. Select settled snow and fair weather.

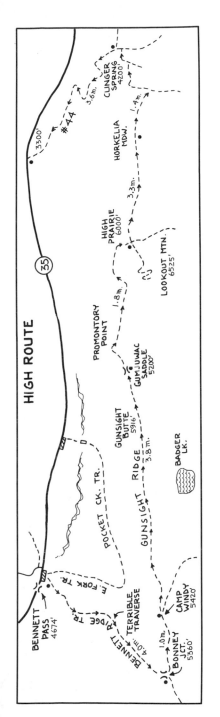

HIGH ROUTE

#44

3300'

3.6 m.

CLINGER
SPRING
4200'

1.4 m.

HORKELIA
MDW.

3.3 m.

HIGH
PRAIRIE
6000'

LOOKOUT MTN.
6525'

PROMONTORY
POINT

1.8 m.

GUNSIGHT
BUTTE
5916'

GUM-JUWAC
SADDLE
5200'

35

POCKET CK. TR.

GUNSIGHT RIDGE

3.8 m.

BADGER LK.

E. FORK TR.

BENNETT PASS
4674'

BENNETT RIDGE TR.

1.0 m.

4.0 m.

TERRIBLE
TRAVERSE

BONNEY
JCT.
5560'

CAMP
WINDY
5420'

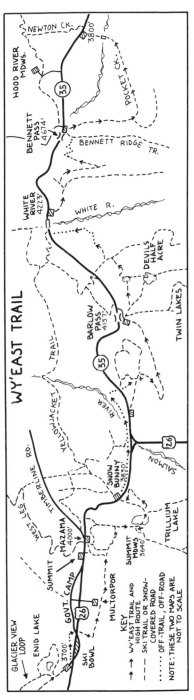

WY'EAST TRAIL

NEWTON CK.

3800'

HOOD RIVER MDWS.

35

POCKET CK.

BENNETT
PASS
4674'

BENNETT RIDGE TR.

WHITE RIVER
4223'

WHITE R.

DEVILS
HALF
ACRE

BARLOW
PASS
4157'

TWIN LAKES

YELLOWJACKET TRAIL

35

RIVER

26

SALMON

SNOW
BUNNY
3820'

WEST LEG

TIMBERLINE RD.

MAZAMA
4000'

SUMMIT

GOVT. CAMP

26

MULTORPOR

SUMMIT
MDWS
3640'

TRILLIUM
LAKE

GLACIER VIEW
LOOP

ENID LAKE

3700'

SKI
BOWL

KEY

WY'EAST TRAIL AND
HIGH ROUTE

SKI TRAIL OR SNOW-
COVERED ROAD

OFF-TRAIL, OFF-ROAD

NOTE: THESE TWO MAPS ARE
NOT TO SCALE

221

WY'EAST TRAIL

Advanced
One way 20 miles
Marked and unmarked routes
Elevation gain 1750 feet cumulative, loss 1400 feet cumulative
High point 4674 feet
USGS Government Camp, Mount Hood South, Badger Lake

Map—pages 73, 119, 151, 156, 168, 221

This twenty-mile trail, extending from Glacier View to lower Pocket Creek, is a composite ski route linking a number of shorter segments to form a unique challenge to the experienced skier. The trail crosses three mountain passes—Summit, Barlow, and Bennett—on its exciting course one-quarter of the way around the base of Mount Hood. The name *Wy'east* was used in Indian myths and is said to be the legendary name for Mt. Hood.

The Wy'east Trail starts at the west end of the Glacier View Loop and ends at the Pocket Creek trailhead. Depending on how you ski this route —and there are several alternative trails—you will cross Highways 26 and 35 two to five times. There are now two creek crossings without bridges, again depending on route selection, and only three off-trail segments totaling less than three miles.

The future, no doubt, will see the undeveloped segments cleared of brush, marked, and bridged. Completion of such a long, unique trail will provide the Mt. Hood region with a remarkable recreational opportunity. Long-distance skiing, like long-distance running, will attain increasing popularity, and this trail will correspondingly grow in importance. That it closely parallels major highways makes it even more available and safe to skiers.

The undeveloped segments at this time are from Snow Bunny to the Pioneer Woman's Grave and portions of the route from Barlow Saddle to Bennett Pass. Although there are a number of route alternatives and variations, such as Boy Scout Ridge, the Barlow Saddle connectors, and the Yellowjacket Trail, the classic as well as most practical route is to follow alternatives closest to the highways.

Eleven sno-parks along the Wy'east Trail permit you to select individual sections rather than the entire trail, thereby allowing you to become familiar with the route and to test yourself against the distance and terrain. The following is but a general description of the route. For details read the appropriate trail descriptions that appear in earlier chapters in Part II and consult maps.

From west to east the classic route begins with the Glacier View Trail, then follows a powerline route on the north side of Highway 26 to the Ski Bowl. From there, the route follows the Summit Trail, Barlow Trail,

Summit Meadows Trail, and Red Top Meadows Trail to Snow Bunny sno-park. The route leads through forest to the Salmon River area (see Salmon River Clearcut), where a segment of the old pioneer Barlow Road (the North Loop) continues to the Pioneer Woman's Grave. The route then follows the old highway to Barlow Pass and the Barlow Saddle connectors to White River. A logging road and an off-road section lead to Bennett Pass, and from there the East Fork Trail and Pocket Creek Trail end the long tour.

Before attempting to ski the full length of the Wy'east Trail, become thoroughly familiar with the various segments. Then, select good snow conditions for your trip. Since many of the segments are already popular tours, much of the total route will probably be tracked for you. The best direction to ski the Wy'east Trail is from west to east, starting at the higher end and saving the descent from Bennett Pass for the last.

Although most of the route is near the highway, the trail should be viewed as a serious undertaking. The length of the tour, particularly in less than ideal conditions, may cause stamina problems for skiers who are not in proper physical condition. There is no difficult terrain along the trail, but route-finding skills are required in several places. Carry maps and repair kit.

FOREMAN POINT

Intermediate   **High point 3498 feet**
Round trip 8.2 miles   **USGS Foreman Point**
Unmarked roads
Elevation gain 430 feet   **Map—page 224**

Foreman Point is located near the north boundary of the Warm Springs Indian Reservation at the edge of the Oregon desert close to the lower limit of forest. The high point of the tour is at the east end of a prominent long ridge jutting eastward into the desert. There is an unusual combination of desert and Cascade views from the tour route, making this a most unusual trip for the Nordic skier. Foreman Point is thirty miles southeast of Government Camp.

From Highway 26/35 interchange near Government Camp drive 17 miles south to the Bear Springs Ranger Station, first on Highway 26 then on Highway 216. Continue another 2.9 miles to Road S-503, the Sunflower Flat road and park at the edge of the highway as Road S-503 is closed to motor vehicles. Take this road past a side road on the right and continue south to a fork 0.6 mile from the highway. Go to the left and follow this road 3.5 miles to the top. Open hillsides with sagebrush, scattered stands of scrub oak, firs and pines surround you on this beautiful tour. Sweeping views are your reward as Mt. Hood, Mt. Adams, Mt.

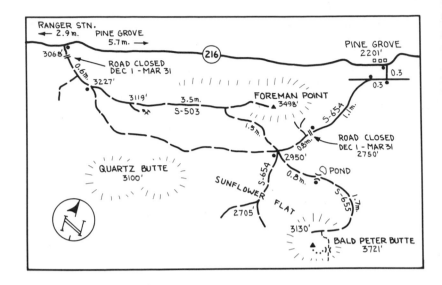

Jefferson, the Three Sisters and Three Fingered Jack appear on fair days. To ski along this long ridge, with the rolling desert extending for miles to the horizon, is a unique experience.

Understanding snow reports and calling the Bear Springs Ranger Station will help you determine if conditions warrant the long drive. Remember, too, that snow depths at Foreman Point (and nearby Bald Peter Butte) may be less than at the ranger station, which is located several miles west, in the forest.

Should the snow be too shallow where you plan to ski, a pair of hiking boots in the car will certainly ensure a successful day in the fresh air. The area is interesting and scenic, and offers many rewards whether you are on skis or on foot.

BALD PETER BUTTE

Intermediate   **High point 3721 feet**
Round trip 9 miles   **USGS Wapinitia**
Unmarked roads
Elevation gain 971 feet   **Map—page 224**

Bald Peter Butte, like nearby Foreman Point (which see), offers an unusual skiing experience. It is not often that a Cascade skier has the opportunity to ski where high desert, Cascade forests, and volcanoes occur within the same vista.

Bald Peter Butte is located 2.5 miles southeast of Foreman Point and 4 miles due south of the small town of Pine Grove on Highway 216. Bald Peter, a partly forested butte, is the highest point in the area and dominates the region. The summit offers even finer views than from Foreman Point. Both of these tours are on Indian reservation land so respect the area and any restrictions that may be posted.

Follow driving instructions for Foreman Point but continue 5.7 miles to the town of Pine Grove. Turn south off the highway at the blue telephone company building, just east of the old school house. Drive south 0.3 mile, turn right and go another 0.3 mile and turn left at a fork near the last houses. If possible, drive up this road through a narrow, wooded valley to a junction at 2750 feet. Park here as the road beyond is closed to motor vehicles. This gate is 1.7 miles from Pine Grove. Hike or ski up Road S-654 0.8 mile through meadows to a three-way junction. Here, go left to a pass with a pond at 3270 feet. The road then rolls along with ups and downs, ending at 3130 feet 1.7 miles from the pass. The road end is 600 feet below the summit of Bald Peter on its northwest side.

The best of several possible routes to the summit is several hundred yards back from the road end at a large, level open area in the forest where a primitive road goes south and up through trees to a pass east of the summit. Climb steeply at first through trees to easier slopes near the top. There are fine views.

North and Middle Sisters from McKenzie Pass

Part III
Central Cascades of Oregon

The Central Cascades west of Bend, Oregon have the most concentrated collection of high quality cross-country ski trails in the state. Skiers outside of Oregon have increasingly recognized the high quality skiing in the area, and some experts reasonably foresee Bend developing into the finest Nordic skiing center in America.

For skiers of all skill levels there are a bewildering variety of trails from which to select. They range from beautifully marked and groomed trails to untracked backcountry tours. The area also has consistent snow depth and experiences more favorable weather and snow conditions than do ski areas on the western slopes of the Cascades. Finally, the unusual natural beauty of the region is a great attraction—sagebrush desert, low-elevation pine woods, alpine old-growth forests, and the incomparable volcanoes of the High Cascades.

The town of Bend, located at 3500 feet in the high desert of central Oregon, is the focus for most travel in the area. To reach Bend from Portland drive Highway 26 through Government Camp and southeastward through the Warm Springs Indian Reservation to Madras, on Highway 97. Then follow Highway 97 south to Bend. Total distance: 160 miles. From the Willamette Valley skiers can drive Highways 22, 20, or 126 to Santiam Pass, then across the pass and down to Bend on Highway 20. Most of the tours described here are west of Bend at the end of snow-blocked Highway 46, better known as Century Drive. In winter this highway ends 22 miles west of Bend, near the Mt. Bachelor Ski Area. A short road continues to the Bachelor sno-park, which provides direct access to the Nordic Sports Center and its excellent groomed trail and track system. In the future, parking at the center probably will be restricted to those using its groomed trails.

Weekend accommodations in Bend are often tight, and reservations are recommended. For information on local accommodations call or write Bend Chamber of Commerce, 164 N.W. Hawthorne Avenue, Bend, Oregon 97701. (502) 382-3221. Overnight parking is permitted at the Mt. Bachelor sno-park, but check first with the night watchperson or information desk. A shuttle bus transports skiers from Bend to the ski area for a fee. A parking lot for cars is located on Century Drive just beyond the ski shops, and the shuttle bus may be boarded here.

Chapter 20
DUTCHMAN FLAT AREA

There are three distinct skiing experiences awaiting the skier at Dutchman Flat—much more than can be savored in one weekend. First, there are 15 miles (25 kilometers) of groomed trails at the Nordic Sports Center, which are well worth the trail use fee and a new experience to many skiers who find they can ski more miles with less effort than is possible on the usual ski trails. Second, there is the complex trail system through the forests and meadows of the Dutchman Flat area. Third, there is the world of the high country. Off-trail tours lead to Broken Top Crater, Tam McArthur Rim, and Tumalo Mountain. The backcountry terrain is generally wide open and gentle, with many impressive views of the nearby volcanoes.

The Nordic sno-park for the trails of the Dutchman Flat-Todd Lake-Broken Top Crater areas is at the south end of Dutchman Flat, where highway plowing ends and where the access road to Mt. Bachelor Ski Area begins. Here both Nordic skiers and snowmobilers mix, for much of the area is used by both groups, although many trails are closed to machine use.

All the ski tours of the Dutchman Flat area proper start at the Nordic sno-park. The trail heads north from the sno-park, branching several times to give access to other trails and connectors leading to various destinations. The trails form more than five main loops, depending on your choice of connector trails and destinations. All the trails are well marked, with excellent directional signs at all junctions. Several large meadows, stands of lodgepole pine, and old-growth hemlock forests offer variety and beauty to the tours.

Touring north of Big Meadows, the northern limit of the marked trail system, is not for novice skiers. Beyond the meadows there are few landmarks in poor weather, and the large open areas and distances only increase the chances of becoming lost.

Routes open to snowmobiles are the Century Drive Highway, Road

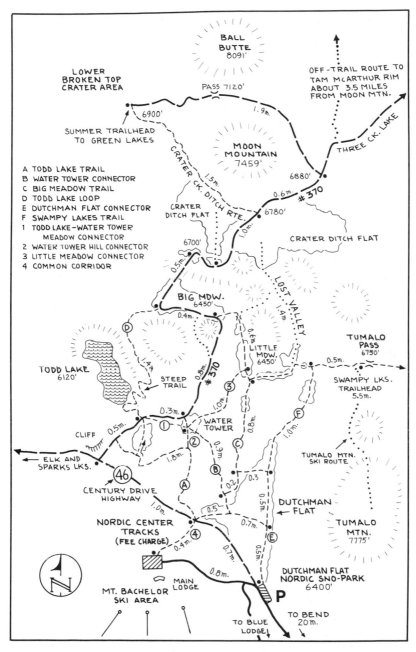

Note: Since the first printing, the Forest Service has opened to snowmobiles an area previously closed, by placing a marked snowmobile trail closely paralleling trails E and F (above) and following Lost Valley off-trail ski route. While this causes a major loss of skiing quality, the area's scenic beauty remains unchanged. This route is still the most direct to Moon Mountain and the lower crater of Broken Top.

370 to Tam McArthur Rim, and the Moon Mountain-Crater Ditch Flat. Closed to snowmobiles is the area south of Century Drive, areas west and north of Road 370, and the Broken Top Crater and Ball Butte areas.

MT. BACHELOR NORDIC SPORTS CENTER

Novice to Advanced	Elevation at trailhead 6400 feet
Round trip distances of loops from	Trail maps available at center
0.6 to 4.2 miles (1 to 7 kilometers)	
Marked trails	Map—page 229

If you have not skied on perfectly set, groomed cross-country ski tracks you have missed a fine experience. Uniform width and depth of tracks assure efficient, controlled skiing, with all energy synchronized to moving forward and skiing with unrestricted, good technique. Fifteen miles (25 kilometers) of machine-groomed trails are maintained daily. They are well marked and double-tracked for side by side skiing. There are loops for every skill level. A reasonable fee is charged for skiing on the tracks.

Drive 22 miles west of Bend to the Mt. Bachelor Ski Area. Go to the main sno-park at the end of the road, where the Nordic Center has a ski school and rental facility at the trailhead.

If you are a beginner or novice, several things will be going for you here. Due to the safe, controlled, one-way skiing layout your first or second try at skiing will be a pleasant experience. By selecting trails with terrain appropriate to your ability, you will feel safer, particularly if you are new to the sport. Downhills are controlled and safe, thanks to the track layout. On flat terrain you will enjoy working on your diagonal stride technique as your skis stay securely in the tracks. With proper technique, skiing in groomed tracks may help you to feel a freedom of movement seldom encountered elsewhere.

FOREST AND MEADOW TOURS

Novice to Advanced	High point 6450 feet
Round trip up to 8 miles	USGS Broken Top
Marked trails	
Elevation gain negligible	Map—page 229

Dutchman Flat Connector. This trail links the Dutchman Flat sno-park with all the other trails of the area. From the sno-park the trail enters the south end of the large meadow, or flat, where poles along the east edge mark the route northward. The trail forks twice in the meadow. The first fork leads to the Todd Lake Trail and to the Common Corridor to the Nordic Center. The second fork leads to the Big Meadow and Swampy Lakes trails.

Another way to reach the Todd Lake Trail is to ski the snow-covered Century Drive from the sno-park, but this route is not recommended as it is the main snowmobile thoroughfare of the area. The junction where the Dutchman Flat Connector joins the Todd Lake Trail is also where the Common Corridor Trail joins the Century Drive, coming downhill from the Mt. Bachelor sno-park and the Nordic Sports Center. Novice; 1.2 miles.

Common Corridor Trail. This connector trail links the Mt. Bachelor sno-park and Nordic Sports Center to Dutchman Flat, the Century Drive highway, and the Todd Lake and Big Meadow trails. Although it crosses the center's trail complex the Common Corridor is a free route. After descending a moderate slope it goes around the east side of a hill (the Old Maid), then through a small valley to snow-covered Century Drive, where you have a choice of skiing in several directions. Signs will guide you to the route of your choice. Intermediate; 0.4 mile.

Todd Lake Trail. This easy trail to Todd Lake will introduce you to forest and meadow skiing while following a scenic road most of the way. Todd Lake, at 6120 feet, is set in a steep-walled cirque with the jagged summits of Broken Top mountain rising above the far rim.

From the Dutchman Flat Nordic sno-park ski north into the flat meadow and take the first trail fork to the left and proceed to the Century Drive junction with the Todd Lake Trail. The marked trail now descends a long, moderate road grade, then follows along scenic meadow like areas paralleling the curving foot of a ridge to the right. The trail eventually curves left, then goes down a short, curving turn before leaving the road. It turns right, into the trees, suddenly emerging into a large, beautiful meadow. The north end of this meadow is only 250 yards from the south end of the lake. To reach the lake, cross Road 370 and follow the lake access road up a gentle grade to the lower end of the scenic lake basin.

The Todd Lake Trail is the most interesting route to the lake. You can also follow Century Drive from the sno-park to the Todd Lake road turn-off at a meadow below a prominent cliff. These roads, however, are also snowmobile routes, whereas the trail is closed to snow machines. Novice; 3 miles.

Big Meadow Trail. The trail leads gently upward from Dutchman Flat to Big Meadow through magnificent stands of old-growth mountain hemlock to a beautiful, large meadow nestled between ridges.

From the Dutchman Flat sno-park follow the Dutchman Flat Connector northward along the flat for 1.0 mile to the second trail fork. Take the lefthand trail into the trees and in 0.3 mile join another trail. Turn right. Before long you are in old-growth, with picturesque forest scenes at every turn. The trail climbs gently but steadily and about 2.1 miles from the sno-park enters Little Meadow, where you can see South Sister, Broken Top, and Bachelor Butte. The Swampy Lakes Trail and the Little Meadow Connector Trail both exit from this meadow.

From Big Meadow there are several choices for further skiing, including the Todd Lake Loop Trail, Broken Top Crater, and Tam McArthur Rim. Your return to Dutchman Flat can be by way of the Todd Lake Loop, the Little Meadow Connector Trail or by your uphill route (Big Meadow Trail). Which you choose will depend in part on weather, snow conditions, and your stamina. Intermediate; 2.7 miles one way.

Water Tower Connector Trail. Traveling through old-growth mountain hemlock forest, this trail connects the Todd Lake-Water Tower Meadow areas with Dutchman Flat. From Water Tower Meadow ski eastward across the lower end of the meadow and up a short, moderate hill as you enter the forest. The trail winds through the forest, following level terrain and occasional gentle grades to where it connects with the Big Meadow Trail. The trees here near Dutchman Flat change to lodgepole pines.

This is a beautiful trail that forms a part of two basic loops, each of which can be handled by athletic novices: the Todd Lake Trail-Water Tower Meadow Loop and the Little Meadow-Water Tower Meadow Connectors loop (see map). Intermediate; 0.9 mile.

Todd Lake to Water Tower Meadow Connector. From the large meadow just below Todd Lake take the curving Road 370 uphill to a meadow east of the road. This is the Water Tower Meadow. At the south edge of the meadow is the black, monolithic water tower, an anomaly in the area. To avoid snowmobiles on the road, however, there is another ski route from Todd Lake to the Water Tower Meadow. Ski up the road 50 yards from the Todd Lake access road and take a marked ski trail to the right, which winds uphill through the forest directly to the water tower. Novice; 0.3 mile.

Water Tower Hill Connector. This short but steep connector offers an alternative route from (or to) Todd Lake. The hill is about 100 yards long and steep enough to demand considerable skill. From the water tower the trail goes behind or south of the tower on level ground and then eastward to the edge of the hill. At the bottom of the hill is the flat area through which passes the Todd Lake Trail. Advanced; 0.1 mile.

Little Meadow Connector Trail. If you are headed to Big Meadow, this trail offers an alternative to skiing Road 370. If you are already at Big Meadow, this trail offers a return route to Dutchman Flat different from the usual Big Meadow Trail. This trail starts at the Water Tower Meadow, entering the forest at the meadow's north end. Follow the trail to the south end of Little Meadow. From there you can ski to Big Meadow or return to Dutchman Flat via the Big Meadow Trail. Intermediate; 1.0 mile.

Todd Lake Loop. This trail offers an alternative route and permits a loop return from Big Meadow. This trail is best skied from top (north) to bottom (south) due to the moderately steep hillside traverses and switch-backs, which are tedious in the uphill direction. The trail is also less scenic than other uphill routes to Big Meadow. The trail starts at the west end of Big Meadow, entering a fine stand of old-growth forest. There is a view of Broken Top as the trail circles a small butte to where a descending hillside traverse eventually leads to several switchbacks and traverses. These could be difficult with frozen old snow or otherwise crusty conditions. Only skiers with strong downhill skills will enjoy the descent. Advanced; 1.4 miles.

DUTCHMAN FLAT-SWAMPY LAKES TRAIL

Intermediate
Distance one way 8 miles
Marked trail
Elevation gain 470 feet cumulative,
loss 1170 feet cumulative

High point 6750 feet
USGS Broken Top, Wanoga Butte

Map—pages 229, 241

Climbing over Tumalo Pass from Dutchman Flat, this trail offers much variety and some splendid downhill gliding. The old-growth forest at Tumalo Pass is beautiful. The trail is well marked for its full length.

From Dutchman Flat sno-park ski the Dutchman Flat Connector north across the flat to the second fork 1 mile north (see Forest and Meadow Tours). Take the right fork, the Swampy Lakes Trail, which shortly climbs through old growth timber, joining the trail linking Swampy Lakes and Little Meadow. Turn right and climb through forest with many scattered openings. As you cross the flat pass, where the trail passes through alternating open swales and small meadows, the forest becomes almost enchanting. If you do not have time nor inclination to ski the full distance, at least ski this far. For an alternative route to the pass take the Big Meadows Trail, then turn right at Little Meadows onto the Swampy Lakes Trail, thereby adding only 0.5 mile to the tour.

The first two miles of the Swampy Lakes Trail from Little Meadow travel through primeval forest. The third mile is a transition zone to the denser lodgepole pine woods of the lower trail. There are several right angle turns here and a couple short hillside traverses to add interest to the tour. The fourth and last mile to the Swampy Lakes shelter is less attractive, passing through dense stands of small pines, but features a widely cleared trail with many long, smooth downhill runs, the best of the entire route.

From the shelter follow Trail C, the Swampy Lakes Trail, southward 2 miles to the trailhead, first crossing a wide meadow, then climbing a low, easy ridge to the flat on top, and finally making a long downhill run to the trailhead to complete this fine tour.

Big Meadow

The Swampy Lakes Trail is essentially a mid-winter tour. In late winter and spring, conditions are often icy, and tree wells make for difficult skiing, particularly in the last mile to the shelter at Swampy Lakes. The trail should be skied from west to east and then only when conditions are known to be ideal. With a covering of new, velvety powder snow there is no finer tour in the Bend area.

Approximately a mile west of the Swampy Lakes shelter the side trail from Vista Butte is encountered. Skiing up this trail to the butte for the exceptional view, then on to the highway, would be an alternative way to end this tour.

Although the trail is well marked, it is possible to lose it if markers are covered by blown snow or if you miss one of the sharp turns. Always backtrack to the last marker seen, then carefully search for the next marker. Although there are no steep sections, some knowledge of step turns and stem turns is required. Because of long, nearly level stretches, this is a very tiring tour if the snow if heavy and the trail has not been broken ahead of you.

LOST VALLEY OFF-TRAIL SKI ROUTE

Intermediate
Round trip from Little Meadow 3.8 miles
Marked trails and off-trail
Elevation gain 330 feet

High point 6780 feet
USGS Broken Top

Map—page 229

This exceptionally scenic tour from Little Meadow to Crater Ditch Flat is gentle in grade and provides direct access to the Moon Mountain area. From the lower end of Little Meadow ski uphill on the Swampy Lakes Trail through a sinuous meadow to the large meadow at its head. Take the east arm of the large meadow and ski uphill following almost continuous meadows along the east side of a low, forested ridge. You will eventually reach Crater Ditch Flat, a huge, level meadow at the southeast foot of Moon Mountain. You can combine this lovely ski route with the Big Meadow Trail for an interesting loop.

This unmarked route is easy to follow in good weather, but might be confusing if visibility is limited. In the almost ubiquitous meadows there are few reliable landmarks for navigation.

BROKEN TOP CRATER

Intermediate to Advanced
Round trip 12 miles
Marked trail (first 4 miles) and off-trail
Elevation gain 500 feet

High point 6900 feet
USGS Broken Top

Map—page 229

This is certainly one of the most scenic ski tours in Oregon. With good snow the tour does not require an unusual amount of effort, and the scenic rewards of the lower crater are ample compensation. The terrain of the lower crater is quite gentle, and it is possible to ski in several directions with no danger of avalanches. Although all of the terrain of this tour is gentle, the large, open areas of the Crater Ditch Flat and lower crater areas could be a problem in adverse weather. Map, compass and emergency gear should be carried.

Follow the Big Meadow Trail (see Forest and Meadow Trails) to Big Meadow, then along the road around the west end and up to a bluff-top viewpoint for a fine view of Bachelor Butte, Dutchman Flat, Tumalo Mountain, and Big Meadow. From the viewpoint cross the road behind you and penetrate a band of trees to the north into a large meadow at the foot of Moon Mountain, a forested butte. Crater Creek Ditch, usually snow-covered but appearing as a narrow road, flows from Broken Top Crater along the very foot of the butte and is quite unmistakable and easy

The broad Tam McArthur Rim, with view of Broken Top (left) and the top of South Sister

to follow. Crater Creek Ditch is actually a man-made ditch built at the turn of the century to carry water eastward for irrigation.

Follow the ditch route around the west side of Moon Mountain into the open terrain of the lower crater, a wide and open gently sloping basin with magnificent views. The impressive crags of Broken Top dominate the remarkable scene.

Part of the area you traverse is open to snowmobiles. Respect their rights to use the areas open to them. They often stray, however, and if they do flag them down and advise them that they are in a closed area. If the violation warrants it, record the snow machine registration number and report it to the Forest Service. Closed to motorized vehicles are the areas west of Road 370, the Broken Top Crater from the foot of Moon Mountain, and the Ball Butte area. Although Road 370 serves as a snowmobile corridor to Tam McArthur Rim and across to the town of Sisters, there are areas west of Road 370 that are exceptions to the closure. All of Crater Ditch Flat is open to snowmobiles, including the flats west of Road 370 at the south foot of Moon Mountain. Also open are Big Meadow, Moon Mountain and a narrow route around it and across the pass north of it back to Road 370. If you see snowmobiles on the Crater Creek Ditch route, they are there legally.

TUMALO MOUNTAIN

Advanced
Round trip 9 miles
Unmarked route
Elevation gain 1375 feet

High point 7775 feet
USGS Broken Top

Map—page 229

The summit of this deceptively gentle looking volcanic cone just east of Dutchman Flat offers a panoramic view of the entire region, including several volcanoes. From the Dutchman Flat sno-park take the Dutchman Flat Connector north across the flat and ski up the Swampy Lakes Trail toward Tumalo Pass (see Dutchman Flat–Swampy Lakes Trail). At or near the pass turn right, off the trail, and ski around the west side of an intermediate butte to Tumalo Mountain. Ski through forest and meadows to the upper northwest slopes, the preferred route to the top.

There are no landmarks on the tour to the summit. From Dutchman Flat the mountain appears as a low forested ridge, but that is only the lower part of the mountain. Dress warmly for what could be a very cold, exposed climb. Carry map and compass, and do not attempt this climb in adverse weather.

TAM McARTHUR RIM

Advanced
Round trip 16 miles
Marked trail (first 4 miles) and off-trail
Elevation gain 1400 feet

High point 7800 feet
USGS Broken Top

Map—page 229

Just two miles east of the jagged summit of Broken Top mountain is the flat-topped, broad ridge of Tam McArthur Rim, which affords extensive views up and down the Cascade range. Some think this is the most spectacular viewpoint on any ski tour in Oregon. For a description of the northern approach to the rim, see Three Creek Lake/Tam McArthur Rim.

From the Dutchman Flat sno-park ski to the open flats south of Moon Mountain (see Broken Top Crater). The most direct route from there is along the east sides of Moon Mountain and Ball Butte. An alternative route is to follow Crater Creek Ditch into the lower crater area west of Moon Mountain, then ski north along the gentle, open slopes west of Ball Butte, crossing the saddle north of the butte and traversing the long slopes to the rim.

From Tam McArthur Rim there are dramatic views of the Three Sisters, Mt. Jefferson, Mt. Hood, Mt. Adams, numerous smaller volcanoes, and, of course, the sky-piercing outline of Broken Top. The precipitous north face of Broken Top falls in a complexity of colored cliffs to the small glacier far below, from where the timberline meadows slowly blend into the sweeping forested expanses spreading northward. On a clear day the scene is breathtaking.

Many skiers agree that the best time to do this tour is in spring, when the snow is consolidated, the weather is more predictable, and the days are longer and warmer. The long, relaxing downhill return to the trailhead is a just reward for the long uphill trek to the rim.

The tour from Dutchman Flat in the higher areas crosses vast, open slopes. Do not undertake this tour in adverse weather. It is only for strong skiers who are experienced with off-trail skiing. Carry survival gear, repair kit, maps and compass.

Historical Note. Tam McArthur Rim is named for Lewis A. ("Tam") McArthur, writer, newspaper reporter, and member of the Oregon Geographic Board. He is well known as the author of Oregon Geographic Names, a definitive listing and analysis of Oregon place names.

Swampy Lakes Shelter

Chapter 21
SWAMPY LAKES

This unique Nordic ski trail complex is located north of Century Drive (Highway 46) 16 miles west of Bend. There are five primary trail loops ranging in length from 2 miles to 8 miles. There are a total of about 25 miles of skiing trails in six square miles of area. The terrain is gentle, rolling forest land, with several meadows and clearcuts and two high points for views. The skiing is on marked, well-designed trails and roads. Trail junctions are clearly signed with trail names, destinations, and distances.

Most tours start at the Swampy Lakes sno-park, although the Snowmobile sno-park to the east may be used for the Emil Nordeen Shelter tour. A roadside sno-park to the west provides access to Vista Butte. Four open-sided log shelters with stoves provide comfortable tour goals and lunch spots. Although the tours do not abound with viewpoints, the natural beauty of the area and the high quality of the skiing trails provide more than adequate compensation.

The Swede Ridge tour is the longest and the most demanding in terms of skiing skills, although an intermediate skier would have few problems. The trail loop to the Emil Nordeen Shelter has a number of views on the south leg, and the shelter offers a view. The tour to the Swampy Lakes Shelter is popular and often crowded. The tops of Telemark Hill and Vista Butte provide fine views.

The quality of skiing at Swampy Lakes is high, and although the area is lower in elevation than Dutchman Flat, the snow is usually good. There is no other trail complex in Oregon at this time to compare with Swampy Lakes for the miles of quality trails particularly suited to beginner skiers. For more experienced skiers, distance skiing and some of the more challenging hills will be rewarding. Maps of the trail system are usually available at the trailhead bulletin board. The Forest Service restricts the use of the area to skiers only—no dogs and no snowmobiles!

The Swampy Lakes area is complex, with many trail and road junctions. Although there are excellent directional signs everywhere, you should always carry a trail map to better plan your tour as you ski along. There are only two trails that offer challenging terrain: Loop A, and the Swede Ridge Shelter Trail east of the Swampy Lakes meadow. Depending on snow conditions, both would normally be safe for intermediate skiers. Be honest about your limitations. If snow and weather are not good, stay to the shorter tours.

Note: The letters used to designate ski trails in the Swampy Lakes area are those of the U.S. Forest Service.

SWAMPY LAKES SHELTER LOOP

Novice
Round trip 4.4 miles
Marked trails
Elevation gain 160 feet

High point 5960 feet
USGS Broken Top, Wanoga Butte

Map—page 241

This loop, the most popular tour of the area, is formed by combining trails A, C, and E. The trail goes through open stands of lodgepole pines, climbing a low divide then descending onto the open flats of the Swampy Lakes. The shelter sits across this wide meadow and 100 yards into the trees. From the shelter, return to the meadow and ski east almost to the far end, where a signpost on the flat indicates a right turn and a southward direction onto trail E, which climbs gently through the pines, crosses a divide, then descends a road to the trailhead. East of trail E is Telemark Hill (6238 feet) where open hillsides offer a tempting ascent to the fine views from near the top. It is a great hill on which to practice downhill turns. The view includes Vista Butte, Bachelor Butte, and Broken Top.

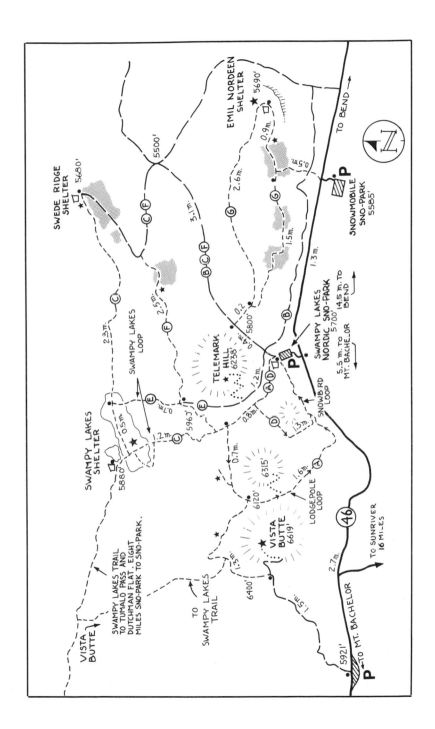

241

LOOP A (LODGEPOLE LOOP)

Intermediate
Round trip 3.1 miles
Marked trails
Elevation gain 340 feet

High point 6140 feet
USGS Wanoga Butte

Map—page 241

Traveling entirely through forest, this is an interesting and challenging 3.1-mile loop. From the sno-park ski the main trail toward the Swampy Lakes Shelter. In 0.8 mile turn left onto trail A. The route climbs a moderately steep sidehill, then passes a short side trail to a view of Broken Top. The trail continues climbing, passing the Vista Butte Trail junction, then making a long descent to the trailhead sno-park.

There is only one short, moderately-steep section on the descent, with an adequate amount of space to maneuver. This loop should be skied in a counter-clockwise direction to take advantage of the easy to moderate, long downhills. Hillside openings beyond the high point, leading east to a butte summit, up a 150-foot climb, can be explored for views.

Loop D (Snowbird Loop). This beautiful 1.7-mile novice trail climbs easily through lodgepole forest, then turns and returns to the starting point down a long, gentle hill. From the Swampy Lakes sno-park ski the trail toward Swampy Lakes Shelter as it travels through scattered pines and openings. In about 0.4 mile turn left at a trail junction, follow Trail D and continue through the lovely pine forest across a low divide. The trail then descends gently, joins the Lodgepole Loop (Loop A), where you turn left, and continue downhill. The last 0.5 mile is a wonderful rolling downhill run. Ski this loop in a counter-clockwise direction.

VISTA BUTTE

Intermediate
Round trip 4 to 6.6 miles
Marked trails and road
Elevation gain 698 to 919 feet

High point 6619 feet
USGS Wanoga Butte

Map—page 241

The summit of the 6619-foot butte on the western edge of the Swampy Lakes area is a wide, windy snow ridge and the finest viewpoint of the area. The sweeping scene includes desert, wide expanses of forest, Bachelor Butte, Tumalo Mountain, Broken Top, Ball Butte, and Tam McArthur Rim. The Swampy Lakes meadow appears far below with the Tumalo valley as a backdrop. Dress for summit winds in cold weather.

There are two routes to the summit. The most direct and scenic is the 2.0-mile trail from the roadside sno-park located 2.7 miles west of the Swampy Lakes sno-park. Follow a primitive road through forest and

Vista Butte summit

across meadows, then up moderate grades on the side road to the summit, a total climb of 698 feet.

The other route starts at the Swampy Lakes sno-park and follows trail C, then trail A for 3.3 miles to the summit, a climb of 919 feet. Just west of the Broken Top view side trail, the Vista Butte Trail leaves trail A and takes off to the right (west), crossing undulating forest country to some easy sidehill skiing with views. The trail turns, passes a junction with a trail that descends northward to the Dutchman Flat–Swampy Lakes Trail. The trail then climbs gently to its high point west of the butte. Just beyond the high point is a primitive road going left to the summit. Follow this up until it is lost then switchback upward to the ridge and summit.

SWEDE RIDGE SHELTER LOOP

Intermediate
Round trip 9 miles
Marked trails and roads
Elevation gain 460 feet cumulative

High point 5960 feet
USGS Broken Top, Wanoga Butte

Map—page 241

This is the longest and most challenging loop in the area. Partly on trails and partly on roads, the loop offers the most varied skiing and scenery of the Swampy Lakes loops. Ski first to the Swampy Lakes Shelter (Trail C), then across the beautiful, long meadow eastward and follow the trail into the trees at its east end for a variety of forest skiing. From there ski some sidehills and descending traverses that require care if the snow is fast. You arrive eventually at the edge of a clearcut. The shelter is located at its northeast corner in the trees.

To continue the loop, descend the clearcut near the shelter, skiing to its far end, where you meet a road. Follow the road a short distance to where Trail F joins it. Follow the trail into pine forest. The way climbs gently but steadily, then passes across a clearcut with views. The trail then crosses a divide and meets Trail E, the return leg of the Swampy Lakes Shelter Loop. Turn left onto Trail E, which soon turns into a wide snow-covered road descending gently along the west foot of Telemark Hill, then on to the trailhead. A scenic alternative return route is not to turn left onto Trail E but to continue across it on Trail F for 150 yards to the main Swampy Lakes Shelter Trail. Turn left there and follow the trail south on mostly downhill grades to the trailhead.

EMIL NORDEEN SHELTER LOOP

Intermediate   **High point 5860 feet**
Round trip 6.2 miles   **USGS Wanoga Butte**
Marked trails and roads
Elevation gain 260 feet cumulative   **Map—page 241**

The highlights of this tour are the scenic route through several clearcuts and the bluff-top setting of the shelter, which provides sweeping views to the east of rolling forests, volcanic cinder cones, and the city of Bend. This tour may begin from either the Swampy Lakes sno-park or the snowmobile sno-park just east on the highway. From the Swampy Lakes sno-park the northern leg of the loop (trail G) passes through lodgepole pine forest along a winding trail. The southern leg of the loop goes through pine forest, as well as several scenic clearcuts, the easternmost one on a gently rolling, open ridgetop. The trail then enters and winds through lovely forest to the outstanding shelter site. Road B can be used as a return to the Snowmobile sno-park, but the south leg of the loop is certainly more scenic and rewarding.

Although the Swampy Lakes sno-park is the usual trailhead for this loop, the Snowmobile sno-park, 1.3 miles east and on the south side of the highway is a good alternative. From this sno-park, ski or walk to and across the highway, where a marked trail leads through forest to a wide road, trail B. Cross this road to a hillside of mixed forest and open areas that leads upward to a clearcut, where trail G passes through on its way to the shelter. This direct, interesting route to the loop trail and shelter provides good downhill skiing on the return. To avoid this hill, however, you can return on the road (Trail B), which descends gently from near the Swampy Lakes trailhead, an easier but less interesting route than the south leg of the loop.

Chapter 22
OTHER TOURS

McKENZIE PASS LAVA FIELDS

Advanced
Round trip 12.4 miles
Unmarked road
Elevation gain 1284 feet

High point 5324 feet
USGS Three-Fingered Jack, Sisters

Map—page 245

Ending at McKenzie Pass, the very crest of the Cascades, this road tour offers unusual lava-flow scenery and views of nearby Mt. Jefferson, Mt. Washington, and the North and Middle Sisters.

From Bend drive 22 miles northwest on Highway 20 to the town of Sisters. From Sisters, drive 8.4 miles west on Highway 242 to the snow gate — or as far as possible, depending on the snow line. McKenzie Pass and Highway 242 are not plowed in winter and remain closed until late spring.

Follow the road through forest as it climbs gently toward the pass. Three miles from the snow gate, at Windy Point (4909 feet), the first views of Mt. Jefferson and Mt. Washington appear. The road is fairly obvious as you near the pass, cutting through shallow valleys in the lava flow, which covers the area for miles. At the pass a small, unusual stone building—an observatory for summer tourists—sits on a prominent point on the south side of the road. Although the pass is the official end of this tour, you can explore in many directions across the immense lava fields and cinder cones.

The view from the pass is outstanding, across vast snow fields to the solitary, high volcanic peaks of the central Cascades. This tour is particularly enjoyable in the spring, when the snow is consolidated and the weather more stable and predictable. The pass area in bad weather offers serious route-finding problems. This is not a tour for days when snow is falling and blowing.

Historical Note. The John Craig Memorial cross-country ski race and tour is held along this route each year in April to commemorate the

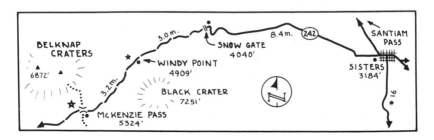

memory of John Craig, who carried mail on skis across McKenzie Pass in the late 1800s. Like Snowshoe Thompson of California legend, John Craig made many remarkable trips across the pass before dying in a winter blizzard. The race and tour is sponsored by the Oregon Nordic Club, a cross-country skiing club with several chapters throughout the state. There are usually several hundred participants each year for this interesting and historic event.

THREE CREEK LAKE/TAM McARTHUR RIM

Intermediate to Advanced
Round trip to lake 10 miles, to Tam McArthur Rim 14 miles
Marked and unmarked road and trail
Elevation gain to lake 1310 feet, to rim 2050 feet
High point 6560 feet at lake, 7300 feet on rim
USGS Broken Top

Map—page 248

Exceptional views are the rewards for the road tour into the lake. If conditions are good, the tour to Tam McArthur Rim above the lake provides views of nine major Cascade peaks and panoramic views of the entire region, with its rolling forests and countless cinder cones and buttes.

In the small town of Sisters (3184 feet), 22 miles northwest of Bend, turn south onto Elm Street, which becomes Road 16 south of town. Continue south on Road 16. At 5.0 miles the road climbs a high ridge with fine views and at 8.0 miles reaches the Black Pine Springs (4330 feet) area. The snow line normally fluctuates between here and the snow gate, 2.8 miles farther along the road. Three Creek Lake is either 4.9 miles or 5.9 miles from the snow gate at 5340 feet, depending on your route selection.

Because snowmobiles use the entire area, a 4.0-mile old road west of and paralleling Road 16 has been marked for exclusive use by skiers, snowshoers, and other quiet visitors. The road adds 1.0 mile to the tour but offers an esthetic alternative to the relative monotony of Road 16. This old road rejoins Road 16 2.9 miles from the snow gate. From there it is 0.8 mile to Three Creek Meadow for the first view of Tam McArthur Rim. Continue on the road 0.4 mile to the obvious junction with the road that goes directly to the north end of the lake. The view of the rim 1200 feet above is impressive: rimrock cliffs, large cornices, snow bowls, and rolling open slopes.

From the lake it is possible to explore the snow benches above for better views of the volcanoes to the north. Or ski 1.0 mile westward to Little Three Creek Lake. The best tour from the lake, however, is to climb to the east end of Tam McArthur Rim (7300 feet), where you can see nine

Rest break at Three Creek Lake. (Photo by Bill Kerr)

volcanoes from Mt. Adams to Broken Top, lined up in an inspiring array
of forms and heights.

If snow and weather are good, the tour to the rim provides an exciting
and scenic adventure for the advanced skier. The best route from the lake
is along the moderate, tree-covered ridge immediately to the east. This
ridge leads to the east end of the rim. A more challenging route leaves the
southwest lake shore and climbs through forest, over consecutive snow
benches, and across small basins to the crest. Watch for cornices above
and stay away from beneath them, climbing to the east of a prominent
rock buttress.

From the rim crest it is possible to follow gentle, vast snow fields
through scattered stands of alpine trees. At 7800 feet, a flat ridge northeast of Broken Top offers the finest views of the entire area, including the
great snow basins at the north foot of Broken Top, and the Three Sisters,
all rising over a mile above their bases. It is about 3.0 miles from the lake
to this viewpoint, which can also be reached from Dutchman Flat eight
miles to the south (see Tam McArthur Rim, Chapter 21).

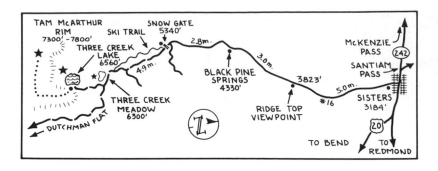

Depending on snow line elevation, the tour to Three Creek Lake can be fairly long (7.7 miles from Black Pine Springs, or 4.9 miles from the snow gate). The tour to the rim is 2.0 miles or longer. One reason to take these tours in the spring is to take advantage of the receding snow line, which shortens the skiing distance. As a compensation for the long approach to the lake and rim, the return tour is all downhill. Snowmobiles often provide packed skiing surfaces and thus save you a lot of energy.

The longest but easiest route to the rim is to follow Road 16 around its east end along gentle grades, then cut off the road to the rim top. The road ultimately leads to Dutchman Flat, but is usually deep in snow and will be lost in the higher areas.

The slopes above the lake range from moderate to steep and much of the rim is corniced, meaning avalanche potential below. In places the rim is precipitous, with spectacular cliffs west of the buttress. The extent of cornice overhang is impossible to reckon from above. Do not go near the edge of the rim. In limited visibility the large open spaces of the rim area and south slopes are difficult to navigate due to lack of landmarks. The rim area should not be skied in bad weather.

*"Something hidden. Go and find it. Go and look behind the Ranges—
"Something lost behind the Ranges. Lost and waiting for you. Go!"*
—Rudyard Kipling
"The Explorer"

Appendix A
WHERE TO SKI: SELECTED TOURS

Sheltered Tours (for bad weather)

Summit Trail
Enid Lake Loop
Giant Trees Loop

Elk Mountain Trail (to Newton Ck)
Lower Twin Lake
Bennett Ridge Trail

Tours With Views

WASHINGTON

Cinnamon Peak
Marble Mountain
Muddy River
Upper Outlaw Creek Clearcuts

Hardtime Creek
Lower Loco Pass
Burnt Peak

MOUNT HOOD AREA

Multorpor Meadows
    (Summit Trail)
Timberline Lodge Area
Trillium Lake Loop
Mud Creek Ridge (and Overlook)
    (Salmon River Overlook)
Snowbunny Clearcut Tours
Raven Rock
Old Burn/Perry Point Tours

Clear Lake Butte
Bonney Butte
Barlow Ridge
Heather Canyon
Elk Mountain
Cloud Cap Inn
White River/Moraine Tour
Weygandt Basin

BEND

Emil Nordeen Shelter Loop
Vista Butte

Todd Lake
Broken Top Crater

CLACKAMAS

High Rock/Low Rock Tours

Beginner Tours

First or Second Time on Skis: Third or Fourth Time on Skis:

WASHINGTON STATE

McClellan Meadows
Old Man Connector (Trail 150)
Hardtime Creek Trail
Rush Creek Tour
McBride Lake

Old Man Loop (to the foot bridge)
    or Shortcut Loop
Skookum Meadow

Beginner Tours (Continued)

First or Second Time on Skis: Third or Fourth Time on Skis:

MOUNT HOOD AREA

Glacier View   Mud Creek Ridge
Summit Trail/Multorpor Meadow   Trillium Lake Loop
Frog Lake/Road 2610   Giant Trees Loop
Clear Lake (Lake Shore)   Timberline Lodge Area
White River (The Bowl)   Enid Lake Loop
Hood River Meadows-Sahalie Falls   Bennett Ridge Trail
Pocket Creek   Horsethief Meadows

BEND AREA

Swampy Lakes Shelter Loop   Emil Nordeen Shelter Loop
Nordic Sports Center tracks   Big Meadow
Dutchman Flat
Todd Lake
Snowbird Loop (A)

Appendix B
RESOURCES

Ski Information

I. Southern Washington Cascades

Gifford Pinchot National Forest Headquarters
Vancouver, Washington (206) 696-7500
Toll free from Portland, Oregon 285-9823
Snow report (206) 694-1586

Upper Wind River, Crazy Hills
Wind River Ranger District
(509) 427-5645

Mt. St. Helens
St. Helens Ranger District
(206) 247-5473

II. Mt. Hood and Vicinity

Mt. Hood National Forest Headquarters
Portland, Oregon (503) 667-0511

Lolo Pass to White River
Zigzag Ranger District
(503) 622-3191, 224-5243

Barlow Pass, Frog Lake, Clear Lake
Bear Springs Ranger District
(503) 328-6211

Brooks Meadow, Lookout Mountain, Camp Windy
Barlow Ranger District
(503) 467-2291

Hood River Meadows, Bennett Pass, Pocket Creek, Cooper Spur
Hood River Ranger District
(503) 352-6002, 223-4690

Clackamas high country
Clackamas Ranger District
(503) 630-4256, 834-2275

III. Central Cascades of Oregon

Deschutes National Forest Headquarters
Bend, Oregon
(503) 382-6922

Dutchman Flat, Swampy Lakes
Bend Ranger District
(503) 382-6922

McKenzie Pass, Three Creek Lake
Sisters Ranger District
(503) 549-2111

Mt. Bachelor Nordic Sports Center
(503) 382-8334

Outdoor Clubs

Oregon Nordic Club — Portland Chapter
P.O. Box 3906, Portland, Oregon 97208
call Bob Ross 246-8048

Mazamas
909 N.W. 19th Avenue, Portland, Oregon 97209
office 227-2345

Trails Club of Oregon
P.O. Box 1243, Portland, Oregon
call Liz Daeges 657-9996

Sierra Club
2637 S.W. Water, Portland, Oregon 97201
call Jim Gifford 775-6759

Chemeketans
360½ State Street, Salem, Oregon 97301

Obsidians
Box 322, Eugene, Oregon 97401

Recommended Reading

Brady, Michael. *Cross-Country Ski Gear.* Seattle: The Mountaineers, 1979. *Nordic Touring & Cross Country Skiing.* Fifth edition. Oslo & Baltimore: Dreyers, 1979.

Brady, Michael & Lorns Skjemstad. *Waxing for Cross-Country Skiing.* Sixth edition. Berkeley, California: Wilderness Press, 1981.

Caldwell, John. *The Cross-Country Ski Book.* Brattleboro, Vermont: Stephen Green Press, 1981.

Gillette, Ned and John Dostal. *Cross-country Skiing.* Second edition. Seattle: The Mountaineers, 1983.

Kjellstrom, Bjorn. *Be an Expert with Map and Compass: The Orienteering Handbook.* New York: Charles Scribner & Sons, 1976.

LaChapelle, E.R. *The ABC of Avalanche Safety.* Seattle: The Mountaineers, 1978.

MOFA Committee of The Mountaineers. *Mountaineering First Aid.* Fourth edition. Seattle: The Mountaineers, 1984 (in press).

Murie, Olaus. *A Field Guide to Animal Tracks.* Boston: Houghton Mifflin Co., 1954.

Peters, Ed, editor. *Mountaineering: The Freedom of the Hills.* Fourth edition. Seattle: The Mountaineers, 1982.

Wilkerson, James A. *Medicine for Mountaineering.* Second edition. Seattle: The Mountaineers, 1978.

INDEX

Other books from The Mountaineers that you'll enjoy:

CITIZEN RACING
By John Caldwell and Michael Brady
Fully illustrated text on techniques, planning, training, equipment and clothing, waxing, physiology of the inner racer, and how races are operated.

MOUNTAIN SKIING
By Vic Bein
A fast-paced technique book, with instructional photos, covering level and uphill techniques, basic and advanced turns, freestyle, going beyond Nordic and into extreme skiing, mountain hazards, wilderness ethics.

THE ABC OF AVALANCHE SAFETY
By Ed LaChapelle
How to spot potential avalanche areas, how to avoid them in mountain travel, to survive if caught, to rescue victims.

CROSS-COUNTRY SKI GEAR
By Michael Brady
Complete technical information on design, construction, care and use of all types of cross-country ski equipment.

SNOWSHOEING
By Gene Prater
How to choose, use and care for snowshoes. Techniques for easy, flatland walking, for rolling and wooded terrain, for mountaineering.

Write for illustrated catalog of more than 100 outdoor titles:
The Mountaineers • Books
306 2nd Avenue W., Seattle, WA 98119